Resources for the Knowledge-Based Economy

THE ECONOMIC IMPACT OF KNOWLEDGE
Dale Neef, G. Anthony Siesfeld, Jacquelyn Cefola

THE KNOWLEDGE ECONOMY
Dale Neef

KNOWLEDGE IN ORGANIZATIONS
Laurence Prusak

KNOWLEDGE MANAGEMENT AND ORGANIZATIONAL DESIGN
Paul S. Myers

KNOWLEDGE MANAGEMENT TOOLS
Rudy L. Ruggles, III

RISE OF THE KNOWLEDGE WORKER
James W. Cortada

THE STRATEGIC MANAGEMENT OF INTELLECTUAL CAPITAL
David A. Klein

Rise of the Knowledge Worker

James W. Cortada
Editor

Butterworth-Heinemann
Boston Oxford Johannesburg Melbourne New Delhi Singapore

Recognizing the importance of preserving what has been written, Butterworth–Heinemann prints its books on acid-free paper whenever possible.

 Butterworth–Heinemann supports the efforts of American Forests and the Global ReLeaf program in its campaign for the betterment of trees, forests, and our environment.

Library of Congress Cataloging-in-Publication Data
Rise of the knowledge worker / James W. Cortada, editor.
    p. cm.—(Resources for the knowledge-based economy.)
    Includes bibliographical references and index.
    ISBN 0-7506-7058-4 (alk. paper)
    1. Knowledge workers. 2. Knowledge management. 3. Intellectual
capital. I. Cortada, James W. II. Series.
HD8039.K59R57 1998
658.3′124—dc21   98–14157
                                      CIP

British Library Cataloguing-in-Publication Data
A catalogue record for this book is available from the British Library.

The publisher offers special discounts on bulk orders of this book.
For information, please contact:
Manager of Special Sales
Butterworth–Heinemann
225 Wildwood Avenue
Woburn, MA 01801-2041
Tel: 781-904-2500
Fax: 781-904-2620

For information on all Butterworth–Heinemann books available,
contact our World Wide Web home page at: http://www.bh.com

10 9 8 7 6 5 4 3 2 1

Printed in the United States of America

Table of Contents

Introduction to the Series—
Why Knowledge, Why Now?

Why is there such an upsurge of interest in knowledge? Every year there are numerous major conferences on the subject; new journals focusing on knowledge (sometimes loosely called "intellectual capital" or "organizational learning") are published; and many major firms in the United States and Europe are adding positions such as chief knowledge officer, organizational learning officer, and even vice president for intellectual capital!

Why the focus on a subject that, at some levels, has been around since the pre-Socratic philosophers? Is it yet another one of the multitudinous management enthusiasms that seem to come and go like some random natural phenomena? We don't think so! Many of us doing research on this subject have seen the rise and fall of many of these varied nostrums—each of which attempted to offer firms a new road to achieving a sustainable competitive advantage. However, when the shouting dies down, we conclude that, excluding monopolistic policies and other market irregularities, there is no sustainable advantage other than what a firm knows, how it can utilize what it knows, and how fast it can learn something new!

But this still does not answer the questions "Why knowledge?" and "Why now?" Let us list some very broad trends that seem to be playing a significant role in the current development of knowledge:

a) The globalization of the economy, which is putting terrific pressure on firms for increased adaptability, innovation, and process speed.

b) The awareness of the value of specialized knowledge, as embedded in organizational processes and routines, in coping with the pressures of globalization.

   c) The awareness of knowledge as a distinct factor of production and its role in the growing book value–to–market value ratios within knowledge-based industries.

   d) Cheap networked computing, which is at last giving us a tool for working with and learning from each other.

While many can argue for and against the significance of these trends, we feel that the preponderance of evidence points to the increasing substitution of brain for brawn within our organizations and our social lives. Yet we have developed few conceptional tools to better work with this "wetware."

   It is with these forces in mind that we offer the following volume to you. While there are, as yet, few agreed-upon standards and analytic frames and definitions, there are enough serious articles and books to help managers get some real traction in dealing with the crucial, yet elusive, subject of knowledge.

   After all, we have had about five hundred years of thought concerning the other major factors of production—for example, land, labor, and capital. Let these volumes start the process of codifying knowledge about knowledge in order for us to better manage in the twenty-first century.

Laurence Prusak, Series Editor

Preface

A generation of magnificent scholars and managers, from Peter Drucker to Jack Welch, have taught us that business issues and the profound changes the world's economy is undergoing make sense if set in historical context. Today the best managers in the world demand to know how things came to be as they are. In short, historical perspective, with a heavy dose of sound economics, has become a crucial part of all good business practices.

This collection of readings is designed to give you historical perspective on the fastest growing sector of the workforce in the world—what we today call "knowledge workers." This insight will allow you to understand how knowledge-based positions evolved from manufacturing and agricultural jobs and will permit you to begin appreciating what their future role will be. Sociologists have also been very influential in helping to define the rise of the modern knowledge worker. A combined historical, economic, and sociological perspective is crucial in identifying long-term trends and the characteristics of this new workforce.

The history of this topic is very interesting. For example,

- Did you know that knowledge workers first and foremost came into being where technologies were most advanced?
- Did you know that the shift to knowledge work began in earnest before World War I, but by the end of the 1920s had become a major trend?
- Did you know that the ability of a woman to work in professional careers was made possible mainly by the rise of knowledge work rather than through any altruistic change in the attitude of male managers?

These questions call attention to topics of great interest to historians, economists, and sociologists. Answers to these and many other questions allow managers and employees at the dawn of the twenty-first century to make considerable sense out of what is happening to them. In a study sponsored by the National Planning Association, and done by a team at MIT, we learned that more change was occurring in the workplace now than at any other time in this century. The study's key finding was "that the traditional methods of managing employees and developing skilled workers inside companies are breaking down."[1] To a large extent the positive parts of the future of work belong to knowledge workers. The readings that follow will help you understand how knowledge work became so important and will give you a sense of confidence about how it is evolving.

The selected readings come from a variety of sources normally not looked at by managers and business executives worried about the changing nature of work. There are reports by historians, sociologists, and economists. Representative writings from highly influential authors shed light on the evolution of knowledge workers. The very good news is that since the 1950s, and in particular in the United States, a small group of outstanding scholars have been studying the rise of the knowledge worker. While most of their work has focused on U.S. experiences, their findings apply to all industrialized societies. Most of what is presented in this book is based on the American experience because it was in the United States that most of the forces driving business change and the rise of the knowledge worker initiated.

While this book focuses on landmark studies and on the recent history of knowledge work, it will end with a view to the future. To put everything in this book into perspective, Chapter 1 will set the stage for the key issues to be addressed. Every chapter has a short introduction on its content, its significance, and the context in which it was written and includes brief biographical comments on the authors.

This book is intended for people working in business and government, for scholars looking at the issues related to knowledge management and business at large, and for students trying to understand the world they will have no choice but to work in. The profound changes under way in the world's economy will lead—if history is any guide to coming events—to continued increases in standard of living for many around the world. It is given only rarely to a generation to witness the birth of a new world and the death of an old one. This is such a time and place, so we had better understand the historic forces at work if we are to ride the wave well. This book is designed to help you achieve that insight, fitting in nicely with the other volumes in this series.

Selecting what to include and what to leave out, then working through the process of getting published, required the help of many people. I would like to first thank Larry Prusak, the series editor and, in his own right, a leading expert on all aspects of knowledge work, for encouraging me to participate in the series. I also want to thank Professor Alfred D. Chandler, the dean of American historians of

1. Peter Capelli et al., *Change at Work* (New York: Oxford University Press, 1997): 4.

business, for teaching me much about the subject and for being such a wonderful collaborator on a related project. Both Prusak and Chandler are knowledge workers *par excellence* but also two of the most wonderful colleagues to work with. I also want to acknowledge our editor, Karen Speerstra, for having the foresight to launch this series at a time when knowledge work was just getting some recognition as being crucial to the future of business success—a bold and risky move on her part—but now so obviously the right time to publish this set of books. I also want to recognize the good work of Susan B. Prusak, production editor for this book, and her team at Butterworth-Heinemann. While I have acknowledged the permission of so many publishers for allowing us to reprint material at the start of each contribution, I want to thank them as a group for also having had the wisdom to publish so many wonderful studies on the subject.

If you find this material interesting and would like to see us publish more on the subject, let us know through the publisher or directly by contacting me at IBM. Call any IBM office in the world for my most current phone number or address, or write to me at jwcorta@us.ibm.com.

James W. Cortada

Introducing the Knowledge Worker

James W. Cortada

What is a "knowledge worker?" What is "knowledge work?" How are those questions different from "What is an Information Age worker?" or simply, "What is the 'Age of Information'?" Is knowledge work tasks that require people to talk, write, think, and apply knowledge? Doesn't a farmer talk, think, and apply knowledge? What about a factory worker operating a CAD/CAM system driven by a computer with more capacity than all the computers built in the 1950s? Is a foreman on a construction job using a laptop to read blueprints and specifications not a knowledge worker? Or, are knowledge workers simply ministers, teachers, lawyers, accountants, librarians, some managers, and consultants?

The answer is, quite simply, increasingly everyone is a knowledge worker. For what historians, economists, and sociologists are discovering is that the amount of information and skills that everyone needs to perform their work has been rising steadily all through the nineteenth and twentieth centuries. Increasing proportions of workers in the industrialized world have come to make their living by performing tasks that do not require them to plant and harvest crops or to work in factories manufacturing items, although they might work on a farm or at a manufacturing site. An historian can live on a farm in Maine, write books there using the Internet and a PC, but also teach at a university in Boston. Today, some 90 percent of workers at a factory making computer chips do not make any product or component; they provide support and related services to those who do. The common vision of a knowledge worker is that of a person dealing in data and ideas. These can include a growing number of professions, such as business consultants, merchants of information (e.g., database managers and publishers); agents who, through their knowledge of a subject, bring buyers and sellers together (e.g., stock brokers and mortgage lenders); and customer service representatives who can explain how bills were calculated or can advise a taxicab driver how to get to a destination. Clerks, particularly those in offices, are considered knowledge workers by some. Secretaries, who came into their own in the last quarter of the nineteenth century thanks to such information handling equipment as typewriters and adding machines, make a favorite example for the gender-interested scholar.

There have always been knowledge workers. Priests, shamans, and medicine men were knowledge workers. Witches, professors, and lawyers were too. Teachers are the preeminent example of the knowledge worker. All of these examples share the common feature of having worked in agricultural and industrial societies. Every culture in every age has had workers whose stock in trade was information and intellectual activity. As service sector activities increased, the number and variety of knowledge workers simply grew. It is that process of expansion and diversification that has created the need to understand better who is a knowledge worker. As the number of office clerks increased through the early decades of the twentieth century, along with a new class of mandarins known as managers, the need to determine their contribution and role expanded.

The process of expansion and diversification went through waves. We can use the United States as an example to illustrate the process at work. In the 1700s and early 1800s, as the population of Europeans in North America grew, so too did the actual tiny number of knowledge workers. Newspaper editors, writers, ministers, teachers, and lawyers increased. They dominated the nonexistent knowledge industry, "nonexistent" because they did not see themselves as knowledge workers. They identified with their own niche; they were teachers, lawyers, or ministers. With the industrial take-off in the United States, beginning in the 1840s and moving through the 1920s, in addition to more of these kinds of knowledge workers, new waves of knowledge workers surged in the economy. These included office clerks, operators of information handling equipment (e.g., telegraph operators, telephone operators, secretaries, and other office appliance clerks), and people who made their living with information, such as novelists, poets, freelance writers, consultants (by 1910), and experts on topics that had been of minor concern a century earlier (e.g., engineering).

Expansion in their number and variety mirrored what had happened earlier with waves of knowledge workers in the 1700s and early 1800s. As the economy grew in size, it could support more people in the same profession (e.g., increasing numbers of secretaries or accountants), and a variety of disciplines and specialties (e.g., teachers in elementary schools versus high school, professors of modern history versus ancient history, or those in such new fields as engineering and, later, computer science). The phenomenon occurred in government, nonprofit organizations, and in businesses, both large and small. New industries led to new knowledge workers. For example, in 1800, there was an industry that cut ice out of New England lakes and shipped it to the southern United States for ice cubes for drinks. By World War I that industry was gone, replaced with another that made motorized ice makers and refrigerators. Staffs of knowledge workers for each industry were different. Old knowledge thus gave way to the new. For example, a wholesaler in whale oil could make a handsome living as a knowledge worker in Boston in the 1840s, but would have starved in the 1890s. By then, wholesalers in crude oil extracted from Pennsylvania and other parts of the United States were in business, brokering the black gold of a new class of industrial workers, called drillers. They relied on a new class of knowledge workers, known as geologists, to figure out where to drill.

Expanded reliance on science and technology, which began to influence American and European economic activity after 1865, created not only whole new knowledge professions, but also new fields. The most dramatic examples include over one million information processing (e.g., computer) workers who were employed by the 1990s in the United States alone. Add to this atomic energy scientists, the modern medical professions, and even the late-twentieth-century warriors (e.g., fighter pilots and submarine commanders), and we see additional waves of diversity and volume.

Over the years, as societies became larger, more complex, and varied, knowledge work became a larger part of the landscape. Globalization of economies and, at a slower but nonetheless relentless pace, culture, took the role of knowledge work and spread it around the world. Increasingly, knowledge work is being internationalized. For example, today the most widely used language for conducting business is English; it is used on all continents. Two continents banded internally to create large economic markets (e.g., NAFTA in North America, the Common Market in Western Europe); now both are broadening to include new countries. Valued knowledge about specific topics makes it possible to cross borders to earn a living.

Complexity brought with it a related surge of knowledge work: services. As it became easier to make a good product, differentiating these with services (often knowledge work) became crucial to a company's success. As our reliance on science and technology kept increasing over the past two centuries, the need for experts, or specialists, became imperative. Gone, for instance, was a once almost total reliance on a medical general practitioner. Today a general practitioner will not even remove a simple mole—one has to go to a dermatologist; a dentist will not remove a molar—one is sent to an oral surgeon. One cannot even go to a librarian to ask a simple question; they will be sent to the reference librarian. IBM salespeople in the 1920s knew the entire product line, today there are product specialists who sell and service segments of the company's offerings.

In fact, IBM is a good example of what has happened. In 1924, the vast majority of its revenues came from leased hardware (96 percent) and sale of punch cards (4 percent). Fifty years later, about 80 percent came from hardware sales, another 15 percent from software, and the rest from services. Barely a quarter of a century later, a third of the company's revenues came from services—almost all knowledge work. In 1924 an IBM salesman was typically a high school graduate, although many were not. In the late 1950s, the company recruited only college graduates, ideally with science and engineering backgrounds. By the late 1990s, advanced degrees in such fields as computer science, engineering, and business administration were deemed minimum requirements just to have an application taken seriously.

Perhaps the first important scholar to appreciate the changing nature of work was Fritz Machlup, professor of economics at Princeton University, who, in the 1950s, began identifying knowledge work. He looked at knowledge much the way any economist would examine a product, by documenting its creation, distribution, and significance. In 1962, he published his now classic book, *The Production and Distribution of Knowledge in the United States,* in which he introduced the notion that knowledge was a major item of production within the U.S. economy. Simultaneously, he argued that there was a new type of worker responsible "for the entire spectrum of activities, from the transporter of knowledge up to the original creator." He included in his new type of worker teachers, clerks, and researchers. By the time of his death in 1983 Machlup had completed an additional three volumes on the same subject. His research led others to view knowledge work as something distinctive; many of these new students of knowledge work are represented in the readings in this book. But as historians have also noted, what Machlup identified in the 1950s and 1960s was not so much new workers (although there were many new types of work) as more knowledge workers, because there had always been knowledge work. His contribution was distinguishing knowledge work from other types of work.

By his definition, Machlup estimated that by 1958 information activities absorbed 29 percent of the U.S. GNP and 31 percent of the workforce. He demonstrated that between 1947 and 1958 that sector had grown at twice the rate of the GNP. Others began looking at this sector, with consensus growing that by 1970, the new sector accounted for 40 percent of the GNP. As scholars began looking at who was a knowledge worker, the percentage of the workforce tagged as knowledge workers increased. Machlup's figures began to look too conservative. Economist William J. Baumol and his team noted that "between 1960 and 1980, data workers increased relative to total employment in all industries except trade and the government sectors, where they declined slightly in percentage terms." He disclosed that "information workers increased in number relative to noninformation workers in all sectors except trade." Complexity of business processes and the need for better-educated and -trained employees drove growth in the new professions.

Jorge Reina Schement and Terry Curtis conducted the most recent work on the size and dimensions of knowledge work in the United States. They concluded that information activities were being broadly incorporated into ever wider sets of jobs than previously. For instance, supervisors were doing more data handling and reporting than had supervisors in their parents' generation. Equally interesting, they demonstrated that information workers began to outnumber agricultural workers as early as the mid-1920s, overshadowing industrial workers by the start of the 1930s.

People who created knowledge had less technological support than data workers who relied directly on such machines as computers and telephones, and they often relied on a more varied technical or industry-related body of literature. The purpose of these aids was to facilitate the accumulation, assessment, and dissemination of information as part of their regular work. These tasks created an enormous demand for reports and documents beginning in the 1880s, and, later, for computers. The PC was simply the latest tool, jumping from U.S. sales of less than one hundred thousand units in 1979 to over a million in 1982, and to a cumulative global population of over one hundred million in 1997. Baumol studied the relative growth rates of knowledge workers versus other types of workers (e.g., manufacturing), concluding that the number of knowledge workers expanded largely because of their substitution for other types of workers within the economy. They accounted for some 70 percent of growth in the 1960s and 84 percent in the 1970s. There is a raging debate under way about how productive these new workers became. But the general increase of knowledge and information content in activities of the U.S., West European, and East Asian economies is unmistakable.

Why we needed more knowledge work has already been suggested above—work became more complicated or additional services were needed to differentiate a product—but the debate is not closed. For example, James R. Beniger suggested that with the arrival of large organizations such as corporations (e.g., national railroads and governments controlling huge tracts of land) came a "Control Revolution, a complex of rapid changes in the technological and economic arrangements by which information is collected, stored, processed, and communicated," to which one could add the computer. Beniger made the case that as manufacturing and distribution sped up and became more complicated, the need for information with which to control economic activities drove up demand for information and knowledge. He said this process began after the end of the American Civil War (1865) and continued to the present. Schement and Curtis agreed, arguing that by the end of the 1980s, over 50 percent of the American workforce could be called knowledge workers. Their statistics are dramatic: "Clerical and kindred workers increased by nearly 500% between 1900 and 1930 and then increased again by 220% between 1930 and 1960." They calculated that "the numbers of professional, technical, and kindred workers increased by nearly 270 percent from 1900 to 1930; between 1930 and 1960, their numbers increased by 220 percent."

Reasons for the rise of the knowledge worker suggest why we are interested in knowledge work. Larry Prusak in his introduction to this book of readings states the case in a straightforward manner. But we can add to the discussion by pointing out that every new kind of work requires new tools and techniques, different understandings, information, and insights, and leads to new experiences, values, and economic dynamics. Put in other words, the rise and recognition of knowledge work is leading to a redefinition of what work is, along with the tools, insights, and technologies needed to make knowledge productive, enjoyable, and profitable. That is why knowledge management and knowledge work are not simply the latest management fad. As economists and historians have clearly demonstrated, knowledge work is now a dominant feature of industrializing and postindustrial societies.

Just as humans had to learn about farming when we made agriculture the basis of our economy, and later we had to learn about manufacturing when manufacturing became the basis of our economy, so too do we face the prospect of learning how to function in an information-rich service-based economy. More readily than economists, sociologists recognized this truth. That is why such experts as Manuel Castells study the role of network societies in large urban settings, and why Shoshana Zuboff interviewed so many workers using computers and other forms of automation to understand what they do, why, and how it effects them and society at large.

But now what of the present and, more importantly, of the future? Contemporary literature on present trends in labor, knowledge, economics, politics, and future business focuses on a variety of issues that can neatly be summed up as the changing nature of work, the reconfiguration or desagregation of industries, the increasing role of technologies of all types, and the emerging new patterns of electronic commerce. Business managers are increasingly redesigning their companies to exploit various telecommunication and computing technologies and changes in how employees work. Relative to knowledge work, a fundamental trend of the past twenty years, first evident in Japan, then later in North America, and now increasingly in Western Europe, is delegation of authority to make decisions to ever lower echelons in organizations. As companies downsized, reduced levels of management, and streamlined major work processes in the late 1980s and early 1990s, it became necessary for executive management to give more decision-making responsibility to employees. For example, in the 1970s, to provide a customer a credit on a disputed bill, a clerk would have gone to her supervisor or the supervisor's manager. Today, that clerk is probably authorized to make that decision on the spot because (a) she has been taught the guidelines of the company that originally would only have been understood by a supervisor and (b) she would have access to information about the specific customer and the bill in question through a computer-based system.

A second development has been the continued expansion of computer systems, with their massive databases of information, which allow both individuals and organizations to have information, insight, and collective experiences. The case of the billing dispute illustrates the process. By collecting information about bills, management can study trends in disputes and, for instance, determine what the break-even point in cost is between granting a credit (regardless of cause) and investigating its merits. Thus, for instance, in the United States, many corporations know that a dispute of under $75 is more expensive to argue over than simply to credit out. That insight comes from analyzing data in billing systems and sharing that insight with employees, followed by altering policy to permit credits of up to $75 with no debate with customers.

The twin developments of empowered employees and expanded use of computers clearly made it possible to reengineer the nature of work, a process now well underway. While the outlines of the changes remain unclear, some features are obvious. Increasingly, work requires employees with greater skills in the use of computers, particularly search capabilities, and a deeper understanding of how they can improve and manage work as collections of processes. At the heart of process management is the need for knowledge about how the process works, insight often obtained by using statistical process control techniques. A willingness to assume responsibility, and not simply authority, at ever lower levels of an organization appears to be a growing requirement of the new workforce. Confidence and willingness to assume responsibility rises as workers know more about what they do and why and how they do it. For those reasons, we are entering an era when corporations are placing a great premium on skills and investment in training. Traditional configurations of companies into set industries appears to be shifting. Firms that clearly were in one industry are increasingly participating in others, with the result that industry boundaries are changing. For instance, there was a time when television production companies only made and broadcast programs. Today such a company might be owned by a larger firm that also operates movie studios in Hollywood and makes music CDs. This same firm may be working with a local utility or a telephone company to deliver entertainment into people's homes via cable. Is it still a television production company? Which industry is it in? Who are its competitors?

Better telecommunications are allowing firms to participate in many markets globally with minimal capital. A book dealer operating on the Internet can sell products around the world using only electronics. Software can be written to track patterns of purchases, tailoring offerings to individual customers around the world. For example, if a person were to buy only books on gardening, it would be possible for the on-line book dealer to know that and subsequently to send that individual notifications about the publication of new gardening books, or even put them on an automatic delivery program for these books.

This example also illustrates a new trend, known as e-commerce, in which companies are selling to their customers via electronic means, mainly through on-line sales using the Internet or telephones. In the United States, for instance, mail order merchants sell everything from clothes to wine over the telephone, using computers to track sales and individual accounts. Payments for goods are conducted using credit cards or electronic deductions from customers' bank accounts. A prerequisite for these kinds of sales, of course, is knowledge of technology and its possibilities. Sharing that insight tacitly across the enterprise is crucial. Having skills to develop, maintain, and exploit e-commerce is more than just an obvious requirement; it simply is quite a different world than a worker faced twenty years ago.

But if there is one general statement that can be made about the present and future, which is linked to historic trends, it is that our dependence on information and knowledge in order to do our work has been steadily increasing since the middle of the last century. It is no accident that knowledge content in work kept rising, and that eventually economists, historians, and sociologists were able to identify "knowledge workers." Knowledge work has a very long history, knowledge content has been rising across all professions, and one can expect this process to continue deep into the future. Understanding, therefore, the dynamics of how knowledge work came into being in the first place is itself a good practice in managing knowledge work. That is why a book of readings on the rise of the knowledge worker makes sense for those who must be successful in today's workplace.

Part One

A New Profession Is Born: The Knowledge Worker

1

Where Did Knowledge Workers Come From?

James W. Cortada

Today, management throughout the industrialized world has become wary of new management concepts, calling new ideas "fads" and wondering where it will all end. Into this stew of suspicion many are pouring "knowledge work," "knowledge management," and "knowledge workers." But not all concepts are fads; some have staying power. Knowledge work is one of those—it is not a fad. How do we know? We look to history—rather than to some academic management theorist—for the proof. It turns out knowledge workers have been around for thousands of years, and knowledge work (complete with its tools, such as brushes, tablets, books, pens, and other data handling items) for an even longer period of time. What is very new is the categorization of these people, activities, and tools into a discrete field—knowledge work—binding together practices and professions that were previously considered separately. By clustering these together, we do not create a new fad; rather, we gain the opportunity to learn how different types of people have worked well. One can carry over from one profession or activity to others some of the best practices that allow organizations to exploit information and insight to better run their operations. Again, history helps because this is exactly what successful leaders and organizations have been doing for centuries. We just never gave that set of activities a name until after World War II.

Even the act of naming the work has a history. Knowledge management is not a 1990s concept. In the 1950s, economists at Princeton University were busy at work studying the production of knowledge in America. In the 1960s, economists, biologists, and psychologists were continuing the work of their predecessors of the 1930s through 1950s in looking at biological feedback mechanisms and how they worked in people, animals, society, and business. To a large extent, competitive analysis, even strategic planning, of the 1960s and 1970s were formalized as part of the process of capturing and exploiting knowledge.

But perhaps the one circumstance over all others that brought knowledge work to our consciousness has been its exposure in business and, more specifically, to management. Professors, witch doctors, lawyers, and priests have been around for a very long time. These have always been "knowledge workers." But until knowledge work—a new concept but old work—came to business, the whole notion of knowledge work and the theories and practice of knowledge work remained the preserve of educators, philosophers, and other academics. Only rarely did the term rear its head in business, usually in training or by the odd manager who, for example, happened to have started his or her career as an historian or priest.

Because the current interest in knowledge work is coming most aggressively from the business community, the history of what has long been going on outside of commerce in the area of knowledge is being brought to business—this book is an example of that—while the managerial practices of commerce are being applied to the collection, use, and assessment of knowledge. It is this latter set of activities— from Michael Porter and his assessments of the behavior of industries, to Laurence Prusak and Thomas H. Davenport in their concerns about how to exploit knowledge in corporations—that has informed students of business practices. But the history of knowledge work and its workers has much to teach us about the nature of knowledge and how to exploit it. In fact, the highly respected guru of business gurus, Professor Peter F. Drucker, may have coined the phrase "knowledge worker" in the late 1950s, but the point is, the notion of this new class of workers has been drawing the attention of scholars and managers at an increasing rate over the past half century as an economic trend of historic proportions.

There are three convenient ways to look at the history of knowledge and knowledge workers. First, information and knowledge have a history of their own, with long standing patterns of behavior, use, and convenience for humans that are of practical concern in business, government, and in our private lives. Second, there is the history of the knowledge worker, that is to say, of people in many walks of life whose primary professional function is gathering and using information or knowledge. Third, knowledge management and knowledge workers as a subject has its own history, although a much shorter one than the first two. These three sets of historical experiences teach us much about the nature of knowledge. These findings increasingly are becoming important as we continue to evolve into an economy in which knowledge drives development and distribution of products and services, and in which growing numbers of workers make their living in the creation and exploitation of information and knowledge for profit.

As we move through what is becoming increasingly apparent as a new industrial revolution, and away from the second industrial revolution, we are exploring ways to understand it. Various observers are attempting to help by giving it a label, often calling the new world the "information age," the "third industrial revolution," or the "postindustrial age." What we see with some certainty at this point, however, is that the value of ideas in the running of organizations is enjoying newfound prominence. Historical experience sobers us by calling to our attention the fact that knowledge has been with us a very long time. Understanding its history holds out the promise of improving our ability to run corporations, universities, and government agencies in what is an emerging new economic world order. That is why the topic is of such importance.

INFORMATION AND KNOWLEDGE:
A HISTORY OF THEIR OWN

The literature on the history of information and knowledge would fill a building. But some basic observations can be made that are of use to managers today. Perhaps the most basic observation is that from the beginning of recorded time, some basic patterns of behavior have remained consistent down to the present concerning the role of information and knowledge. This observation suggests what the value and use of knowledge can be.

History provides many examples. There is the British stock broker who in 1815 made a fortune just by learning hours before his fellow countrymen that Napoleon had lost the Battle of Waterloo. More recently we have the example of information on how to use personal computers making it possible for high school students to hold well-paying part time jobs in corporations, helping the rest of us use these new tools. Knowledge also had held value for many people. American General George S. Patton constantly relied on this insight to plan his highly successful campaigns during World War II. Earlier, Thomas Jefferson—the quintessential renaissance man of colonial America—sought lessons from history to inform all his political actions, from writing the Declaration of Independence to defining the role of an American president. Emperors of China always surrounded themselves with advisors who were scholars first, politicos second. Roman emperors, like the ancient Greeks, consulted educated priests to gain insight on the possible future. Today in business, we see technocrats doing "data mining," the act of drawing insights from mountains of information stored in computers. The American government routinely calls in historians and experts on various regions of the world to advise the White House on how to deal with Cuba, Iran, and Iraq. The Cuban missile crisis of the 1960s and the unification of Germany in the early 1990s are two well-documented cases where national leaders turned to historians for advise on what to do. So what are some of the insights about the use of knowledge?

First, from the beginning of time for humankind, people have recognized the value of consciously collecting and using information. They have unceasingly continued to do this to the present. The development of language made it possible to pass on one's experiences to children so that they did not have to reinvent existing knowledge through repeated experiences, the way animals usually have to. Language also made it possible to exploit the cognitive capabilities that were expanding in the human brain to deal with ideas and abstract notions; in other words, to engage in discussions about intangible things, such as love, faith, and ethics. With language humankind experienced, and possibly enjoyed, the birth of tacit knowledge. Our growing knowledge about how people learn has been tremendously augmented in the past century thanks to studies on linguistics, biology, and computing, and, in the past half century, through studies of the brain and of DNA encoding. Today, many students of the brain and nervous system speak of these in much the same way that computer scientists think about computers: data input, processing, data output, and data storage. The history of computing clearly demonstrates that it was the work of biologists more than the work of engineers that informed computer science. Mathematics and physics influenced computer science a great deal too. Yet it was the description of how computers work that so energized much understanding about the nature of feedback (a knowledge-driven process) in machines and in all living organisms. In fact, the biological metaphor is rapidly replacing the old Newtonian concepts of society and organizations operating like machines. This thinking has led to a more complex analogy in which people and institutions take in data about the environment, make sense of it, and then react advantageously to what is going on: fear (e.g., stay out of a market, or avoid a war), fight (enter a market, occupy a rival nation's territory).

Second, humans have always tried to augment human memory with writing to aid in their preservation of information and knowledge for subsequent use. Cave drawings of bison may have been painted for religious purposes. But even more basic is the fact that they were painted for whatever reason. A painting of a bison is information (an image in this case) that had some value; otherwise, it would not have been created. Historians have done yeoman work in documenting the history of language and writing; both emerged almost one upon the other. From very early times humans have found ways to record pieces of information outside of their memories. In other words, from almost the beginning, humans looked for ways to store information outside their heads. These approaches ranged from assortments of rocks and sticks to clay tablets, to complex languages like that of the Egyptians and later that of the ancient Greeks, to today's languages. Thousands of languages and writing systems litter the history of humankind.

Even today, while linguists complain that the world is becoming so homogeneous that indigenous languages and writings of primitive tribes are disappearing, they ignore the reality that new writing systems called programming languages are appearing all the time. In the half century since the invention of computer programming, several thousand languages for writing software have been created; in any given year there are about 250 in use. So the process of developing and using written languages as tools to store information for subsequent use has continued unabated. Alphabets from Assyrian times, through the grammar of Chinese and Romance languages, to the rules of programming in effect today, are the prime tools and practices that control the effective application of language and writing. Again, we see need for information followed by standards and conventions to ensure effective use of the tools.

Third, humankind has constantly developed physical objects in which to store and manipulate information. The first letters ever mailed were clay tablets that usually served as receipts for transactions carried out by traders in the Middle East. Centuries later, Roman soldiers received pay stubs, also made out of clay, with their salaries. The Egyptians invented papyrus to record data while the Chinese were busy at work inventing paper. Neither was invented to wrap up food bought in the market place. That came many centuries later! Tablets, papyrus, and paper were invented to augment human memory by allowing the recording (storing) of information for use later or by individuals other than the original author. Over time, thousands of other tools appeared to carry out similar functions: notched sticks, paintings, carvings on stone, mechanical devices, movable type in printing (in the 1400s), adding machines (1600s), typewriters (1700s and 1800s), calculators (1820s forward), and, beginning in the mid-1800s, a vast array of electronically based tools: telegraph, telephone, radio, television, tape recorders, phonograph, and, of course, the computer. Within each category of devices, inventors and engineers developed hundreds and often thousands of variations.

The volume of tools invented is staggering. In ancient times, the great library of Alexandria reportedly had 700,000 volumes of manuscripts. By 1500 in Europe alone, there were 35,000 titles which resulted in publication of between 15 and 20 million books that had been published. Today, over 40,000 books are published annually in the United States; and even in Spain—a country only 13 percent the size of the United States—publishers bring out over 30,000 new titles yearly. The world has spent over $4 trillion on computers since 1950. Just before the start of World War I, eighty-two manufacturers were busy at work in the United States manufacturing tens of thousands of typewriters each year. As we became more numerically sensitive throughout the twentieth century, people began to count more, and one of the things they counted were such aids to information as the number of books, libraries, adding machines, TVs, and computers. In our lifetime we have seen the process continue.

As the variety and number of tools for storing and using information increased, so too did the amount of data available to humankind. The phrase "recorded knowledge" came into use in the nineteenth century to capture the essence of people's desire to accumulate knowledge that they could use. Creation of the great modern libraries of the world, such as the British Museum and Library, the Library of Congress, Harvard University's library, and the national libraries of France and Spain, reflect a modern version of a very old pattern of behavior. A library's standing is still measured by the number of volumes in its collection. We are impressed with Alexandria's ancient library because of its size—an analogy for valued information—and no self-respecting librarian would be ignorant of how many millions of volumes are in his or her collection. The same type of numerical shorthand for how much information exists can be seen in the world of computers. Every manager of a computer data center can recite how much information storage capacity they have in the form of disk drives in total volume of bytes of storage.

Collection of information (or knowledge) has also long been a prestigious activity of the wealthy. The essence of the definition of the "renaissance man" is someone who knows a great deal about many subjects. Often the manifestation of that interest, or display of an acquisitive nature, is the private library. The great merchants of Renaissance Italy amassed great libraries of manuscripts and, later, of books. Look at a wealthy noble family estate in Britain and you will find a private library of thousands of volumes. In the New World, the plantation owners along the James River in Virginia in the 1600s and 1700s, despite living at the edge of a violent and rustic frontier, nonetheless built libraries with thousands of volumes. In the late nineteenth century, steel magnate Andrew Carnegie endowed hundreds of public libraries in the United States, while the leading banker of the day, J. P. Morgan (on the East Coast), and railroad magnate Henry E. Huntington (on the West Coast), built some of the finest collections of books in the history of mankind.

The process continued unabated to the present. Histories of book collecting catalog collections of enormous size and variety being put together by people from all walks of life down to the present. In other instances, and for a variety of reasons, contributions to information continue in new ways. For example, Bill Gates, CEO and founder of Microsoft, and reputed to be the wealthiest man in the world, in the 1990s began to provide public schools in the United States with free access to the Internet. In short, at all levels of society and over a very long period of time, individuals and institutions made the collection of information and knowledge a high priority, despite the enormous expense involved.

Fourth, every major institution in society has collected, preserved, and exploited information. Indeed, as many historians have demonstrated through their studies of the Catholic Church, various national governments of Europe and Asia, and, more recently, such large geographically dispersed industries such as railroads and large-scale manufacturing, without information one could not control, let alone expand, operations. These institutions have always been the best customers for whatever new information handling tools came along. The Catholic Church was incontestably the largest buyer of manuscripts and books for centuries, and it may still be in certain parts of the world. Every major government in the world for the past two thousand years has supported centers of knowledge such as libraries, universities, monasteries, and departmental libraries and archives. Often these were administratively linked to the function of teaching, as occurred for centuries in monasteries and in universities. Every complex and large society has had what today are fashionably called "centers of learning." Priests taught seminarians around the world, often creating new knowledge in the process in such diverse fields as agriculture, business, medicine, science, military tactics and strategies, religion, and government practices. The "best practices" have been to create these centers to consolidate large bodies of knowledge and then to use them to disseminate this information through education, research, business, and consulting. Benedictine priests in the Spanish Pyrenees often advised Catholic popes on liturgical matters. In the ancient Chinese Empire, administrators began their professional lives as scholars, then moved on to become managers and bureaucrats. Jesuit priests whispered advice into the ears of the emperors of the Hapsburg Empire in the 1600s, while today consultants from IBM, A. Andersen, McKinsey, and many other firms do the same to CEOs of corporations.

Fifth, information begets more information. Information normally leads to deep insight, to knowledge. It is a canon of knowledge gurus that bits of data can lead to a higher-order insight, which then can be applied to advantage. They call that higher order of insight "knowledge." But the notion of a hierarchy of valued information is an old one. Recognition that it takes time and effort to create that knowledge is also an ancient notion. Most religions, for example, recognize that ultimate knowledge comes through years of study. Nirvana is not a gift to the new Asian believer, while in Europe mysticism was the preserve of the hard-studying and long-praying faithful. Formal study and application has long been recognized as the road to higher knowledge.

Credentialing early on became a way to recognize someone, or some organization, for having knowledge. Awarding an MBA or Ph.D. today serves essentially the same purpose that ordination of priests and rabbis did over the centuries. Certification of organizations also has an ancient history. ISO 9000 certification in the 1990s tells a potential customer that there are certain bodies of knowledge and practices in an organization that hopefully result in quality products. In ancient Greece, not just any citizen could build their own temple and open shop as a priest and prophet; they had to go through a certification process, just like doctors have to be taught their trade before most governments will allow them to practice. For a thousand years, from London to Moscow, from northern Europe to the warm Mediterranean, guilds certified the ability of craftsmen making everything from jewelry to armor.

Development of a base of knowledge in individuals caused people to spend increasing amounts of their time working with knowledge and, in the process, to create more of it. In turn, that led to the development of professions that were, for all intents and purposes, filled with full-time knowledge workers. We can think of many obvious examples: witch doctors, priests, medical practitioners, lawyers, government officials, and later accountants and computer programmers. As the world got wealthier it could afford full-time writers, painters, speakers, teachers, and consultants. Part-time knowledge workers became full-time knowledge workers. In the nineteenth century, many European inventors invented on weekends or evenings while holding day jobs. Today, very few important inventions appear this way. More often, inventors work full-time for corporations, government agencies, or universities in well-stocked laboratories. As full-time work and many types of workers increased, the amount of time they could devote to the creation of new information, and hence knowledge, expanded. That is why today, for example, engineering knowledge doubles every five years, whereas a hundred years ago, even the concept of an engineer was still new; why medical knowledge doubled every ten years two decades ago and now doubles in less than four. Like coat hangers in closets and rabbits left alone, information seems to breed more information.

A direct corollary to this process concerns the influence of wealth and economic strength in any society. The richer, and simultaneously the more complex and large, a society has become, the more information, knowledge, and knowledge workers it has needed and, thus, acquired. That is why wealthy civilizations such as Rome, Greece, ancient Egypt and China, and later Western Europe, all with exponential growth to match expanding wealth, had scholars, and knowledge-creating priests, accountants, and full-time teachers. Nowhere has this process been more documented than in Western Europe following its rapid economic growth after 1500, and in North America after 1850, where the standard of living normally rivaled or exceeded that of its mother countries. Thus, one could expect to see a growing community of knowledge workers in East Asia at the end of the twentieth century as that area grew more prosperous. Looking to the future, it is why we may see fewer knowledge workers in Africa and in parts of the Indian subcontinent.

Sixth, collections of information have normally led to the creation of knowledge. The process of moving from bits of data to insight as a result of that data existing and being used has normally been carried out by experts, or what we would today call knowledge workers. From the perspective of the historian of information, it is important to recognize that a higher order of usefulness often lies in the insights generated by data; hence the value of knowledge. Histories of information invariably capture data on the collection and use of information, while often it is the philosophers and sociologists who have done a better job in documenting the evolution of information into knowledge. Historians have studied specific professions that use knowledge—lawyers, teaching professions, scientists, and engineers—but have not reached a definitive point of being able to describe the overall pattern of metamorphosis. They are only just now beginning to attempt to generalize about the role of knowledge workers and what they do, and similarly are only starting the process of characterizing the role of information, knowledge, and knowledge workers by era, nation, or type of economy. As some of the papers in this book demonstrate, however, at least the process of analysis has begun and is generating fascinating insights of use to scholars, knowledge workers, and managers.

Seventh, over time, respect for the value of information and knowledge has increased. In a study currently under way by a team of American historians, sociologists, and business professors led by Professor Alfred D. Chandler, Jr., of the Harvard Business School, the whole notion of the role of information in North America's economy from the 1600s to the present is being examined. Their findings so far show the great value Americans have always placed on information, its availability and free flow through the economy, and public support through constitutional provisions (e.g., the First Amendment right to free speech), government support for infrastructure (e.g., the creation of a national postal delivery system), and legal protections (e.g., copyright and patent laws) to encourage the use of knowledge. They see this emphasis on the use of information as a basic competitive advantage for the U.S. economy. It was in this nation, for example, that literacy rates since colonial days have normally outpaced those of the countries from which the colonists came. It was in this nation that basic information handling technologies were invented (or most aggressively exploited) the fastest: telegraph, telephone, typewriter, radio, television, and, of course, every form of computer from mainframes to PCs. It was also in this country that from earliest times public education and the necessary infrastructure of schools, colleges, universities, research facilities, and libraries were created with public and private funds. It is a country in which the wealthy routinely contribute to public institutions of higher learning. In the nineteenth century, the fashion led to contributing to libraries.

Even governments participated. The U.S. Congress, during the depths of the Civil War, found the time to pass legislation that made it possible to establish dozens of land-grant universities, some of which have become world-class institutions of higher education. Today, a local American community spends nearly 80 percent of its budget on education. During the Cold War (1940s–1990s), up to 85 percent of all R&D in the United States was funded by the American government. Western European governments also invested heavily in creating knowledge. In short, there existed multinational cultures that from their beginnings understood the value of knowledge.

The U.S. economy exploited information aggressively. Faster than either Europe or Asia, the percent of American employees who became what we eventually learned to call knowledge workers was always the highest. Historians today believe the shift to a knowledge-based economy in the United States and Canada began sometime in the middle of the nineteenth century, while the historic shift to clerks and office workers at the expense of the percentage of workers in manufacturing dates back to World War I. As historical studies on knowledge work are done, the actual start date gets pushed back further.

RISE OF THE KNOWLEDGE WORKER

Where did knowledge workers come from? More important, how did they come into existence? Social historians also want to know what causes the rise of a new class of knowledge worker and what are the common features of knowledge workers in general. Definitive answers to these questions do not yet exist because the subject is still a cathedral under construction. However, we know some things.

We have already suggested who knowledge workers are, and we see them all around us; indeed, they have always been around. Some knowledge workers have done the same kind of work for centuries, but only recently have they been characterized as knowledge workers. The obvious suspects include scholars and professors, teachers, priests, ministers, and other clerics, lawyers, accountants and bookkeepers, government office–bound employees (we began calling them clerks and bureaucrats in the eighteenth century), politicians, writers, witch doctors and all manner of medical personnel (not just doctors), and specialized experts on such things as forecasting the future (witch doctors or palm readers; sometimes a duty of priests, as in Greece and the Roman Empire). These professions were added to once the industrial revolution of the eighteenth century came into full blossom: social critics who supported themselves on their writings, inventors who put food on the table through business or patent activities, then clerks, accountants on tax laws and cost accounting, secretaries, office workers, consultants in the early 1900s, and punch card and, later, computer operators and programmers. When one starts to catalog all the types of knowledge workers, all of a sudden the list becomes quite long. It begins to represent a substantial part of the population of any community, despite the observation of economists that for the majority of humankind's modern history, people have been employed first in agriculture and, in the past two centuries, in industry. Even here, we have some curiosities. For example, by the 1980s in such high-technology industries as microprocessors (computer chips) and pharmaceuticals, the number of employees in a factory who directly made a product (i.e., bent metal) often hovers at 10 to 15 percent of all workers at the plant site. Everyone else serves in some support function, many in knowledge work, such as in human resources, work schedulers, and plant management.

By now you might begin to think that everyone is a knowledge worker; we will deal with the implications of that observation later in this essay. However, the more immediate question is "Do knowledge workers share some common characteristics and patterns of behavior?" I would like to propose several that make it possible for one to be called a knowledge worker.

First, a class of knowledge work comes into existence when a body of related information must be collected, applied, and built on for subsequent actions. The expert is the obvious example. As bodies of knowledge on a particular subject come into existence that require substantial investments of time to understand and apply, we see the opportunity for a knowledge worker. When a field of science comes into its own, for instance, you might have a new class of professors or scientists (e.g., physicist, molecular biologist, professor of information science). Does the rise of a particular body of knowledge create the new profession or does the establishment of new knowledge work lead to new knowledge careers? This is a chicken-and-the-egg question. Which comes first? Sociologists studying knowledge work in the late twentieth century would argue that both occur. For example, foreman directing the work of men installing metal girders in a new skyscraper today spend more time entering data into a laptop computer in their pickup trucks than a foreman a hundred years ago spent simply filling out a sheet on workmen's hours. Clearly the iron worker foreman of the 1990s is doing some knowledge work, as is his manager who is trying to figure out what progress is being made on the project and in planning next steps. But would we consider the foreman of a construction crew to be a knowledge worker? Knowledge work is present—tactic and implicit learning and knowledge is alive and well—and this insight is needed to handle the growing complexity of the work. Students of knowledge work, thus, have to deal with our questions about the foreman and with what that means for doing work better and smarter.

As the volume of information about a subject grows, so does the possibility of new specialized workforces to work with that data and its resultant insights. Experts on sources of new funding for home mortgages in the United States or travel agents in nineteenth century Europe have shared the common feature of understanding a body of language and bringing that to others when they need that insight. Travel guides fall into this category too. Complicating the picture is the fact that one can be of a particular profession yet also be a knowledge worker in a related field. A professor of ancient history is a knowledge worker, but he can also be a different type of knowledge worker when he serves as a tour guide to the Holy Lands for European and American tourists during his summer off from teaching. In both circumstances, essentially the same body of information is used, often with similar insights, but also with others drawn from the same information.

Second, knowledge work is often created by the introduction of some new knowledge handling technology. This truth is massive in application. Examples are everywhere. Telegraph operators became a class of workers after the telegraph was invented in the 1840s. Telephone operators came into being after the invention of the telephone. Women could become secretaries in large numbers after the invention of the typewriter and a variety of other office equipment, such as adding machines and calculators. With the invention of computers and software, it became possible for men and women to make a living as computer programmers or as systems analysts.

The central features of this kind of work includes:

- an intimate understanding of how the technology works (e.g., the worker knows how to type, answer the phone, and advise a boss)
- appreciation of how to apply that technology to create new information or knowledge for someone (e.g., using an adding machine to do new forms of acccounting, or the telephone to advise a client when to buy and sell stock)
- expansion of the overall culture and insight of a body of knowledge (e.g., improving the ability of a doctor to perform a specific type of operation).

These workers, in turn, create new bodies of information and more sophisticated levels of knowledge. Into this class we can put scientists and engineers, who are continuously adding to humankind's understanding of many issues.

Related to this is the growing body of knowledge about how to increase and improve knowledge. For example, scientists' training is different (hopefully better) than was the case in the fifteenth century. The use of specific technologies makes it possible to entertain new pedagogical techniques, which is a fancy way of saying that there are now, for instance, new ways to use television to teach students with fewer teachers (distance learning).

Third, knowledge workers increase in number in environments where complexity of work expands at the same time that either the volume of work or the size of the organization in which it is done grows. Historians now understand very clearly that one of the primary causes of the enormous increase in the number of clerks in offices in the twentieth century is a direct result of the expansion in the size of organizations, such as the rise of corporations on the one hand and the expanded role of governments on the other. The same occurred with the success of the new Christian Church late in the history of the Roman Empire, making it possible for the Vatican to come into existence. The expansion of the Chinese Empire into its final unified entity by 1400 A.D. had been an historic process of growth lasting over a thousand years. Expansion and control called for vast armies of knowledge workers who could govern the empire in an efficient manner consistent with the wishes of the central administration. That government improved its understanding of China and of government administration over the centuries— classic knowledge work—but would not have done so if the early emperors had not been ambitious conquerors.

Complexity of work creates new knowledge work. A very recent example involves the personal computer. Prior to the arrival of the PC in the late 1970s, a user of such a device had little or no support. A decade later, these machines were in wide use in government and business by people who knew little about the technology; thus their organizations began to populate offices with experts who could help them use the equipment. In the 1990s, when these disparate machines were linked together in networks, the need for telecommunications and PC experts rose. In fact, this happened so fast that there are now "rules of thumb" about how many of these "help" functions you need (e.g., one for every fifty users in a network). Programmers of software tools were generalists in the 1950s, but by the end of the 1960s had become specialists in specific languages, applications, and types of software tools (e.g., database managers, systems analysts). Complexity caused people to invest significant amounts of time, effort, and other resources in order to be effective. That is how complexity contributed directly to the creation of more knowledge work.

Those who needed more information, but did not necessarily spend all their time with that data (e.g., our foreman of iron workers) provided a profound incentive for the expanded hiring of knowledge workers. But the key sources of these jobs invariably were growing job complexity and the need for information to control operations.

THE HISTORY OF THE STUDY OF KNOWLEDGE WORK

The term "knowledge work" first appeared in the late 1950s—during the first decade of commercial use of the computer—and owes its origins as much to Fritz Machlup as to anyone. While Peter Drucker may have popularized the term in the same period, it was the hard analytical work done by Machlup that firmly established the reality. Machlup was a distinguished economist who spent from 1950 until his death in 1983 studying knowledge and its creation, distribution, and economic significance. In 1962, he published *The Production and Distribution of Knowledge in the United States,* in which he presented the idea that knowledge was a major item of production within the U.S. economy. He also described a new kind of worker who was responsible "for the entire spectrum of activities, from the transporter of knowledge up to the original creator." Machlup included clerks, teachers, and researchers as knowledge workers. In a series of subsequent books, he refined his definition of what knowledge workers did and who they were. His definitions have influenced students of the subject down to the present.

Machlup estimated that by 1958, information activities absorbed 29 percent of the GNP in the United States—considered at the time to be the leading home of knowledge workers. He also estimated that 31 percent of the workforce were knowledge workers and that between 1947 and 1958 this sector had grown at twice the rate of the GNP as a whole. Other economists began documenting this sector for subsequent years, with consensus forming that the information sector occupied about 40 percent of the GNP in the 1970s. In other words, as people began to look at who was a knowledge worker, they increased the percentage of the workforce fitting this new category.

William J. Baumol and his team of American economists, while identifying the dynamics of U.S. economic productivity, also noted the enormous increase in the number of individuals who spent their time exchanging information: "Between 1960 and 1980, data workers increased relative to total employment in all industries except trade and the government sectors, where they declined slightly in percentage terms." Baumol further observed that as a whole, "Information workers increased in number relative to noninformation workers in all sectors except trade" in these decades. Driving this growth was the complexity of business processes that required both more information with which to function and better-educated and -trained workers.

The most recent work done to analyze the size and dimension of the knowledge worker community in the United States has been done by Jorge Reina Schement and Terry Curtis. Their research has led them to conclude that information activities are being broadly incorporated into a much wider set of jobs than previously thought. For example, supervisors increasingly have data handling work (i.e., paperwork) to do. Second, their analysis of the workforce indicates that information workers outnumbered agricultural workers in the 1920s and overshadowed industrial workers by the start of the 1930s, and then continued to grow after the end of the depression of the 1930s. What these and other students of the American workforce are beginning to teach us is that workers who created knowledge had less technological support than data workers who could rely directly on computers, telephones, publications, and so forth to transmit and manipulate information. Those tasks largely drove demand for computers and, later, to creation of more knowledge worker jobs (e.g., computer programmers). Baumol studied the relative growth rates of knowledge workers versus other types of workers (e.g., manufacturing) for the entire period, concluding that the number of knowledge workers expanded largely because of their substitution for other types of workers within the economy. They accounted for some 70 percent of the growth in the 1960s and 84 percent in the 1970s. While there is debate about how productive these people were, what is unmistakable is the increase of knowledge and information content in the general activities of the American economy. Over time, growing numbers of these workers relied on computers to perform their jobs. Baumol demonstrated that by the second half of the 1980s, knowledge workers occupied 52 percent of the workforce. We do not have any comparable studies on knowledge workers in Asia (particularly Japan) or for Western Europe, so for the time being, American patterns have to serve as starting assumptions for any projection of non-U.S. knowledge work.

While the question of why there has been such a shift in the workforce is still subject to much controversy, one popular argument, put forth most forcefully by James R. Beniger, is that there occurred a "Control Revolution, a complex of rapid changes in the technological and economic arrangements by which information is collected, stored, processed, and communicated" to which the computer contributed, along with a wide array of office appliances of the last third of the nineteenth century and all of those of the twentieth. He argued effectively that as manufacturing and distribution sped up and became more complicated, the need for information with which to control economic activities drove up the demand for information and knowledge. He documented that this process began soon after the U.S. Civil War (post-1865) and continued to the present.

Beniger has allies. Schement and Curtis have argued that "profitability of large corporations depended on efficient management, and that efficient management depended on information. As a result, the number of information workers employed in large corporations grew rapidly in the first decades of the twentieth century." They noted that the increase of clerical and kindred workers grew by nearly 500 percent between 1900 and 1930. An additional growth of 220 percent occurred in the next thirty years. Growth rates for professional, technical, and kindred workers were similar in the same period.

These are constrained views of knowledge work, because they leave out religious workers, lawyers, teachers, and probably other professions, although Machlup included some of these in his analysis. But regardless of whose numbers one uses, we are presented with a workforce in the post-World War II United States that expanded in an age when, for a variety of reasons, work had become more complex, and hence was in need of more sophisticated forms of control. Information content—for performance of work and then for the manufacture, use, and service of products—became a fundamental feature of U.S. business activity during the past half century.

Other sources of knowledge workers are appearing around the world. At the risk of being too U.S.-centric, one could argue that the uptick in the globalization of the world's economy—a clear and widely acknowledged feature of the economy at the end of the twentieth century—has been driven largely by two American developments: global implementation of computers and telecommunications on the one hand and, on the other, the enormous expansion of American corporations and their national subsidiaries around the world.

Economic historians would eagerly rush in and add that a long-standing historic pattern of behavior has included waves of economic prosperity that swirled around the globe periodically over the centuries. That means, for example, that the impetus has been toward economic equalization around the world, barring some momentary peculiarities of a government's economic policy (such as a local trade barrier), inflation-fighting monetary reform, or excessive import tax. The fact that this does not occur exactly as implied does not necessarily mean that the influence of global trade or the transfer of technologies, for example, does not occur. Beginning with the great French historian Fernand Braudel in the 1940s, and continuing to the present, historians have been able to document massive volumes of traffic in global trade occurring for centuries, even in neolithic times. Historians of technology have also demonstrated a global propensity to distribute knowledge and technologies. So the globalization of the economy, which everyone seems to be saluting at the end of the twentieth century, is really not-so-new news. That long-standing pattern suggests knowledge work probably has developed around the world in ways similar to those detailed in cases available in the United States.

When knowledge workers were "discovered" by the academics, one could suppose it would be inevitable that the nature of knowledge work would come under the microscope. Nowhere has this been more so than among professors of business administration and management consultants. Their literature on the subject just from the past two decades can only be described as substantial, and for the past half dozen years, vast. It is, to put it crudely, a "hot topic" as this essay is being written (1998). But the issues are familiar because they have concerned students of knowledge work for some time. Using the American experience simply helps to frame the subject.

Several students of the changing nature of work illustrate how knowledge began to increase its role in economic activity over the past two decades. A highly respected professor of business administration at Dartmouth College, James Brian Quinn, published in 1992 an important description of how knowledge- and service-based practices were beginning to change the structure of corporations, government agencies, and even the configuration of the world's economy. In *Intelligent Enterprise,* he presented the case for why and how corporations could be competitive in the future only if they exploited their core competencies. To do that required companies to leverage their intellectual assets, and Quinn cited many examples of the process at work. Through his cases, drawn from companies around the world, we had solid proof that knowledge work was rising in importance and had been for well over a decade prior to the publication of his book.

Next, business managers began using the work of Gary Hamel and C. K. Prahalad who, in 1994, published *Competing for the Future.* They argued that the key to future economic success for a firm lay in creating and controlling emerging opportunities. What made the message novel was the fact that they viewed corporations less as clusters of financial and physical assets, and more as collections of skills. Relying on intellectual assets to define and dominate new markets was the key. Their message and examples reinforced Quinn's, but with the added effect of wide endorsement because their book became a best-seller, cited by many executives as influential.

The messages delivered by these two books made the whole notion of knowledge work a very conscious issue by the mid-1990s in East Asia, Western Europe, and the United States. That consciousness also came on the heels of a decade-long process of corporations and national governments adopting what came to be known as "quality management" practices. Originated in the United States through the work of W. Edwards Deming and Joseph Juran (among others) in the 1940s and 1950s, but most embraced and substantially refined by Japanese companies in the 1950s and 1960s, underlying principles included fact-based decision-making, having employees understand how processes were working through application of quantitative measurement techniques, and empowerment of lower-level workers to make decisions based on those facts. This development applied to both white- and blue-collar workers. Western companies resisted adopting these practices until the early 1980s, only to find that they did frequently improve efficiency of operations. As an unintended consequence, however, the value of knowledge work received another energizing jolt. This new interest built nicely on the increasing availability of information made available by expanded use of computers all through the 1960s and 1970s. By the mid-1990s, we, thus, faced a situation in many parts of the industrialized world where corporations and many government agencies viewed skills and institutional intellectual capital as assets at least as valuable as the raw materials, inventories, buildings, and cash of old.

As this realization spread, it seemed inevitable that scholars and consultants would attempt to define knowledge work not so much the way Machlup and his colleagues had in earlier years in macroeconomic terms, but in tactical operational language. Much of this new work involved merging the power of computers with analytical practices of quality management and a growing body of scientific and pedagogical research on the nature of learning, knowledge, and application of skills.

The work of Thomas H. Davenport and Laurence Prusak demonstrated the codification of what many were touting as the new age of knowledge work. While their operational recommendations were new, those who would be doing the work had been in the workforce for decades. Davenport, a professor at the University of Texas and a former consultant, brought to his interest knowledge of information technology and quality management practices. Prusak, also with a consultant's heritage, had been formally trained as an historian, thus, bringing a sound liberal arts background to the task at hand. They took the strategic messages of Quinn, Hamel, and Prahalad down one level to tactics. They documented how organizations created knowledge and codified it for employees to use. They described how to share it, what technologies to use, and how to manage the process. Deming and Juran would have been very pleased with their message because they saw it as central to any organization's success. Davenport and Prusak also acknowledged the obvious: it was a "new emphasis on an age-old subject." In their book, *Working Knowledge* (1998), they illustrated the tactical application of knowledge work with examples from around the world, providing yet additional evidence that knowledge work is expanding globally. Like Quinn and the others, their cases were from various industries and continents.

THE FUTURE OF THE ORIGINS OF KNOWLEDGE WORK

I have suggested that knowledge work, and the study of knowledge workers, is nothing less than a growth industry for academics, consultants, and business managers. My expectation is that this will remain the case for some time to come because:

- the world's economy continues to evolve into an increasingly complex and technical form
- consequently, the amount of information needed is rising, not declining
- new proven ways of applying knowledge to generate profits in business or improve quality of life by governments is increasing.

Analysis of knowledge work will follow, as does all academic study of new trends, promising a greater understanding of knowledge work and knowledge workers.

This last point—that analysis and study will increase—in addition to following the same pattern of all knowledge work, promises to inform managers of companies, universities, and governments about how to apply knowledge to their core activities. Like the thousands of generations before ours, each contributed to humankind's stockpile of information, knowledge, and knowledge work.

The growing interest on the part of historians in the subject of knowledge workers is novel, particularly as concerns the subject of those employed in making a living. As we have seen above, historians studied the careers and work of lawyers, ministers, teachers, and librarians as purveyors of information and knowledge. But the historical analysis of knowledge work in business and government is relatively new. Unlike traditional labor history—which does have a long history of its own—this new history concentrates less on the contractual relationships between management and unions, and more on the tasks performed outside of the traditional scope of manufacturing, agricultural, and retail clerking. The process by which historians are coming to the subject is no different than for other aspects of business history.

Study in this area began with economists finding new patterns of employment and work content. Then came the sociologists who examined work environments, taking the macroeconomic activities down to the level of specific case studies of people at work. Next, business professors began to identify strategic implications of this changing nature of work. They normally paid less attention to the sociologists and more to the economists for their background data. Consultants are usually hired in droves when organizations are experiencing change. Therefore, it was no surprise that management consultants would begin to turn their attention to the tasks of knowledge work at about the same time that business management professors were describing its strategic implications. The two began merging together. Then came the historians.

The questions of concern to historians are broad. In many instances, the original motivation for studying knowledge work revolved around three issues:

- roles of community leaders, such as politicians, doctors, and teachers
- political and intellectual values and practices of a nation, such as American democracy
- gender themes, leading to examination of the role of working women, often leading to the study of secretaries, clerks, and telephone operators.

Related areas of research that have long captured the interest of historians include intellectual history (usually the history of different philosophies, literature, or disciplines), the history of education and pedagogy, the evolution of technology, the history of science, and the histories of military and political work. Each of these broad themes have their own questions, issues, and research concerns. However, they all are roads into the broader subject of knowledge work.

Historians are looking at a number of issues related to the theme of knowledge work:

- Who were the knowledge workers of different times and places?
- What did they do at work?
- How were they rewarded and punished, and when were they considered successful?
- What effect did they and knowledge work have on the success or failure of companies, government agencies, and specific industries and national economies?
- How did knowledge work come about and why?
- What effect did knowledge work have on the values of individuals, companies, and nations?

CONCLUSIONS

Futurists, journalists, economists, sociologists, and business professors writing about the future of work are enthusiastic students of the contemporary features of knowledge work. However, their efforts are not yet well-informed by the history of knowledge work. As a result, we can, as we have learned about other aspects of modern work and technology, continue to expect that they will not "get it right." What we have learned by looking at how, for example, contemporaries forecasted use of computers, atomic energy, process reengineering, and global competition, is that their predictions were invariably incorrect and often overstated. Those who have grounded their work in historical experience, like Peter Drucker, have fared much better over the course of the twentieth century.

This is the harsh reality that we can bring to bear in learning about knowledge work. The faster we can appreciate patterns and practices of knowledge work, the easier and more effective it will be to implement what is rapidly emerging as a central component of the third industrial revolution. Change, as historians are willing to point out, is never quite the same as in the past, but not so dissimilar that we can't recognize what to do from earlier experiences. While historians like to tell us what did not work in the past, and always avoid predicting the future, we can learn about the nature of knowledge work from them. We can learn how companies, industries, and even whole economies evolved over time, applying those insights in three areas:

- lowering the risks of failure as our organizations become more service-based
- relying increasingly on intellectual capital to be competitive
- deploying a workforce that houses many of the crucial assets of the corporation in their heads.

Harnessing those realities is, after all, the whole reason we are interested in knowledge work in the first place.

The selections presented in the rest of this book were chosen with the purpose of suggesting the origins of knowledge workers, what their work has been and continues to be, and how their activities influence organizations and whole economies. They are few because we wanted to keep them within the confines of one book. So we did not include, for example, descriptions of how Catholic bishops work, or how the Roman Empire communicated with all its provinces in an age before the telephone and airplane. In selecting material for this book, nearly ten times as many pieces were candidates for inclusion, suggesting how much useful information has already been put together on the history and practice of knowledge work. Other volumes in the series in which this book is published suggest what some of that material contains. However, the book you are holding in your hand is one of the first that looks at history for practical lessons on the management of modern knowledge work.

2

Gender and the Masculine Business Professions

Sharon Hartman Strom

Two selections are presented here on the history of two major new knowledge jobs created in the second half of the 1800s, bookkeepers and professional secretaries. Professor Strom has studied various women's professions and in her book, *Beyond the Typewriter,* from which these selections come, she explores the evolution of women's work in offices during the period 1900 to 1930. She demonstrates that knowledge work opened new opportunities for women's work beyond farming, household chores, and teaching.

MORE AMBIGUOUS GROUND: ACCOUNTING, STATISTICS, AND BOOKKEEPING

Business administration seemed to emerge out of whole cloth in a single decade, but bookkeeping and accounting had a long history and an enormous constituency. Although some firms had to be sold on the importance of executives trained in business administration, accounting's importance to the new methods of doing business and to government was undeniable. The expansion of accounting and the collection of statistics lay at the heart of changes in office work after 1900. As accounting procedures surged during World War I, demand for statisticians, accountants, and bookkeepers was intense. The growing number of human computers reflected these trends. In 1900 there were nearly 23,000 accountants and 232,000 bookkeepers; by 1930 there were 191,600 accountants and more than 738,000 bookkeepers. The sexual division of labor in bookkeeping and accounting was pronounced but not as absolute as in most other office occupations. Bookkeeping was not as feminized as stenography and typing, and accounting and auditing were not as exclusively male as engineering. By 1930 about 63 per-

From *Beyond the Typewriter: Gender, Class, and the Origins of Modern American Office Work, 1900–1930* (Urbana and Chicago: University of Illinois Press, 1992): 82–93, 342–349. Reprinted with permission.

cent of bookkeepers were women, as were nearly nine percent of accountants (See Table 2.1).

The goal of those committed to the professionalization of accounting was to develop and maintain distinctions between bookkeeping and accounting. Because computing clerks and bookkeepers could claim a role in doing accounts, the professionalization of accounting required the separation of theories of accounting from the mere techniques of bookkeeping. But accountants were not as successful as other professionals in separating "technique" from "theory."

Part of the difficulty in determining who might designate themselves as a professional accountant was in defining exactly what accountants did. There were two main categories of accounting.

Public accounting (initially a form of auditing, or checking account books for errors or fraud) became important at the turn of the century as the financial records of large institutions were subjected to more extensive scrutiny by management, stockholders, and government. The public accountant's job was to vouch for the accuracy and integrity of books, to advise on taxes, and to offer independent consultations. The states began to certify some public accountants, and public accounting firms in large cities offered the services of these licensed experts.

By 1910 a second kind of accounting emerged: managing the finances and cost accounting systems of corporations. The National Association of Cost Accounting was formed in 1919 to link managerial and system designing accounting with the scientific management movement. Comptrollers and treasurers were now more likely to be college-educated accountants who assembled staffs to provide and interpret reams of bookkeeping detail for future planning. Joseph Sterrett of the prestigious public accounting firm Price, Waterhouse told a New York reporter in 1921 that he thought it was still possible for ambitious young men to take up accounting with a high school diploma, but would prefer to see those who wished to enter the profession take a "full college course in general subjects, followed by post-graduate work in accountancy."

TABLE 2.1   Accountants and Bookkeepers in the United States, 1900–1940 (in Thousands)

	1900	1910	1920	1930	1940
Accountants/auditors	29.9	39.2	118.5	191.6	238.0
Male	21.5	35.6	105.1	174.6	218.3
Female	1.4	3.6	13.4	17.0	19.7
Bookkeepers/cashiers	232.0	446.8	615.5	738.2	721.1
Male	159.2	263.3	269.8	272.5	248.4
Female	72.7	183.6	345.7	465.7	472.8

Source: David L. Kaplan and M. Claire Casey, "Occupational Trends in the United States, 1900–1950," Bureau of the Census Working Paper no. 5, Washington, D.C.: Department of Commerce, 1958, 6.

Those who claimed an administrative role for accountants staked out a claim that went beyond what some perceived as the "glorified bookkeeping" of public accountants. The executive accountant, they insisted, was an essential complement to engineers and business administrators in the proper execution of scientific management. Sterrett, a promoter of this view, sought to explicate the differences between public and managerial accounting: "One is analytic as typified by the audit and the examination. The other is synthetic or constructive, instances of which are found in the construction and installation of cost and other systems of accounts. . . . Accountancy . . . will, if those in whose hands its fortunes are entrusted fulfill their part, expand . . . until it will stand shoulder to shoulder in the estimation of the public with those older professions whose courses have been a laborious evolution of years and centuries."

Whether managers or CPAs, accountants continued to articulate what they thought made them different from bookkeepers. Bookkeepers were often described by accountants and managers in the same way that doctors described nurses. Like nurses, bookkeepers were to stay in their place and not entertain ideas of self-importance. The office management expert William Henry Leffingwell thought that the importance of bookkeeping, which was really just "a series of checks and counter-checks on accuracy," was often "overexaggerated." Bookkeepers should realize their mission was to assist professionals who had an overall sense of how things actually worked. Bookkeepers had to keep accurate records but should never aspire to interpret them. The accountant must be the one to confer with the business executive when plans and decisions were to be made. Knowing this fact, Leffingwell claimed in 1917, might enable the bookkeeper to "read into the dull, uninteresting rows of figures real romance and exciting narratives," because "in their books lie valuable data on the solution of almost every business problem." But whereas nurses were clearly female and doctors male, bookkeepers and accountants could be either.

Nor could accountants always define the boundaries between bookkeeping and accounting. George E. Bennett, an advisor on the installation of accounting systems, admitted that the difference between bookkeeping and accounting was often a matter of size and complexity, not a distinct difference in technique: "Bookkeeping records business transactions in Journals and Ledgers. Accounting analyzes and interprets these records. Hence, it is the bookkeeper who compiles data for the accountant. The terms 'bookkeeping' and 'accounting,' therefore, are not synonymous." But as a practical proposition, it is not always possible to make the above sharp theoretical distinction or separation, since frequently the bookkeeper acts as an accountant; in general, it is only in a business that is at least of fair proportions that the fields of bookkeeping and accounting are rather sharply divided.

Accountants turned to the states for licensing legislation in their ongoing effort to separate themselves from bookkeeping technicians, to "raise standards," and to exclude undesirables. Because most early public accounting firms were in New York City, New York was the first state to institute examinations for the licensing of "certified public accountants" in 1896. But in response to intense lobbying from those already calling themselves accountants, the examination was waived for those who had practical experience. By 1914 thirty-three states had CPA licensing laws, but most allowed "grandfathering," or the substitution of a sufficient number of years of experience for the test. A new professional organization, the American Association of Public Accountants, later the Institute of Certified Public Accountants (AICPA), was formed in 1916 to advocate examination, college training, and experience as requirements for certification in all of the states. By 1921 examinations prepared by the AICPA were used in thiry-six states, but resistance to the examination continued. Only thirteen percent of all those who took the examinations in 1921 passed. While the low passing rate might have been an indication that many would-be CPAs had inadequate training and were probably better trained in bookkeeping than in auditing, it also lent credence to the "undesirables'" claims that high-placed public accountants were using the examination's difficulty and arbitrary grading to maintain a monopoly on business for themselves.

The way in which the new professional standards might elevate an accountant into an illustrious career appeared in Hermon F. Bell's progression from lowly bookkeeper to prestigious cost accountant. Bell grew up in New England, where his father owned a retail furniture store. The younger Bell graduated from Amherst in 1901 with a liberal arts degree and took postgraduate courses at Yale in philosophy and religion. In an abrupt departure from his college work, he entered business in 1905 as a sales clerk in a New York department store and then drifted into bookkeeping. In 1908 his employer's books were audited by a small accounting firm, and he recalled that "one of the staff told me that I was wasting my time in bookkeeping and that better jobs would be available in public accounting." He took some accounting courses at a business college and lessons from a downtown accountant to prepare for the CPA examination, which he repeated three times before passing. Meanwhile, he had also gained the practical experience required for certification. After taking some additional courses at the recently established Pace Institute, Bell took a new job at a better firm on Wall Street in 1911 but was still forced to spend most of his time on the road, auditing. In 1913 he moved to the prestigious firm of Lybrand, Ross Brothers, and Montgomery, whose owners were actively involved in the formation of the National Association of Cost Accounting. Bell's firm developed uniform cost accounting for department stores, created a specialty in income tax consultation, and, during the war, worked out cost accounting methods for war contracts. Bell's trajectory to the top of his profession remained exceptional. Most accountants continued to ignore Sterrett's advice to gain a college degree. Application to take state-certified public accountant examinations did not indicate any standard form of education or training. The AICPA found that of its members admitted between 1917 and 1926, only 22 percent were college graduates, and as many as 40 percent did not even have high school diplomas. New York State, which continued to be among the most rigorous CPA licensors, passed legislation requiring college degrees in 1926, but allowed for a twelve-year phasing-in of the new requirement.

Accountants were unable to develop the distinctions that would clearly set accounting off as an elite profession. Accounting continued to be taught in correspondence courses, night schools, private business colleges, and universities. The failure of the elite accountants to exclude the irregulars, some thought, led to lower salaries than in the other professions. "In view of the fact that for many years past such large numbers of college men have been entering the rather limited field of accountancy *per se*," said one observer, "there is some question as to whether there has not been some overcrowding in this occupation." Even accountants trained at the more prestigious business schools felt the effect of an open-door policy. Graduates of the Wharton School of Business, for instance, reported "substantially lower" incomes than their peers in other lines of business. Accounting remained one way for individuals from nonelite groups to enter the business professions just as other doors were closing. Given the rapid growth of the profession, the need for expert accountants, the insatiable demand for computing clerks, and the blurring between bookkeepers' and accountants' tasks, the outright exclusion of women from accounting education and accounting jobs was impossible to maintain. Because increasing numbers of bookkeepers were women and accounting frequently descended into mere bookkeeping—or bookkeeping often turned into sophisticated accounting—the division of labor in business computing was not as clearly delineated as it was in either engineering or medicine. As a result the sexual division of labor in computing remained imprecise, never a good sign for the establishment of an elite profession.

Women seized on the ambivalence in accounting with enthusiasm, partly because occupational advisors urged them to do so. As early as 1914 advisors argued that a woman stenographer or bookkeeper in a public accounting office might "gain sufficient experience in accounting methods to become an assistant accountant," and that "if she were sufficiently interested and able in accountancy and possessed those inborn qualities which inspire confidence, a new field might be hers to develop." The Intercollegiate Bureau of Occupations agreed that "bookkeepers who possess initiative are sure to press on into the more highly specialized fields of expert accounting and cost statistics."

Business college entrepreneurs immediately grasped the extent of the potential market for teaching accounting to women as well as to men. Pace Institute added women accountants to its teaching staff and advisory board, and openly encouraged women to enter the field. Mrs. Florentine D. Goodrich, a Pace graduate and an accountant with the Reo Sales Motor Company of New York, was quoted in Pace advertising brochures specifically aimed at women: "My own commercial experience has shown me that there is a growing demand for Accountancy. . . . I constantly recommend Pace Institute's course of training to women, who, in my opinion, have natural accounting and executive ability."

Despite these opportunities for education in accounting, no woman could expect to follow Hermon Bell's starlike trajectory in the profession. Public accounting had first emerged in England, with a distinct antifemale bias. Most of the English professional societies excluded women, a matter that became a controversy in the British suffrage campaign and was resolved in 1918 when the Incorporated Society of Accountants and Auditors reluctantly amended its charter to admit women. Although "women might make excellent bookkeepers," contended one English accounting expert, "there is much in accountancy proper that is, we think, altogether unsuitable for them." American firms, many of which began as British transplants, continued these prejudices. Hermon Bell recalled that his first employer, a crusty Scotsman, would not even employ women as typists, let alone as accounting clerks. The more prestigious public accounting firms in the United States refused to hire women as junior accountants. Women's exclusion from public accounting firms was critical because practical experience as well as passage of the CPA examination was required for state licensing. In New York, for example, public accountant candidates had to practice accounting for five years, at least two in the employ of a practicing CPA with the rank of at least "junior accountant."

The life of an accountant was initially considered unsuitable for women. In the early years of the century, public accounting was mainly auditing. Accountants spent days or even weeks away from home in boardinghouses and hotels, where they could conceivably gamble, drink, and seek out prostitutes. But by World War I it was possible for professionals to work all year in their home offices. Women accountants, like women architects, could establish their own businesses and compete for clients. Some women did manage to take and pass the CPA test and find jobs with public accounting firms or establish their own; by 1920 there were a handful of women certified public accountants. Alice M. Hill, once a clerical assistant, was a Massachusetts CPA and a supervising accountant with Jordan, Marsh, and Company. A woman named Lowenstein who had passed the New York State bar examination had also recently taken the CPA test and decided to go into accounting because she thought the profession offered fewer obstacles to women than did the law. Her Manhattan office suite was said to be located "in one of the finest buildings in lower Manhattan," and she was said to have "so many clients that a half a dozen busy assistants are necessary to do the work." The appeal of accounting as a more open profession than many others had clearly played a role in Lowenstein's choice.

She said that it is one of the new professions in which women are absolutely unhandicapped by their sex. "For one thing, they can receive the same preparation as men, and that is not true in many other connections. When, for instance, three of five law schools in New York are closed to women and most of the foremost medical schools still reject women students, a woman desiring to enter either profession finds herself handicapped at the very outset. Many women have made conspicuous successes in both fields, but this discrimination against them by schools and colleges is an obstacle that turns many bright women to other fields of endeavor. Accountancy is also one of the few professions in which a woman can reach the topmost pinnacle."

These claims for accounting's acceptance of women were far too sweeping. Only a handful of women took and passed the CPA examination before World War II. But because many men passed themselves off as professional accountants without taking the test, some women did too. Extraordinary success stories surfaced from time to time. Mrs. Caroline Wylie of Sioux City, Iowa, spurned her family's advice to take up teaching and became an office worker in the stockyards instead. The *New York Evening Post* reported in 1921 that her employer insisted she keep a loaded pistol on her desk in case she faced trouble from "the rougher elements." Although she never had to use her gun, she did learn to handle cash inflows of $100,000 a day. Later, when she lived in New York and her husband became ill, she went to work for a lawyer and "gradually became recognized as an expert accountant, and her responsibilities have increased until now she is a recognized public accountant in downtown New York and regularly handles the books of several large corporations."

Most women who studied accounting became accounting or statistical clerks in the employ of business or government and never attempted to become CPAs or to set up their own firms. Business schools cleverly incorporated this reality into their advertising. While an advertisement for the Walton School of Commerce in Chicago in 1918 was clearly aimed at men—"Be a Walton-Trained man"—an advertisement from Pace was aimed at both sexes: "The demand for trained accountants, both men and women, is increasing daily, hourly." The Walton School boasted that many of its students had successfully passed the CPA examination in Illinois and received top-level jobs with corporations and public agencies. Pace did not even mention training for the New York CPA examination and described its graduates as "business technicians," not as professionals. Women who inquired about Pace's courses might also not be directed into accounting but to a "shorter course in accounting for women," which was in reality a glorified bookkeeping course. Nonetheless the advertisement for this course vaguely implied it might lead to something big: "Mastery . . . prepares women for successful entrance into Business through the avenue of accounting records. . . . Women who have this kind of knowledge are in growing demand and are rapidly winning promotion. Beginning as bookkeepers and clerical employees, they can soon aspire to positions of executive consequence."

Accounting remained a profession to which office clerks and bookkeepers, including those who were women, could aspire. The explosion of new accounting systems by 1910 required the hiring of vast numbers of "computers" at every level of the office hierarchy. The widespread availability of accounting instruction combined with the sudden surge in demand for accountants and computing clerks during World War I opened the profession to women in ways that were unheard of in engineering or business administration. While corporate managers did not view women as potential executives, they did hire them as assistants to accountants and statisticians. Smaller businesses might find it to their advantage to hire women as bookkeepers or accounting clerks; discrimination had created a large pool of college-educated women who were qualified for much higher-level work.

Some women bookkeepers did make their way into interesting jobs that bordered on accounting. A survey of "Opportunities for Trained Women in Cleveland Factories" in 1919 found that women headed four of the cost accounting departments of the 125 factories surveyed, and in several were the heads of payroll departments. A middle-aged bookkeeper who lived in Los Angeles worked in a small factory in 1925 and had duties that made her the president's chief assistant. She supervised the plant when the president was away, prepared income tax reports, and handled all financial matters. An unidentified investigator sent out by the Bureau of Vocational Information to observe women working in accounting, auditing, and statistical offices in New York and Pittsburgh in 1919 was disappointed to find only four who could be classified as professional statisticians or accountants. "Financial men," she concluded, "do not seem inclined to give to women the responsibility of final figures." But she uncovered hundreds of women clerks compiling, computing, graphing, and summarizing data.

The federal government hired several thousand women statisticians during World War I. Elizabeth Kemper Adams observed that women graduates of coeducational business programs came to Washington with their professors, "who were acting as experts in various capacities for the government. They collected and organized information. . . . They constructed price tables; they made shipping and tonnage charts. . . . They grew to be authorities on wool and leather and sugar and wheat." It was claimed that these positions were largely beneath the dignity of male business graduates, who could expect to find much better-paying jobs in the private sector.

Wartime shortages of labor and the new importance of figures landed women in statistical and accounting jobs, both in industry and government. A 1909 graduate of Cornell with a degree in history worked as a teacher for a year. She spent the next eight years as a statistical clerk and examiner for the Board of Education of New York City. After taking a year of accounting at Pace she became a statistician for the U.S. Shipping Board in 1919 and then when the war ended moved to a private firm, Arthur and Walter Price Inc. of Paterson, New Jersey. A geology major from the University of Iowa prepared and analyzed cost data at Consolidated Steel Corporation in 1919. A woman who had attended Wellesley College for two years began working in the collection department of Lee Higginson and Company in Boston in 1917. After taking night courses in income tax and corporation finance at Boston University, she was promoted to statistical and income tax clerk.

The most prominent woman to be found doing accounting work in the federal government was a career civil servant who received an appointment to head a division of the Internal Revenue Service. She had been educated at Indiana State Normal but had never worked as a teacher; she came to Washington in 1900 instead to work in the census office. She obtained a B.S. degree from George Washington University in 1910 and a law degree from the Washington College of Law in 1912. After a five-year stint in the Children's Bureau between 1914 and 1919, she was promoted to a $5,000 a year position with the Internal Revenue. But this case was exceptional. A woman supervisor in the U.S. Office of Agricultural Insurance knew of many women employed as statistical clerks by the federal government, but was "convinced that not more than one percent of these women get beyond the drudgery stage in statistical work." Most of the employees at the U.S. Bureau of the Census in 1921 were women, but of the 2,024 women employed, only ten percent were "expert chiefs" or "statistical experts" earning $2,000 or more a year; the rest were stenographers, clerks, and operatives earning $1,800 or less.

Once in jobs and performing them well, these women resented their inability to go further. A woman with a Ph.D. from Cornell had worked at the New York City Department of Finance since 1913. Although she had taken the civil service examination with almost two hundred men and placed at the top of the list, she was categorized as a "statistician" instead of as "examiner" or "investigator." The result was her appointment "at the minimum salary of the next lower civil service salary grade," although she claimed she did work "similar to men who have titles of examiner and investigator." Other women interviewed by the BVI in 1919 believed that they earned less than men doing similar work and that they were passed over for advancement to higher positions despite their qualifications. An actuarial clerk at the New York State Insurance Department reported in 1919 that the chances of "using initiative or taking responsibility . . . are very little for a woman. . . . Men are given opportunity for advancement but women are kept to details and are given poor salaries." "There is no particular method in assigning work here," said one of her co-workers, "nor any particular method of advancement nor of paying salaries. . . . Men are usually paid from one and one half to twice what women are for the same work." A statistician at the Port and Zone Transportation Office said "men make *at least 50 percent more*." A woman who worked at the National Industrial Conference Board in Boston complained that "men are put ahead of women, even knowing less and of much less ability."

The complaints, however, need to be put into context. These largely college-educated women felt entitled to complain because their expectations had been heightened. Many preferred their accounting and statistical jobs to their old occupations, because their new ones were better paying and more interesting. The psychological climate induced by the suffrage movement and changes that made the Civil Service more open to women reinforced a sense that things had to improve eventually. A statistical clerk with the Children's Bureau agreed that men were paid more than women, but emphasized, "this is better than social work!" A statistical clerk in the Department of Commerce thought things were "becoming more favorable in government positions since the federal clerks formed their union and demanded equal pay for equal service regardless of sex." Many hoped that widening opportunities for women might some day include positions of real importance. The IRS department head who earned $5,000 year was predictably optimistic: "perhaps *highest* places [are] not open to women yet, but that is more a question of time." Such optimism was understandable, given the progress women had already made. But the 1920s would not see any significant gains for women at the upper levels of management.

THE PROFESSIONAL SECRETARY

Whether long- or short-term employees, college-educated women in office jobs thought they were entitled to both interesting work and a professional identity. While women with less elaborate educations were certainly often as ambitious as college women, they did not seem to feel they deserved promotions and enhanced responsibilities by virtue of their education alone. College women had been led to expect these things as a result of their college degrees. College women were, perhaps, more vulnerable than most office workers to the expectation that secretarial work was a springboard to more responsible positions.

Sometimes these expectations came true. Jean Aiken Reinke, a 1907 graduate of Wellesley and a widow with two children, returned to the workplace in 1920 as a secretary and office manager in a lawyer's office. She had been able to arrange her hours so that she could work in the afternoon and attend Fordham Law School in the morning. "This came about," she said, "from the fact that I felt I could not progress much farther in my present position, and yet enjoyed law work." She expected to go into partnership with her boss once she was admitted to the bar. Bertha Ives found fulfilling work as the executive secretary for the Republican Women's Committee of New York: "I came here as my first venture with no special secretarial training other than the foundation of a college course and the special training in organization and politics which was gained through work in suffrage. I have been seemingly successful and have enjoyed the work. I have one secretary who is a stenographer under me in my special department. . . . I come and go as the work requires and am out of town and attending meetings in the city a good deal." Both Ives and Reinke had obtained what their college advisors had promised that secretarial work might deliver; interesting, independent work, freedom to arrange their work day as they sought fit, a chance for self-improvement, and a setting appropriate to middle-class women. In these circumstances it was enormously tempting to label the private secretary or office manager a "professional," especially if she had a college degree.

But these experiences were atypical. As reality set in and the grim awareness that talent, hard work, and college education would do little to crack discrimination against women in executive positions, some college women became dismayed and embittered. They had expected careers, not just jobs. Louise Nail, who had a 1923 business degree from the University of Chicago, expressed outrage over her disappointments. Fired from her last job because "she bawled out the vice president," she had gone to work as a secretary at a garment factory. Within months the employer let go the male credit manager making $75 a week and added his duties to hers; she was currently making $40 a week. "I have . . . deep feelings on the lack of opportunities for women in business," she wrote, "and especially those who get in the routine office work positions . . . the possibilities in secretarial work are so limited that I doubt if I would list it as an occupation. About four women graduate from the school of commerce and administration each June, and I hope you will follow their success, or rather lack of success. They all change around a number of times until they come to the conclusion that nowhere will they find an 'opportunity' (that word about which we have heard too much for four collegiate years) and they resort themselves to some position such as mine and wait for anything—matrimony, another equally stupid position, and perhaps a better, more remunerative one."

Money was not the main issue, but rather the right to expect meaningful and rewarding work as the result of a college education. Kathryn Martell of Brooklyn echoed similar themes in the letter she fired off to the BVI in 1925: After several years of experience as private secretary . . . it is my honest opinion that secretarial work at the present time is anything but desirable, and so sincere am I in this opinion that I have prevented two nieces from entering this field. . . . Even ten years ago a capable stenographer was really understudy to some particular individual of standing in the larger corporations and . . . later had a prospect of working into either an executive position or acting as confidential secretary. . . . One has but to glance into the "stenographic departments" of these same corporations today. Efficiency . . . but in what way differing from clean factory work, and with just about as much prospect of a future.

Martell's assumption that there had once been a time when the secretary (especially the woman secretary) was destined to rise to a position of importance was not correct. But the hold of the myth persisted in the advice literature and for individual women. As scientific management techniques took hold, the myth seemed more and more unattainable. Its failure could also be increasingly pinned on the working-class clerk, who supposedly undermined the position of the "educated" secretary.

Others were less angry and judgmental, but felt they had strayed from their original goals and somehow fallen into clerical work and could not get back out again. A woman who had worked as a clerk in an architectural firm in Washington decided to get an architectural degree at George Washington University. She had never managed to work in her profession: "Unfortunately, a number of young women in Washington followed my course, but like myself, were obliged to seek employment elsewhere, because of the inadequate salaries paid and the uncertainty of steady employment . . . one of these young women is now working on maps for the Geological Survey. I have recently secured a Government position, entering at the very bottom, as a stenographer." A BVI interviewer reported that a Smith graduate claimed there were "very few attractions in this field of work, except that it has given her some inside knowledge to managing of the organization. . . . Does not think secretarial work wears well—becomes boring. Is perhaps too easy. Many positions give no chance of initiative." A former Barnard student ruefully commented that "I might be a more contented secretary if I hadn't gone to college."

Both the advice literature and individual clerks struggled to resolve the dream of individual success with the mundane reality that most women in office work might expect. Women who worked in offices but who wanted to think of themselves as professionals had to find some way of distinguishing themselves from what they perceived to be more ordinary workers. The professional secretary, not to be confused with the order-following "mechanical" stenographer, emerged from most discussions of career work in the office as a model for the aspiring middle-class woman.

The choice of the adjective *professional* to modify secretary indicated the status that much of the middle class coveted. There was considerable confusion, not just among college women, over how to think about American professions after 1900. Most people in the newer professions such as engineering, hospital nursing, personnel management, and accounting worked for salaries paid by institutions and corporations and had relatively little control over their own working conditions. What did, exactly, distinguish these professionals from salaried workers like salesmen and stenographers? While a comptometer operator who worked on a strict schedule for wages on a bonus plan under intensive supervision was clearly not a professional, the college-educated secretary who worked for an important executive and had a variety of tasks to do, many of them requiring writing and managerial skills, did seem to do what many professionals did. On the other hand, defining secretaries by educational levels alone remained problematical. The secretary did not need college training to secure or do her job. Could the secretary with a college degree from Simmons really differentiate herself from an office worker with only two years of high school? And once she got her job, could the secretary, whatever her class or educational background, really hope for the individual responsibility and decision-making powers traditionally associated with the professions? Both the overqualified college woman and the upwardly mobile high school woman found themselves in an occupation that might be done professionally, but that in and of itself would never be a profession.

Elizabeth Kemper Adams agreed that the temptation to label a secretary a professional was overpowering, but she advised that doing so was stretching the use of the term. She described ordinary clerical work as "stereotyped, monotonous, . . . humanly deadening, and exhausting," and warned that with newer systems of business training in place, "secretarial work ceases to be an exclusive or preferred line of advancement for either men or women." While the secretary had "a trained mind, an acquaintance with sources of information, and a knowledge of the operations of the business with which she is connected," she remained an "intermediary without final responsibility and with limited independence. . . . Her opportunities even for intellectual development depend largely upon the personality of her employer; and she lacks the stimulus of sharing in the working out of group plans of action. Her position is somewhat like that of the bedside nurse." Adams's solution to this dilemma was again to make the class boundaries clearer between kinds of clerical workers. If one could differentiate between the stenographer and the secretary precisely, then it might be possible "to establish the professional character of the secretarial worker." The Bureau of Vocational Information put Adams's suggestion into practice when it interviewed two thousand office workers in 1925 and began its list of in-depth questions with the chief differences between stenographic and secretarial work. The possibility of settling the issue now seems impossible, but its centrality to the 1925 study reveals the mind set of an earlier generation. It remained critical before 1930 to middle-class women to confine the term *secretary* to those who did secretarial work and to distinguish secretaries from those who allegedly did assembly-line work like stenography.

The answers of the BVI respondents demonstrated the passion with which many secretaries delineated the boundaries between stenographic and secretarial work and the realism with which others analyzed them. Most in the survey agreed that while the stenographer was a "dictating machine, taking and transcribing notes," there was "more elasticity to a secretarial position—a wider scope, a variety of duties—the feeling that one is part of an organization; there is no monotony about the work; greater opportunity for self-expression."

Others observed that in real practice the duties of the stenographer and secretary usually overlapped, and job titles were often the only actual difference between the two occupations. A 1915 graduate of Wellesley who had been at work since 1917 claimed there was "no difference at all" between secretaries and stenographers. The secretary was a "high sounding name which some stenographers assume." She had noticed that some stenographers actually doing secretarial work were stuck with stenographer job titles because they worked for "a parsimonious company" seeking to avoid the payment of "high salaries." Anna Raymond, supervisor of a large stenographic department, agreed that "the line of demarcation between secretaries and stenographers is often very negligible" but also believed it was very important to many women's sense of self-worth. "I know most excellent stenographers who while called stenographers are really secretaries," she commented, "and I have known secretaries who were merely clerks who scorned stenographers, yet the latter commanded a higher salary than the so-called secretaries. . . . I must interview many applicants and I have noticed a certain sneer at the term stenographer with the remark, 'I am looking for a secretarial position.'" "Because of the gum chewing stenographer of newspaper jokes and cartoons," continued another secretary, "many people look down upon stenographers, but the greatest disadvantage is the low salary usually paid. A stenographer is expected to dress well, have a knowledge of English and a more professional knowledge that requires brains and money to acquire. They should be more adequately rewarded." A 1923 high school graduate with six months of training in business college who had already left five jobs, including one where dictaphones had been installed, agreed that "individuals do treat 'secretaries' with more respect than a typist, store clerk, waitress, etc., regarding them more as a co-worker than someone who is doing a service for them."

Some women who worked as secretaries decided that secretarial work was not a real profession. They argued that "a real professional" originated and took responsibility for her or his own work and, most importantly, was never confused with a stenographer. The disdain felt for office work by some women who passed through it on their way to bigger and better things emerged in a lengthy BVI interview with "Miss H." Unable to afford college, she had taken commercial training and then a position with a law firm in California. She managed to save enough to study law at Stanford; with her "finances again at low ebb" in 1920 she became secretary to a prominent California attorney and also did much of his legal work. Having finished her law degree and passed the bar examinations in Kentucky and California, she was currently a law clerk in New York, where she hoped to be admitted to the bar. Miss H. described her own history in strictly individualistic terms. She thought most secretaries remained secretaries because "they hesitate to take on responsibility and in this way waste the time of their employers." For herself, she could never envision returning to secretarial work, which now "looks very small . . . almost menial. It's like being married," she said; "you have always to adapt yourself to someone else's mood. . . . You feel almost as though you prostitute (that may be too strong a word) yourself to making money—for you must sacrifice yourself and approach everything through the point of view of your employer." H's allusion to prostitution grappled with the ever-present dichotomy of the private secretary's (or the stenographer's) job. She was supposed to do her job independently and resourcefully, but she was also supposed, if not to provide sexual services to her employer, then to give him the services of her gender: domesticity, passivity, charm, and endless patience.

It became easier and easier for middle-class women to fall into clerical work, at least temporarily. As office jobs expanded during the war and through the 1920s, well-educated clerical workers with middle-class manners were in demand in towns and cities throughout the country. For women whose parents could not or would not send them to college, clerical work was often the only reasonable choice of employment. Turned away from most of the well-paying professions and no longer willing to settle for teaching, many college graduates decided to break into office work and were enthusiastically advised to do so by their college counselors. Some would rise to important positions within the office or go on to managerial positions, especially in personnel work. A few would be able to use their office job contacts and earnings to secure further professional training and become part of the tiny percentage of women competing in the male-dominated professions.

With office jobs available for the asking, clerical work did become the way in which middle-class women enacted fantasies of their future lives. Mothers' or grandmothers' advice that girls should take typing in high school so they would have "something to fall back on" was not so misguided; women used clerking jobs to support themselves as students, to finance careers as artists and writers, to bide their time until something better came along.

Take, as a final example, the case of the Herbst sisters, Josephine and Helen, who were high school students in Sioux City in 1910 and dreamed about becoming writers. The Herbst parents had fallen on hard times and could not afford college educations for their children. Josephine spent two years in a mediocre midwestern college and worked in her father's store, where she saved enough money to attend the University of Iowa for a year. She secured a job teaching seventh and eighth grade. Helen was unable to attend college at all, at least for the moment, and went straight from high school to teach in a one-room schoolhouse in a country town. Both sisters disliked their teaching positions, and Josephine left hers in 1914 to return to Sioux City, where she studied shorthand, took a job in a lawyer's office, and lived at home. By 1915 she had saved enough money to finish college on the West Coast; Helen had saved enough to attend the University of Wisconsin for a year. Over the next four years Josephine held a series of stenographic positions in the Bay area of California while she got a start in writing. By World War I Helen had married a handsome young farmer and become the society reporter at a newspaper office in Sioux City; Josephine headed to New York to the radical writers' community of Greenwich Village. Both women became pregnant but feared the disruption babies would create in their fledgling careers. They both had abortions, but Helen died of complications in Sioux City. Only Josephine lived on to fulfill the sisters' ambitions, supported in her early years as a writer in New York by secretarial and editing jobs, longing still for Helen's companionship.

The Herbst sisters may have appeared as statistics in overall aggregates of teachers and clerical workers in twentieth-century census figures. On one level they were simply two of countless numbers of women who ended up in predictable women's occupations. But teaching and clerking were never the jobs they wanted, they were the jobs they could get, and therein lay not only, as in Helen's case, the rub of woman's condition, but, as in Josephine's, the possibility of salvation.

3

The Role of the Librarian

James Kendall Hosmer

Think of the earliest knowledge workers and invariably we call to mind the librarian. In the late 1800s it became a formal profession, even forming its own American Library Association. At the 1899 annual conference, the librarian at the Public Library at Minneapolis, Minnesota, spoke about the role of this early knowledge worker. In this entry we see an early description of the tasks and management issues related to the subject of helping people use information.

To propitiate the spirit of the moment, let the exordium of my remarks be a naval figure. On the tumultuous sea of a great city's life, the public library, with its branches, stations, and sub-stations swims like the squadron of an admiral, and the enemy which it forever combats may be described as vacant-mindedness. This vacancy of mind is a thing of protean shapes: now it is the dearth of knowledge, felt by the man of scholarly tastes; now it is the ennui of the fashionable lady, coveting a time-killer between the ball of last night and the opera of tonight; now it is the soul-hunger of the child with eyes just opening upon a world quite unknown; now it is the ignorance of the man of affairs which must be done away with if this and that business scheme is to be pushed to success. Vacant-mindedness has many shapes; but whatever shape it takes, it is always in an American community a desperately aching void, and confronts its antagonist, the public library, with an omnipresent and unsleeping energy that makes needful every resource. The squadron, besides its commander, must have its fleet-captain, chief-of-staff, chief assistant; a head also for each department; and crews larger or smaller of catalogers, desk attendants, reference-clerks, delivery-men, messengers, and janitors. If the campaign of the library is to be effectual, the places from commander down must be properly filled; every hand must know its work and be zealous in it.

From *Papers and Proceedings of the Twenty-First General Meeting of the American Library Association Held at Atlanta, Ga. May 9–13, 1899* (Atlanta: American Library Association, 1899): 54–57.

Since every proper assistant hopes to stand at some time in the chief place—is, in fact, a chief librarian in the making, and is always, if he be suitably ambitious, bettering his equipment with that end in view—it is right to ask, at the outset, what the chief librarian should be. Not long since I saw him described substantially as follows: He should, first of all, possess firm health. He should have wide knowledge of men and women, and the power of meeting them with firmness and good-nature. He should have seen the world in various lands through having been to some extent a rolling-stone; provincialism should be polished off from him, his back should possess no lodgment of moss. He should be an administrator, with lively initiative tempered by cool judgment, with a sharp eye for the qualities that tell in the men and women whose work he directs, with persistency tempered by geniality in pushing a policy, with all screws so far from being loose that to rattle him shall be out of the question. He must be a man of thorough academic education, able to read, if not to speak, the great ancient and modern tongues, and as widely read as possible in all literatures. Morally, he must be possessed of lamb-like patience, of lion-like courage, of sunny spirit, of invincible push. The ideal librarian, in fact, should possess wings that drag on the floor. Among poultry of the celestial kind, if he be fully equipped for his work, not Gabriel himself will surpass him in the splendor of his feathers—and all this fine plumage he must be prepared to prink and trim usually upon a very modest stipend.

Since every assistant is potentially a chief and aspires to be a chief, let the assistant have in his eye some such figure as this. But while chiefhood, so to speak, remains in abeyance, what, precisely, is the assistant's field? To recur to the naval figure, in large operations, beside the admiral must always be the fleet captain, chief-of-staff, first assistant; and the chief-of-staff is often scarcely less important than the commander himself. Gneisenau, indeed, in the belief of many, made Blücher; Moltke certainly made the princelings who were in the foreground in the wars of '66 and '70: just so I believe there are fleet-captains that have made admirals, and first assistants who have made librarians. To try to distinguish between the spheres of the librarian and the first assistant, perhaps we may say that the former should be occupied by grand strategy—the latter with tactics. In his warfare against the vacant-mindedness about him, the void that ever aches and keeps him forever on the alert, the chief librarian must take the broad view. In his arsenal of books what deficiencies need to be made good that his fire may be well sustained: where shall he put his branches and stations that assault may be most quickly and effectively met? How shall he replenish the stock of information in his own mind, knowledge growing from more to more, day by day, as it does; and what time can he find to be productive himself, working to stimulate the better tastes of his community, to supply information, to add prestige to his institution by making it a center of scholarship and worthy literary accomplishment? With all this, certainly the hands and the mind of the librarians will be well filled. It is indispensable that he should have at his side one whose function shall be to care for the thousand details of administration, the tactics; and if at the same time that one be a man or woman, broad and keen, capable of surveying the strategic plane and of giving advice in the larger field, it will simply be in accordance with the precedents of the great chiefs of staff, who at the right hand of commanders have been of momentous weight in crises.

As to assistants of lower grade, for each there is the round of duties, narrow or broad, to be fulfilled; but I should say the hope of reaching the highest place should never be lost sight of. A footing once gained in a large library, let no subordinate forget that before fidelity and capacity his path will widen toward the top. And here it is in place to speak of a certain discouragement that seems inevitable in the position of an employee in a large library. I remember once, in the great starch factory at Oswego, I saw a company of young women who had acquired astonishing dexterity in doing up packages of starch. Their fingers as they worked were scarcely visible; in a second or two of time the product was properly enclosed and labelled for the market. My guide said these girls did nothing but this; every other part of the manufacture was as unknown to them as if they were strangers in the factory. This very dexterity was a bar to any enlargement of their sphere of work. It was to the interest of the Kingsfords that they should be kept at the one thing, this deftness increasing all the time through the limitation, but with a sacrifice of all breadth of training.

Political economists have often noticed the trouble which comes in factory life from a close division of labor, each worker having his own little task at which he becomes infinitely dexterous, but knowing nothing else. Division of labor is pushed sometimes to such an extent as to produce even physical deformity. One set of muscles becomes abnormally developed while another set withers—the fingers become quick while the legs shrink. In a large library something approaching this is quite possible. The capable assistant, aspiring to a broad efficiency, feels that it is a misfortune to him to be kept to one task; that it would be far better for his training if he could change his work, discharging in turn each one in the various round of labors. In practice, however, what inevitably comes to pass? A writes a faultless hand, and has a marked spirit of neatness and system. In utilizing his staff the library head, having in view the good of the institution, naturally assigns A to the catalog. B has poise, a ready smile, firmness, combined with a quick eye and prompt mind; B therefore goes naturally to the issue desk. C, having dealt much with books, and possessing a retentive memory, has become deeply read; C goes to the reference-room. D, self-reliant and full of executive force, will, it is likely, be charged with the direction of a branch. A, B, C, and D, once placed, may find it no easy thing to get away from their respective spheres. As years go by the natural aptitude of each becomes more and more fully developed. The little groove of the first month becomes a well defined rut. In his rut the assistant becomes skillful, but his very skill operates to his detriment. With a helper of such marked efficiency in the place, it is not economy to employ there anybody else.

Every head of a large library, I suppose, is more or less beset with petitions from those of his staff who feel that they are side-tracked in corners or lost in these ruts, who weary of the monotony of their tasks, and long to develop in other work powers almost untried. If the librarian, however, is disposed to yield to the pressure, straightway from the head cataloger, from the superintendent of circulation, or the superintendent of branches, comes remonstrance: "Smooth running of the library machine requires that A, B, C, and D shall each stay in his place. To break in new people will cause embarrassment; they themselves, though highly skilled in one way, in other ways are but tyros, and must be broken in with loss of time and patience."

I believe I do not exaggerate the matter. As in a great factory, so in a large library, the most economical utilization of the forces of the employees seems sometimes to require a sacrifice of the individual, for whom rounded symmetry of growth is better than one-sidedness. Many an assistant in a large library has doubtless felt he has had no fair chance, and very likely may have reached the opinion that, as a training-school, a small library is really to be preferred, where work of all kinds must be done; just as I have heard a great banker say that, for a business training, a cross-roads country store was vastly better than a huge city establishment. I can think of no way for fully meeting this difficulty. The welfare of the employees in a large library must perforce be a secondary consideration, the first demand being the efficient and economical service of the public. Something may be done by a well organized system of staff meetings. If these can be regularly held—say once a week during six months of the year—the heads imparting each one the lore of the department which he superintends, the subordinates giving time out of hours to learning the tasks with which, in the daily routine, they have no concern, certainly something can be done toward a well rounded development. Important incidents of such a system of meetings are the fostering in the members of the staff of friendly acquaintance, the springing up of *esprit du corps,* the knitting of the links necessary to proper co-operation. The large library lacks an important, indeed an indispensable thing, which does not make provision for an efficient system of staff meetings.

Let the assistant aspire always to the high places of the profession, and always keep in view the great ideals. And here let me combat for a moment a conception of the librarian's character, which in my judgment is incorrect, and which, if it prevails, I believe will effect seriously the dignity of our profession. Talking not long since with the librarian of a large library in his office, an office which had few suggestions of books, and might as well have been the office of a banker of a manufacturer, he told me that his work was purely administrative. Passing judgment upon books, their selection, classification, cataloging, as well as charging and discharging at the desk—all these functions were in the hands of subordinates. Nor had he time to study or write in any line, his energies being quite absorbed in executive work—the control of his large staff, the oversight of a widely extended and highly complicated system of distribution, the receipt and expenditure of large funds. The librarian referred to did not think it right that his energies should be, thus, exclusively absorbed in administration; it was, however, in his case, inevitable.

I am old-fashioned enough to feel it will be a sad day for our profession when the qualities required in the high places are for the most part the same qualities required for the successful running of a department store. It has been asserted that librarianship had come to that—that it was quite a secondary consideration whether or not the librarian should be a bookish man. Heretofore the heroes of our profession have been a Lessing, librarian at Wolfenbüttel, greatest scholar and critic of his time, giving to the world while discharging his office the "Education of the human race," and "Nathan the Wise"; a David Hume, librarian of the Advocates' Library at Edinburgh, while busy in his place, ranking as the soundest philosopher and best historian of Scotland; a Justin Winsor, while librarian at Boston and Cambridge, rising to be the first authority in America in his great field; a William F. Poole, librarian at Boston, Cincinnati, and Chicago, at the same time in each great city leading as critic and antiquarian. Or to refer to honored men still living who, however, greatly to the loss of our calling, have laid down their professional burden, I point to Richard Garnett, Keeper of Printed Books in the British Museum, and always prolific in the directions of biography and the choicest belles lettres; and to Joseph N. Larned, librarian at Buffalo, but becoming in the widest and profoundest sense a scholar as regards the records of human achievement.

Heretofore such men as these have been our cynosures. Has the time arrived when such ideals are superseded—when the model librarian shall be chiefly a man of affairs, a man to run a department store, while erudition and literary capability are matters of small account? One would say that it was a good thing to have at the head of a large library a man who by achieving something in the realm of literature had gained among his fellows a position of some authority—who naturally would be looked up to to direct in choosing books and following out courses of reading—who placed as he would be at the intellectual center of his city might be a spring out from whom should flow a constant, if not always, perceptible stream of influence, working directly, and also in a thousand subtle ways, for the refinement of taste, the propagation of true learning, the bringing to pass in general of sweetness and light. One would say that capability of this sort should count as much looking toward high position as the kind of capability that provides for the introduction of automobiles and the wireless telegraph in the delivery system at the most expedient time, that the heaviest possible discount shall be knocked off the bills of the bookseller, that the staff, while lavish of skill and labor, shall be always low-salaried and yet always good-natured.

It is not necessary to feel, however, that the scholarly and the administrative faculties cannot be combined in one man. It is much to ask, but as the world evolves, higher and higher becomes the type of man demanded. To recur again to the navy, the distinction between the officers of the line and the engineers has been abrogated; the captain must be able to run the machinery, the engineer must be capable of commanding the ship. The great librarian must have the executive, and also the bookish gifts. There have been such librarians; there will be such librarians hereafter; what is demanded will be provided. If, however, it were the case that such gifts were incompatible, and that in the need for capable administration, scholarship and literary taste should come to be held of small account, the dignity of our profession would be lowered most unfortunately.

4

The Middle Class

C. Wright Mills

This sociologist at Columbia University wrote one of the most important modern works on American society. *White Collar: The American Middle Classes* (1951) quickly became a minor classic because it was a well done and an early look at the new middle classes of the mid-twentieth century. Their careers were built largely out of knowledge work. An important critic of American society, Mills also wrote other books, *The Power Elite* and *The Sociological Imagination.* The selection below comes from his classic, *White Collar,* and is one of the earliest attempts to define the make-up of middle class work.

In the early nineteenth century, although there are no exact figures, probably four-fifths of the occupied population were self-employed enterprisers; by 1870, only about one-third, and in 1940, only about one-fifth, were still in this old middle class. Many of the remaining four-fifths of the people who now earn a living do so by working for the 2 or 3 percent of the population who now own 40 or 50 percent of the private property in the United States. Among these workers are the members of the new middle class, white-collar people on salary. For them, as for wage-workers, America has become a nation of employees for whom independent property is out of range. Labor markets, not control of property, determine their chances to receive income, exercise power, enjoy prestige, learn and use skills.

OCCUPATIONAL CHANGE

Of the three broad strata composing modern society, only the new middle class has steadily grown in proportion to the whole. Eighty years ago, there were three-quarters of a million middle-class employees; by 1940, there were over

From *White Collar: The American Middle Classes* (New York: Oxford University Press, 1951, 1956): 63–76. Reprinted with permission.

twelve and a half million. In that period the old middle class increased 135 percent; wage-workers, 255 percent; new middle class, 1600 percent.

The Labor Force	1870	1940
Old Middle Class	33%	20%
New Middle Class	6	25
Wage-Workers	61	55
Total	100%	100%

The employees composing the new middle class do not make up one single compact stratum. They have not emerged on a single horizontal level, but have been shuffled out simultaneously on the several levels of modern society; they now form, as it were, a new pyramid within the old pyramid of society at large, rather than a horizontal layer. The great bulk of the new middle class are of the lower middle-income brackets, but regardless of how social stature is measured, types of white-collar men and women range from almost the top to almost the bottom of modern society.

The managerial stratum, subject to minor variations during these decades, has dropped slightly, from fourteen to ten percent; the salaried professionals, displaying the same minor ups and downs, have dropped from 30 to 25 percent of the new middle class. The major shifts in over-all composition have been in the relative decline of the sales group, occurring most sharply around 1900, from 44 to 25 percent of the total new middle class; and the steady rise of the office workers, from 12 to 40 percent. Today the three largest occupational groups in the white-collar stratum are schoolteachers, salespeople in and out of stores, and assorted office workers. These three form the white-collar mass.

White-collar occupations now engage well over half the members of the American middle class as a whole. Between 1870 and 1940, white-collar workers rose from 15 to 56 percent of the middle brackets, while the old middle class declined from 85 to 44 percent.

New Middle Class	1870	1940
Managers	14%	10%
Salaried Professionals	30	25
Salespeople	44	25
Office Workers	12	40
Total	100%	100%

Negatively, the transformation of the middle class is a shift from property to no-property; positively, it is a shift from property to a new axis of stratification, occupation. The nature and well-being of the old middle class can best be sought in the condition of entrepreneurial property; of the new middle class, in the economics and sociology of occupations. The numerical decline of the older, independent sectors of the middle class is an incident in the centralization of property; the numerical rise of the newer salaried employees is due to the industrial mechanics by which the occupations composing the new middle class have arisen.

The Middle Classes	1870	1940
OLD MIDDLE CLASS	85%	44%
Farmers	62	23
Businessmen	21	19
Free Professionals	2	2
NEW MIDDLE CLASS	15%	56%
Managers	2	6
Salaried Professionals	4	14
Salespeople	7	14
Office Workers	2	22
Total Middle Classes	100%	100%

INDUSTRIAL MECHANICS

In modern society, occupations are specific functions within a social division of labor, as well as skills sold for income on a labor market. Contemporary divisions of labor involve a hitherto unknown specialization of skill: from arranging abstract symbols, at $1000/hr, to working a shovel, for $1000/yr. The major shifts in occupations since the Civil War have assumed this industrial trend: as a proportion of the labor force, fewer individuals manipulate *things,* more handle *people* and *symbols.*

This shift in needed skills is another way of describing the rise of the white-collar workers, for their characteristic skills involve the handling of paper and money and people. They are expert at dealing with people transiently and impersonally; they are masters of the commercial, professional, and technical relationship. The one thing they do not do is live by making things; rather, they live off the social machineries that organize and coordinate the people who do make things. White-collar people help turn what someone else has made into profit for still another; some of them are closer to the means of production, supervising the work of actual manufacture and recording what is done. They are the people who keep track; they man the paper routines involved in distributing what is produced. They provide technical and personal services, and they teach others the skills which they themselves practice, as well as all other skills transmitted by teaching.

As the proportion of workers needed for the extraction and production of things declines, the proportion needed for servicing, distributing, and co-ordinating rises. In 1870, over three-fourths, and in 1940, slightly less than one-half of the total employed were engaged in producing things.

	1870	1940
Producing	77%	46%
Servicing	13	20
Distributing	7	23
Co-ordinating	3	11
Total employed	100%	100%

By 1940, the proportion of white-collar workers of those employed in industries primarily involved in the production of things was 11 percent; in service industries, 32 percent; in distribution, 44 percent; and in co-ordination, 60 percent. The white-collar industries themselves have grown, and within each industry the white-collar occupations have grown. Three trends lie back of the fact that the white-collar ranks have, thus, been the most rapidly growing of modern occupations: the increasing productivity of machinery used in manufacturing; the magnification of distribution; and the increasing scale of co-ordination.

The immense productivity of mass-production technique and the increased application of technologic rationality are the first open secrets of modern occupational change: fewer men turn out more things in less time. In the middle of the nineteenth century, as J. F. Dewhurst and his associates have calculated, some 17.6 billion horsepower hours were expended in American industry, only 6 percent by mechanical energy; by the middle of the twentieth century, 410.4 billion horsepower hours will be expended, 94 percent by mechanical energy. This industrial revolution seems to be permanent, seems to go on through war and boom and slump; thus "a decline in production results in a more than proportional decline in employment; and an increase in production results in a less than proportional increase in employment."

Technology has, thus, narrowed the stratum of workers needed for given volumes of output; it has also altered the types and proportions of skill needed in the production process. Know-how, once an attribute of the mass of workers, is now in the machine and the engineering elite who design it. Machines displace unskilled workmen, make craft skills unnecessary, push up front the automatic motions of the machine-operative. Workers composing the new lower class are predominantly semi-skilled: their proportion in the urban wage-worker stratum has risen from 31 percent in 1910 to 41 percent in 1940.

The manpower economies brought about by machinery and the large-scale rationalization of labor forces, so apparent in production and extraction, have not, as yet, been applied so extensively in distribution—transportation, communication, finance, and trade. Yet without an elaboration of these means of distribution, the wide-flung operations of multi-plant producers could not be integrated nor their products distributed. Therefore, the proportion of people engaged in distribution has enormously increased so that today about one-fourth of the labor force is so engaged. Distribution has expanded more than production because of the lag in technological application in this field, and because of the persistence of individual and small-scale entrepreneurial units at the same time that the market has been enlarged and the need to market has been deepened.

Behind this expansion of the distributive occupations lies the central problem of modern capitalism: to whom can the available goods be sold? As volume swells, the intensified search for markets draws more workers into the distributive occupations of trade, promotion, advertising. As far-flung and intricate markets come into being, and as the need to find and create even more markets becomes urgent, "middle men" who move, store, finance, promote, and sell goods are knit into a vast network of enterprises and occupations.

The physical aspect of distribution involves wide and fast transportation networks; the co-ordination of marketing involves communication; the search for markets and the selling of goods involves trade, including wholesale and retail outlets as well as financial agencies for commodity and capital markets. Each of these activities engage more people, but the manual jobs among them do not increase so fast as the white-collar tasks.

Transportation, growing rapidly after the Civil War, began to decline in point of the numbers of people involved before 1930; but this decline took place among wage-workers; the proportion of white-collar workers employed in transportation continued to rise. By 1940, some 23 percent of the people in transportation were white-collar employees. As a new industrial segment of the U.S. economy, the communication industry has never been run by large numbers of free enterprisers; at the outset it needed large numbers of technical and other white-collar workers. By 1940, some 77 percent of its people were in new middle-class occupations.

Trade is now the third largest segment of the occupational structure, exceeded only by farming and manufacturing. A few years after the Civil War less than five out of every 100 workers were engaged in trade; by 1940 almost twelve out of every 100 workers were so employed. But, while 70 percent of those in wholesaling and retailing were free enterprisers in 1870, and less than three percent were white collar, by 1940, of the people engaged in retail trade 27 percent were free enterprisers; 41 percent white-collar employees.

Newer methods of merchandising, such as credit financing, have resulted in an even greater percentage increase in the "financial" than in the "commercial" agents of distribution. Branch banking has lowered the status of many banking employees to the clerical level, and reduced the number of executive positions. By 1940, of all employees in finance and real estate 70 percent were white-collar workers of the new middle class.

The organizational reason for the expansion of the white-collar occupations is the rise of big business and big government, and the consequent trend of modern social structure, the steady growth of bureaucracy. In every branch of the economy, as firms merge and corporations become dominant, free entrepreneurs become employees, and the calculations of accountant, statistician, bookkeeper, and clerk in these corporations replace the free "movement of prices" as the co-ordinating agent of the economic system. The rise of thousands of big and little bureaucracies and the elaborate specialization of the system as a whole create the need for many men and women to plan, co-ordinate, and administer new routines for others. In moving from smaller to larger and more elaborate units of economic activity, increased proportions of employees are drawn into co-ordinating and managing. Managerial and professional employees and office workers of varied sorts—floorwalkers, foremen, office managers—are needed; people to whom subordinates report, and who in turn report to superiors, are links in chains of power and obedience, co-ordinating and supervising other occupational experiences, functions, and skills. And all over the economy, the proportion of clerks of all sorts has increased: from one or two percent in 1870 to ten or eleven percent of all gainful workers in 1940.

As the worlds of business undergo these changes, the increased tasks of government on all fronts draw still more people into occupations that regulate and service property and men. In response to the largeness and predatory complications of business, the crises of slump, the nationalization of the rural economy and small-town markets, the flood of immigrants, the urgencies of war and the march of technology disrupting social life, government increases its co-ordinating and regulating tasks. Public regulations, social services, and business taxes require more people to make mass records and to integrate people, firms, and goods, both within government and in the various segments of business and private life. All branches of government have grown, although the most startling increases are found in the executive branch of the Federal Government, where the needs for co-ordinating the economy have been most prevalent.

As marketable activities, occupations change (1) with shifts in the skills required, as technology and rationalization are unevenly applied across the economy; (2) with the enlargement and intensification of marketing operations in both the commodity and capital markets; and (3) with shifts in the organization of the division of work, as expanded organizations require co-ordination, management, and recording. The mechanics involved within and between these three trends have led to the numerical expansion of white-collar employees.

There are other less obvious ways in which the occupational structure is shaped: high agricultural tariffs, for example, delay the decline of farming as an occupation; were Argentine beef allowed to enter duty-free, the number of meat producers here might diminish. City ordinances and zoning laws abolish peddlers and affect the types of construction workers that prevail. Most states have bureaus of standards which limit entrance into professions and semi-professions; at the same time members of these occupations form associations in the attempt to control entrance into "their" market. More successful than most trade unions, such professional associations as the American Medical Association have managed for several decades to level off the proportion of physicians and surgeons. Every phase of the slump-war-boom cycle influences the numerical importance of various occupations; for instance, the movement back and forth between "construction worker" and small "contractor" is geared to slumps and booms in building.

The pressures from these loosely organized parts of the occupational world draw conscious managerial agencies into the picture. The effects of attempts to manage occupational change, directly and indirectly, are not yet great, except of course during wars, when government freezes men in their jobs or offers incentives and compulsions to remain in old occupations or shift to new ones. Yet, increasingly the class levels and occupational composition of the nation are managed; the occupational structure of the United States is being slowly reshaped as a gigantic corporate group. It is subject not only to the pulling of autonomous markets and the pushing of technology but to an "allocation of personnel" from central points of control. Occupational change, thus, becomes more conscious, at least to those who are coming to be in charge of it.

WHITE-COLLAR PYRAMIDS

Occupations, in terms of which we circumscribe the new middle class, involve several ways of ranking people. As specific activities, they entail various types and levels of *skill,* and their exercise fulfils certain *functions* within an industrial division of labor. These are the skills and functions we have been examining statistically. As sources of income, occupations are connected with *class* position; and since they normally carry an expected quota of prestige, on and off the job, they are relevant to *status* position. They also involve certain degrees of *power* over other people, directly in terms of the job, and indirectly in other social areas. Occupations are, thus, tied to class, status, and power as well as to skill and function; to understand the occupations composing the new middle class, we must consider them in terms of each of these dimensions.

"Class situation" in its simplest objective sense has to do with the amount and source of income. Today, occupation rather than property is the source of income for most of those who receive any direct income: the possibilities of selling their services in the labor market, rather than of profitably buying and selling their property and its yields, now determine the life-chances of most of the middle class. All things money can buy and many that men dream about are theirs by virtue of occupational income. In new middle-class occupations men work for someone else on someone else's property. This is the clue to many differences between the old and new middle classes, as well as to the contrast between the older world of the small propertied entrepreneur and the occupational structure of the new society. If the old middle class once fought big property structures in the name of small, free properties, the new middle class, like the wage-workers in latter-day capitalism, has been, from the beginning, dependent upon large properties for job security.

Wage-workers in the factory and on the farm are on the propertyless bottom of the occupational structure, depending upon the equipment owned by others, earning wages for the time they spend at work. In terms of property, the white-collar people are *not* "in between Capital and Labor"; they are in exactly the same property-class position as the wage-workers. They have no direct financial tie to the means of production, no prime claim upon the proceeds from property. Like factory workers—and day laborers, for that matter—they work for those who do own such means of livelihood.

Yet if bookkeepers and coal miners, insurance agents and farm laborers, doctors in a clinic and crane operators in an open pit have this condition in common, certainly their class situations are not the same. To understand their class positions, we must go beyond the common fact of source of income and consider as well the amount of income.

In 1890, the average income of white-collar occupational groups was about double that of wage-workers. Before World War I, salaries were not so adversely affected by slumps as wages were but, on the contrary, they rather steadily advanced. Since World War I, however, salaries have been reacting to turns in the economic cycles more and more like wages, although still to a lesser extent. If wars help wages more because of the greater flexibility of wages, slumps help salaries because of their greater inflexibility. Yet after each war era, salaries have never regained their previous advantage over wages. Each phase of the cycle, as well as the progressive rise of all income groups, has resulted in a narrowing of the income gap between wage-workers and white-collar employees.

In the middle thirties the three urban strata, entrepreneurs, white-collar, and wage-workers, formed a distinct scale with respect to median family income: the white-collar employees had a median income of $1,896; the entrepreneurs, $1,464; the urban wage-workers, $1,175. Although the median income of white-collar workers was higher than that of the entrepreneurs, larger proportions of the entrepreneurs received both high-level and low-level incomes. The distribution of their income was spread more than that of the white collar.

The wartime boom in incomes, in fact, spread the incomes of all occupational groups, but not evenly. The spread occurred mainly among urban entrepreneurs. As an income level, the old middle class in the city is becoming less an evenly graded income group, and more a collection of different strata, with a large proportion of lumpen-bourgeoisie who receive very low incomes, and a small, prosperous bourgeoisie with very high incomes.

In the late forties (1948, median family income) the income of all white-collar workers was $4000, that of all urban wage-workers, $3300. These averages, however, should not obscure the overlap of specific groups within each stratum: the lower white-collar people—sales-employees and office workers—earned almost the same as skilled workers and foremen, but more than semi-skilled urban wage-workers. (It is impossible to isolate the salaried foremen from the skilled urban wage-workers in these figures. If we could do so, the income of lower white-collar workers would be closer to that of semi-skilled workers.)

In terms of property, white-collar people are in the same position as wage-workers; in terms of occupational income, they are "somewhere in the middle." Once they were considerably above the wage-workers; they have become less so; in the middle of the century they still have an edge but the over-all rise in incomes is making the new middle class a more homogeneous income group.

As with income, so with prestige: white-collar groups are differentiated socially, perhaps more decisively than wage-workers and entrepreneurs. Wage earners certainly do form an income pyramid and a prestige gradation, as do entrepreneurs and rentiers; but the new middle class, in terms of income and prestige, is a superimposed pyramid, reaching from almost the bottom of the first to almost the top of the second.

People in white-collar occupations claim higher prestige than wage-workers, and, as a general rule, can cash in their claims with wage-workers as well as with the anonymous public. This fact has been seized upon, with much justification, as the defining characteristic of the white-collar strata, and although there are definite indications in the United States of a decline in their prestige, still, on a nationwide basis, the majority of even the lower white-collar employees—office workers and salespeople—enjoy a middling prestige.

The historic bases of the white-collar employees' prestige, apart from superior income, have included the similarity of their place and type of work to those of the old middle-classes' which has permitted them to borrow prestige. As their relations with entrepreneur and with esteemed customer have become more impersonal, they have borrowed prestige from the firm itself. The stylization of their appearance, in particular the fact that most white-collar jobs have permitted the wearing of street clothes on the job, has also figured in their prestige claims, as have the skills required in most white-collar jobs, and in many of them the variety of operations performed and the degree of autonomy exercised in deciding work procedures. Furthermore, the time taken to learn these skills and the way in which they have been acquired by formal education and by close contact with the higher-ups in charge has been important. White-collar employees have monopolized high school education—even in 1940 they had completed twelve grades to the eight grades for wage-workers and entrepreneurs. They have also enjoyed status by descent: in terms of race, Negro white-collar employees exist only in isolated instances—and, more importantly, in terms of nativity, in 1930 only about nine percent of white-collar workers, but 16 percent of free enterprisers and 21 percent of wage-workers, were foreign born. Finally, as an underlying fact, the limited size of the white-collar group, compared to wage-workers, has led to successful claims to greater prestige.

The power position of groups and of individuals typically depends upon factors of class, status, and occupation, often in intricate interrelation. Given occupations involve specific powers over other people in the actual course of work; but also outside the job area, by virtue of their relations to institutions of property as well as the typical income they afford, occupations lend power. Some white-collar occupations require the direct exercise of supervision over other white-collar and wage-workers, and many more are closely attached to this managerial cadre. White-collar employees are the assistants of authority; the power they exercise is a derived power, but they do exercise it.

Moreover, within the white-collar pyramids there is a characteristic pattern of authority involving age and sex. The white-collar ranks contain a good many women: some 41 percent of all white-collar employees, as compared with 10 percent of free enterprisers, and 21 percent of wage-workers, are women. (According to our calculations, the proportions of women, 1940, in these groups are: farmers, 2.9 percent; businessmen, 20 percent; free professionals, 5.9 percent; managers, 7.1 percent; salaried professionals, 51.7 percent; salespeople, 27.5 percent; office workers, 51 percent; skilled workers, 3.2 percent; semi-skilled and unskilled, 29.8 percent; rural workers, 9.1 percent.) As with sex, so with age: free enterprisers average (median) about 45 years of age, white-collar and wage-workers, about 34; but among free enterprisers and wage-workers, men are about two or three years older than women; among white-collar workers, there is a 6- or 7-year difference. In the white-collar pyramids, authority is roughly graded by age and sex: younger women tend to be subordinated to older men.

The occupational groups forming the white-collar pyramids, different as they may be from one another, have certain common characteristics, which are central to the character of the new middle class as a general pyramid overlapping the entrepreneurs and wage-workers. White-collar people cannot be adequately defined along any one possible dimension of stratification—skill, function, class, status, or power. They are generally in the middle ranges on each of these dimensions and on every descriptive attribute. Their position is more definable in terms of their relative differences from other strata than in any absolute terms.

On all points of definition, it must be remembered that white-collar people are not one compact horizontal stratum. They do not fulfill one central, positive *function* that can define them, although in general their functions are similar to those of the old middle class. They deal with symbols and with other people, co-ordinating, recording, and distributing; but they fulfill these functions as dependent employees, and the skills they, thus, employ are sometimes similar in form and required mentality to those of many wage-workers.

In terms of property, they are equal to wage-workers and different from the old middle class. Originating as propertyless dependents, they have no serious expectations of propertied independence. In terms of income, their class position is, on the average, somewhat higher than that of wage-workers. The overlap is large and the trend has been definitely toward less difference, but even today the differences are significant.

Perhaps of more psychological importance is the fact that white-collar groups have successfully claimed more prestige than wage-workers and still generally continue to do so. The bases of their prestige may not be solid today, and certainly they show no signs of being permanent; but, however vague and fragile, they continue to mark off white-collar people from wage-workers.

Members of white-collar occupations exercise a derived authority in the course of their work; moreover, compared to older hierarchies, the white-collar pyramids are youthful and feminine bureaucracies, within which youth, education, and American birth are emphasized at the wide base, where millions of office workers most clearly typify these differences between the new middle class and other occupational groups. White-collar masses, in turn, are managed by people who are more like the old middle class, having many of the social characteristics, if not the independence, of free enterprisers.

Part Two

Recognition of the New Professions

5

Personnel Resources in the Social Sciences and Humanities

U.S. Department of Labor

In 1954, the American Government conducted the largest survey ever done to that point on the role of social scientists, obtaining feedback from over 25,000 individuals across 14 fields of specialization. These ranged from academics in anthropology, economics, and history, to others in sociology, statistics, and linguistics. The study looked at what they did, their backgrounds, and genders. The excerpt below are highlights from this study.

PERSONNEL INCLUDED IN THE SURVEY

The more than 25,000 social scientists who returned usable questionnaires in response to this survey included about one-third of the total number of men and women estimated to have been professionally employed in 1952 in the following social science fields: anthropology, economics, geography, history, political science, sociology, and statistics. The 7,800 humanists in the survey represented somewhat less than one-fourth of the total personnel professionally employed in linguistics and literatures, aesthetics, art, Biblical literature, musicology, oriental studies, and philosophy. Also included among the respondents were about 2,200 graduate students, not quite one-sixth of all students doing graduate work in the social sciences and humanities in 1952.

The fact that most of the respondents were members of professional associations should be borne in mind in interpreting survey findings, since other studies have demonstrated that members of a professional society tend in general to be an older, more highly trained, and a better established group than their profession as a whole.

From *Personnel Resources in the Social Sciences and Humanities*, Bulletin No. 1169 (Washington, DC: US Department of Labor, 1954): 3–17, 22–23.

FIELDS OF SPECIALIZATION

The men and women in this survey were classified in different specialties on the basis of their own statements concerning the fields in which they had greatest competence. Specialists in linguistics and literatures were the largest group of respondents. Economists, political scientists, and historians came next. Also responding to the survey were smaller numbers of sociologists, statisticians, geographers, anthropologists and archaeologists, and members of several relatively small humanistic professions.

Most respondents in each of these fields had specialized in some subdivisions of the field. In the general field of anthropology and archaeology, for example, the men and women who considered themselves specialists in archaeology were the largest group, and the specialists in ethnology and social anthropology were the second largest. Labor economics was the primary specialty of the largest number of economists. Among geographers, the largest numbers were in economic, physical, and human geography, in descending order. More than two-thirds of the historians reported modern history, chiefly U.S. history, as their first specialty. Among the political scientists, public administration was the specialty of by far the largest group; within this specialty, personnel work and municipal and rural administration were major areas of concentration. Detailed specialties cited by the greatest numbers of sociologists were social organization and applied sociology. Well over half the statisticians reported methodological techniques, chiefly analysis of data, as their first specialty.

In linguistics and literatures, the specialties most often reported were English literature, language teaching, American literature, and literary history. Among the smaller humanistic fields (combined as "other humanities" throughout most of this report), philosophy, Biblical literature, and art accounted for the largest numbers of respondents; musicology, oriental studies, and aesthetics accounted for the remainder.

Age

Since some of the social science professions have grown more rapidly in recent years than the humanities, social scientists have a lower average age than humanists. Median ages for the respondents in the social sciences ranged from 37 years for statisticians and sociologists to 41 years for historians, and were 45 and 43 years for the two broad groups of humanists—linguistics and literatures specialists and other humanists. Graduate students were generally concentrated in the 25 to 29 year age group.

Education

The Ph.D. was the predominant degree in seven of the nine fields of specialization included in the survey; only in statistics and geography did the proportion of respondents with the master's degree exceed the proportion with the doctorate. More than half the respondents in history, linguistics and literatures, and other humanities held doctoral degrees. Most of the surveyed graduate students had received their master's degrees and were working on the doctorate.

Women

Women represented from 20 to 30 percent of the respondents in art, aesthetics, anthropology and archaeology, and linguistics and literatures, but less than 8 percent of the economists and political scientists. A smaller proportion of women than men had the Ph.D. in each of the major fields of specialization. Women included in the survey were older, on the average, than men.

Employment

Since this study was limited to persons who considered themselves specialists in the social sciences or humanities, it was expected that most would be employed in these fields. Thus, about 10 percent of all those working full or part time held jobs of other types—ranging from employment (such as educational administration) which was closely related to their specialties to nonprofessional work. Persons with only the master's or bachelor's degree tended to be employed outside their respective fields of specialization to a much greater extent than did Ph.D.'s.

The majority of social scientists and humanists in most specialties were employed in colleges and universities. For example, over 90 percent of the specialists in linguistics and literatures were so employed. However, more statisticians were employed in government and in private industry than in educational institutions, and nearly as many political scientists were in government employment as on the campus.

The relative numbers of social scientists and humanists in these different types of employment varied markedly with their educational level. Most of the Ph.D.'s in every specialty were employed by colleges and universities, but the greatest proportion of master's in political science and statistics were employed by the Federal Government. In general, greater proportions of personnel with master's or bachelor's degrees than of those with Ph.D.'s were employed in private industry.

Median ages of social scientists employed in colleges and universities ranged from 37 years for statisticians to 43 years for historians. Linguistics and literatures specialists in colleges had a median age of 45 years. Employees of the Federal Government were younger than college faculty members, and the respondents in private industry were, on the average, youngest of all.

The principal function of the college and university employees was, of course, teaching. However, a sizable proportion of the statisticians (25 percent) and of the anthropologists and archaeologists (20 percent) on college faculties, reported research as their chief activity, as did a somewhat lower proportion of sociologists. The majority of the Federal employees were engaged in research—the most notable exception was the political scientists, more than half of whom were performing administrative functions. Of the economists and statisticians who were Federal employees, about one-third were engaged in administrative work, another third in research, and slightly fewer in operational activities. More than 40 percent of the economists in private industry reported research as their major function, and a like proportion of statisticians in private employment reported administrative work as their chief activity.

Earnings

Median annual salaries of survey respondents were as follows for 1952: anthropologists and archaeologists–$5,300, economists–$6,500, geographers–$5,100, historians–$5,000, political scientists–$5,900, sociologists–$5,100, statisticians–$6,800, linguistics and literatures specialists–$4,900, and specialists in other humanities–$5,000. These figures may be somewhat higher than the average for all social scientists and humanists in the country in 1952, since the survey included a disproportionately large number of highly qualified persons.

Salaries tended to rise with increasing experience, up to or near retirement age. However, there were wide differences in salaries of individuals in every age group—especially among the older members of the professions. In general, Ph.D.'s had higher average salaries than persons of comparable age with only the master's or bachelor's degree. Salary levels were also higher among the social scientists and humanists in the Federal Government and private industry than among those of comparable age and education employed by colleges and universities. However, a high proportion of the college faculty members supplemented their regular salaries with income from other sources, such as extra teaching, royalties from publications, lecturing, or consulting. The median salary of college or university employees was approximately $5,000 in 1952, in most fields covered by the survey, and median total annual income was from $400 to $900 higher, depending on the field of employment.

Women social scientists and humanists are less highly paid than male members of these professions. In most specialties, the average salary differential between men and women of comparable age and level of education and the same type of employment was about $1,000 in 1952.

SPECIALTIES AND CHARACTERISTICS OF SOCIAL SCIENTISTS AND HUMANISTS

Personnel Included in the Survey

No classification system of the social sciences and humanities, satisfactory for all purposes, has yet been devised. Classification is difficult owing to the overlapping of fields—not only with other branches of the social sciences and humanities and closely related fields, but also with widely different subject fields such as the natural sciences. For example, many administrative and research positions in welfare organizations are held by sociologists, but welfare service is generally considered the domain of social workers; and specialists in economic and human geography may be classified as social scientists, but persons specializing in other aspects of geography are usually classified as natural scientists. One of the most difficult occupations to classify is that of the statistician. Statistics is a tool used by specialists in many subject-matter fields, and it is frequently impossible to distinguish people who are primarily statisticians from those who are economists, biologists, or other subject-matter specialists. The classification of teachers also presents a special problem—they may be assigned to their major subject field (as is usually done in classifying college teachers) or to the teaching profession as such (the usual method of classifying high school teachers and most school administrators). The basis for classification of all specialists covered in this study was the respondent's own opinion as to his primary field of specialization.

In general, personnel covered by this survey were in basic subject fields, rather than in applied fields. Social scientists were in the following fields: anthropology (including archaeology), economics, geography, history, political science, sociology, and statistics. The humanistic fields covered linguistics and literatures, aesthetics, art, Biblical literature, musicology, oriental studies, and philosophy. (The last six fields are relatively small and are combined in most tables under the heading "other humanities.")

Specialists in applied fields such as psychology, law, social work, education, library science, and journalism are excluded from this report. Also excluded are persons who had not been in any activity in the humanities or social sciences within the past 15 years. (The following groups have also been excluded: (1) nonresident aliens and those who indicated that their residence in the United States was temporary; (2) undergraduate students below the senior year; (3) respondents without academic training or professional experience in the humanities or social sciences; (4) respondents whose questionnaires were so incomplete that it was impossible to determine their fields of specialization; and (5) respondents born before 1870.)

Fields of Specialization

Each respondent to this survey of social scientists and humanists was asked to determine his broad field of specialization and then to select from a list of detailed specialties the one in which he had greatest competence. (The respondents were also instructed to indicate their second and third specialties, in descending order of competence. However, tabulations in this report refer only to the first specialty indicated. For a complete list of detailed specialties used in the survey see, Classifications for Surveys of Highly Trained Personnel, American Council of Learned Societies, 1219 – 16th Street, N. W., Washington, DC 20006.) The largest group had specialized in linguistics and literatures. Next largest fields were economics, political science, and history—followed by sociology, statistics, geography, and anthropology, in that order (See Table 5.1). The detailed specialties most frequently reported by the survey respondents are discussed briefly in the sections which follow. Retired persons and undergraduate students are omitted from these and all subsequent tables.

Anthropology and Archaeology

Archaeology was the field of highest competence of the greatest number of respondents (32 percent) in the broad field of anthropology and archaeology. The second largest group (26 percent) cited ethnology and social anthropology as their first specialty. Between five and ten percent regarded themselves as specialists in each of the following: areas of the new world (especially the southwestern part of North America), applied anthropology, social organization, physical anthropology, and culture and personality.

Economics

Labor economics was the specialty of the greatest number of economists (14 percent). Nearly as many, however, considered themselves to be general economists with no specialty or regarded some aspect of economic theory (most frequently value and distribution theory) as their area of highest competence. From

TABLE 5.1 Employment Status of Social Scientists and Humanists and of Graduate Students, 1952

Field of specialization	Total	Social Scientists and Humanists			Graduate Students			
		Employed Full Time	Employed Part Time	Unemployed and Seeking Work	Employed Part Time	Full-time Student	Under-graduate Students[1]	Other[2]
All fields	25,054	20,870	612	391	1,012	1,150	179	840
Anthropology and archaeology	1,007	660	47	44	73	108	16	59
Economics	4,174	3,735	63	29	143	113	11	80
Geography	1,070	862	23	18	60	58	8	41
History	2,979	2,434	82	46	124	158	12	123
Political science	3,618	3,013	63	71	140	209	52	70
Sociology	2,321	1,778	62	49	171	150	55	56
Statistics	1,476	1,385	11	10	31	12	8	19
Linguistics and literatures	5,535	4,674	147	75	204	181	4	250
Other humanities[3]	2,874	2,329	114	49	66	161	13	142

[1]Seniors only.

[2]Includes retired, others not seeking work, and persons not reporting employment status.

[3]Includes aesthetics, art, oriental studies, musicology, philosophy and Biblical literature.

six to ten percent of the total number of economists were in each of the following specialties: business administration, land and agricultural economics, international economics, and money and banking.

Geography

The greatest number of geographers were specialists in economic geography (33 percent); this broad classification included those who had specialized in such fields as natural resources, agriculture, transportation, and industry. The second largest group was the physical geographers, who represented more than a fifth of the respondents in this profession and included those who specialized in land forms, climate, plants, animals, soils, and related subjects. Human geographers (political, population, social or historical specialists) were the third largest group (20 percent). Other geographers indicated specialization in a technique (such as mapping) or a region of the world.

History

Two-thirds of the historians reported modern history of specific countries (mainly the United States) as their first specialty. Nearly one-fourth had topical specialties—chiefly diplomatic history (including international relations), cultural and intellectual history, and state and local history. Fewer than 6 percent of the historians were specialists in either medieval or ancient history.

Political Science

By far the greatest proportion (40 percent) of the political scientists had specialized in public administration—either in this field as a whole, in personnel work, or municipal or rural administration. The second largest number (14 percent) had specialized in American Government, and nearly as many (12 percent) were international relations specialists. Specialties cited by fewer respondents, but in each case by four or more percent of the total, included public law, international law, area studies, history of political ideas, political parties and public opinion, and comparative government.

Sociology

Social organization, relating mainly to the community, was the specialty of the greatest number (13 percent) of sociologists; nearly as many (10 percent) were specialists in some branch of applied sociology, such as human relations in industry, or penology and corrections. The next largest groups had specialized in intergroup relations, family relationships, or rural-urban problems.

Statistics

In filling out the survey questionnaire, a statistician had the alternative of checking as his first specialty either one of several specified types of methodological techniques or one of a number of fields of application of statistics. The majority (nearly 60 percent) regarded themselves as most competent in methodological techniques—most often, in statistical analysis of data. Approximately 10 percent, in each case, regarded the application of statistics to economics or business and management as their primary specialty; and 16 percent checked the application of statistics to other social sciences and related fields, including education, psychology, and social service. Most of the remaining respondents applied their statistical knowledge to the physical sciences and related fields.

Linguistics and Literatures

More than half the respondents in this field regarded themselves as specialists in the literatures of particular countries or areas—most frequently, English literature. Applied linguistics (chiefly language teaching) was the specialty of the second largest group (16 percent). Other specialties cited by considerable numbers of respondents were literary history, literary types (for example, poetry, the ballad, and the novel), and descriptive linguistics (including phonetics, syntax, and dialects).

Other Humanities

Of the six relatively small humanistic fields grouped under this heading, the largest were philosophy, Biblical literature, and art, each of which accounted for nearly one-fourth of the respondents in the combined group. General history of art, practice of the graphic arts, and the history of medieval art were the fields of highest competence for the greatest numbers of art specialists. Among the Biblical literature specialists more than half regarded some aspect of study of the Old or New Testaments as their field of highest competence, and relatively large numbers reported pastoral work as their first specialty. In philosophy, the most frequently reported specialties were metaphysics and epistemology, ethics, philosophy of religion, and history and criticism of European philosophic systems.

The remaining fields grouped under "other" humanities were musicology, oriental studies, and aesthetics. Historical musicology was the major specialty of the musicologists, while comparative and systematic musicology (particularly the theory of music) ranked second and music in society (including music in education) ranked third. More than half the group of specialists in oriental studies reported China as their region of specialization and more than a quarter reported Japan. The few who regarded aesthetics as their major field of specialization were rather evenly distributed among the specialties within this field, but slightly greater numbers had specialized in the various aspects of theatre arts than in other branches of aesthetics.

Age

Because of recent growth in some of the social science professions, their members tend to be younger than those of other social science fields and of the humanistic fields. The median age of the statisticians and of the sociologists was only 37 years, but specialists in the humanities and in history had median ages of more than 40. About 60 percent of the statisticians and sociologists, but only 35 percent of the linguistics and literatures specialists, were under 40 years of age in 1952.

Within each major field of specialization, there was significant variation in the age composition of the groups in the detailed specialties. These variations reflect the effect of social, economic, political, cultural, and other trends on the development of each profession. For example, within anthropology and archaeology, the specialty reported by the youngest personnel, on the average, was social organization—a relatively new application of the knowledge and methods of anthropology—whereas physical anthropology, a long-established specialty, had the oldest personnel. Among the economists, those who specialized in industry studies and statistics and econometrics were much younger, on the average, than specialists in economic systems, business finance, and population and social welfare. In political science, persons who specialized in international law had a median age ten years greater than those who had specialized in area studies or the history of political ideas. In sociology, specialists in the newer fields of social psychology and public opinion (including market research) were the youngest and the specialists in family problems were the oldest group. Historians who were specialists in modern history had a median age ten years younger than the much smaller group who were specialists in ancient history. The other social scientists and humanists included in the survey did not show any great variation in median ages by detailed field of specialization.

Educational Background

Extent of Education

In most of the social sciences and humanities, the proportion of personnel with doctoral degrees is greater than in many other professional fields. To a large extent, undergraduate training in the social sciences and humanities is regarded as preparation for meeting one's personal and social responsibilities or cultural needs, rather than as vocational training. However, it is possible to enter professional employment in all of the fields—particularly statistics—without graduate training.

The Ph.D. was the degree held by the greatest number of respondents in seven of the nine major fields of specialization included in the survey. (The designation "Ph.D." is used throughout this report to refer to earned doctorates in science or education, as well as those in philosophy.) As previously stated, it is believed that the survey included a disproportionately large number of persons with the doctorate. It is estimated that about one-third of all professional social scientists and humanists in the country had the Ph.D. in 1952, whereas the proportion among those surveyed was approximately 51 percent.

Great variation exists in the educational attainment of personnel in the different fields of specialization. Nearly 70 percent of the linguistics and literatures specialists included in the survey held the doctorate. This was a much higher proportion than in any other field, except history where the proportion was almost 64 percent. Only among the statisticians and geographers were there more respondents with master's degrees than with doctorates. And only in statistics was the proportion of bachelor's degrees (38 percent) greater than the proportion of doctorates (18 percent). The number of men and women with other degrees, such as M.D.'s or LL.B.'s, was insignificant in all fields except political science, where six percent of the respondents—chiefly those specializing in public law—held LL.B.'s. The survey also included a few people in each field of specialization who had attained professional status without holding any college degree; most of these people had some college training.

The educational attainments of persons in the detailed specialties within each broad field of specializaton varied greatly. For example, approximately 60 percent of the economists whose specialty was either economic systems, money and banking, or public finance had the doctorate, but only 14 percent of those who specialized in industry studies and 35 percent of those who specialized in statistics and econometrics had this degree. Similarly, in political science, over 60 percent of the specialists in the history of political ideas and in comparative government held the Ph.D. degree, but only 20 percent of the personnel who specialized in public administration had the doctorate. Such differences in educational level are due, in large part, to the type of work performed by persons in each specialty. For example, those specialties pertaining primarily to basic theory are taught in colleges and universities where the doctorate is a usual requirement for professional employment. On the other hand, high educational attainment may not be a prerequisite for positions in administrative or operational activities in applied fields.

In all fields except anthropology, the majority of the surveyed graduate students had already received their master's degrees and were presumably working for their doctorates. The number of students included in the survey in the various fields reflects to a large extent the policies of the different professional associations in admitting students to membership.

Field of Education

In taking their highest degrees, a few social scientists and humanists in all fields had majored in subjects outside their current areas of specialization. However, most of them held degrees in fields closely related to their specialty. For example, some historians had taken their highest degrees in language and literature, a sizable number of political scientists had taken degrees in economics and history, some geographers had degrees in geology, and a few people in every field had majored in education and psychology. It is not surprising to find that the statisticians took their degrees in the greatest variety of subjects, since statistics is a tool which is applied in many subject-matter fields.

Even among the Ph.D.'s a few respondents had taken their highest degrees in fields outside their current areas of specialization, but the proportion was not nearly so great as among the respondents with less formal training. For example, among the historians, only about five percent of the Ph.D.'s had taken their highest degrees in subjects other than history, but 12 percent of the masters, and 33 percent of the bachelors and the respondents without college degrees, had majored in other subjects.

Women

Women constituted more than a fifth of all the survey respondents in art, aesthetics, anthropology and archaeology, and linguistics and literatures. The proportion of women was smallest (less than ten percent) among the specialists in Biblical literature, economics, political science, philosophy and oriental studies.

Relatively fewer women than men in these professions hold graduate degrees. The Ph.D. was the degree most often held by women in linguistics and literatures (60 percent), history (53 percent), economics (43 percent), and anthropology and archaeology (39 percent). However, in none of these fields was the proportion with the doctorate as great among women as among men. The master's degree was the one most frequently held by women in geography, statistics, sociology, the humanities, (except linguistics and literatures), and political science. Only in statistics and anthropology did more than a fourth of the women have only the bachelor's degree.

Among women graduate students the majority already had master's degrees, but in anthropology and the humanities (except linguistics and literatures) more than half the women students had not yet attained a graduate degree.

Type of Employer

The majority of social scientists and humanists are employed in colleges and universities. The proportion of college faculty members was highest (93 percent) among the respondents working in the field of linguistics and literatures. About three-fourths of the historians, sociologists, and "other" humanists were also employed in institutions of higher learning. In only two fields—statistics and political science—were more than half the respondents employed outside colleges and universities.

The Federal Government is the second largest source of employment for social scientists. More than a fourth of all the statisticians, political scientists, economists, and geographers in the survey were on Federal payrolls in 1952. (The proportion of federally employed social scientists included in the survey appears to be somewhat lower than for all social scientists. Data in Bureau of Labor Statistics Bulletin 1117, Federal White-Collar Workers—Their Occupations and Salaries, June 1951, showed that about 30 percent of the estimated total number of social scientists were employed by the Federal Government in 1951.) In addition, State or local governments employed significant proportions of the political scientists (13 percent), statisticians (nine percent), and sociologists (five percent). Nonprofit foundations including museums were major sources of employment only for anthropologists and archaeologists. And statisticians and economists were the only groups with substantial proportions employed in private industry.

The importance of the Ph.D. degree for employment in colleges and universities is well known. Among the college faculty members in the survey, the proportion with doctorates was over half in every major field of employment—ranging from about 55 percent of the statisticians and geographers to 76 percent of the historians. (The proportion of Ph.D.'s may not be as high among all social scientists and humanists employed by colleges as among those in this study because of the survey's relatively high coverage of Ph.D.'s.) In the Federal Government and private industry, however, less emphasis is placed on advanced academic training. Fewer than 20 percent of the Government-employed political scientists, geographers, and statisticians held the doctorate, and approximately 27 percent of the economists and 7 percent of the statisticians employed by private industry held that degree.

6

Knowledge Production and Occupational Structure (1)

Fritz Machlup

For most people interested in knowledge work, Princeton economist Machlup was and is the first source to turn to. Machlup was the first to look at how information was created, distributed, and used in the American economy, working in the period when computers and other knowledge-based professions expanded rapidly (1950s–80s). The selection below is drawn from his first, and foremost, his seminal work, published in 1962. This selection is his first analysis of occupations. He subsequently went on to write several more books on knowledge work in America.

At last we are ready to take up the "occupation approach." The focus of our attention will now be on the worker, his activity and occupation, rather than on the industry in which he is employed. The question is whether, how, and to what extent the occupational composition of the labor force and of employment has changed, and how this change is connected with the changing role of knowledge-production in the economy.

TECHNOLOGY, DEMAND, AND OCCUPATIONAL STRUCTURE

It may seem "self-evident" that great advances in technology and great shifts in demand lead to changes in the occupational composition of the labor force—but actually it is neither self-evident nor necessary in any sense. It is conceivable that all sorts of technological progress and shifts in demand leave the occupa-

From *The Production and Distribution of Knowledge in the United States* (Princeton, NJ: Princeton University Press, 1962): 377–400. Reprinted with permission.

tional structure of the economy unchanged, provided occupations are not too narrowly defined.

Inevitable, Impossible, and Probable Changes

Assume that a technological revolution in an industry allows the same output to be produced with half the quantity of physical labor, or twice the output with an unchanged work force. Even if demand is not sufficiently elastic to permit the same work force to be kept on to produce the doubled output, the workers released from this industry may find jobs requiring very similar kinds of work in other industries. If they cannot find such jobs at their accustomed wage rates, they may find them at relatively reduced wage rates.

Assume next that a drastic switch in demand occurs which, at given price relations, would call for more output of a product made with one type of labor, and less output of a product made with another type of labor. If workers are not flexible and cannot change over from one occupation to another, wage rates will rise in the one industry and fall in the other, and the prices of the products in question will do likewise, until the quantities demanded, despite the changes in demand, will be adjusted to the supply "dictated" by the inflexible occupational structure of the labor force.

Thus, neither changes in technology nor in demand *necessarily* result in changes in the composition of the labor force. With inflexible skills and preferences on the part of labor, and flexible relative wage rates, the employed labor force can remain unchanged in composition. Its composition will change only where the labor force is adaptable and adjusts to the "requirements" of changed technology or changed demand.

In the United States, the labor force has been adaptable to a high degree. Workers, by and large, follow the monetary incentives created by changes in relative earnings; even where the wage rate is not sufficiently flexible, they respond to the stimuli of open job opportunities. For this reason it is highly probable that changes in technology or demand will result, with a natural time lag, in a corresponding change in the occupational structure of the labor force. (Incidentally, there can be considerable adaptability in the long run even without any workers changing their occupations: all that is needed is that new entrants into the labor force go into the occupations now favored by the changes in technology or demand, and allow other occupations decline through death and retirement.)

Even with a highly adaptable labor force, it is not certain that every technological change releasing physical labor in a given industry will necessarily result in a decline in the ratio of physical labor to the labor force as a whole. Consumers, having more of their incomes left to spend on other things when one product becomes cheaper owing to improved technology, may well choose to buy goods and services produced with an even greater share of labor of the type displaced—so that no change in the composition of the labor force may be called for. But to say that not every technological change needs to have an effect upon the occupational structure is one thing; it is another to say what is likely to happen when many technological changes occur. If physical labor is displaced in a large number of industries, the probability is great (1) that some of the consumers' purchasing power will be used for things made with less physical labor and more of other types of labor, (2) that, on balance, therefore, demand will change in favor of these other types of labor, and (3) that consequently there will be a change in the composition of the labor force such that the share of physical labor is reduced.

It helps in the interpretation of observed statistical trends if one clearly understands the difference between what is logically necessary and what is logically probable. The "logic" in this connection refers to the concepts formed and their interrelations posited within the explanatory models of the economy.

Mechanization and Automation

Much of the technical progress of the past has consisted of the replacement of men by machines in particular production processes. This will undoubtedly be true also for the technical progress of the future. In recent years much has been heard about "automation" and how it threatens to depopulate entire industries. Automation and mechanization are often confused with each other, though it should not be too hard to keep them apart. Mechanization saves the use of human muscles, automation saves the use of human judgment. Mechanization, therefore, displaces physical labor, while automation displaces mental labor. These displacements occur in particular processes, not necessarily in the economy as a whole. The reabsorption of the displaced labor in other processes, industries, or sectors of the economy, may or may not be causally related to the displacement.

It is not possible to draw a clear and inconvertible line between "physical" and "mental" labor. Almost every kind of operation requires both physical and mental effort. Even pressing a button, pushing a pen over a piece of paper, or dictating an order call for some muscular activity; on the other hand, lifting a bag, shoveling snow, or carrying loads cannot be done without some mental activity. Yet, for theoretical as well as practical purposes it is possible to make the distinction between physical and mental operations, and between predominantly physical and predominantly mental labor. The frequently-used distinction between blue-collar and white-collar workers is designed precisely for this purpose.

When an "automatic control" device reaches "conclusions" and makes "decisions" which even the best human brains could not achieve with the same accuracy and/or the same speed, things become possible which brain power alone simply could not do. In these cases, automation does not "replace" mental labor hitherto employed, but merely permits things to be done that had not been possible before; the "thousands" of brains that are replaced in such instances are only hypothetical brains hypothetically employed. In other cases, however, there is actual replacement of human labor as a result of automation. Masses of clerical workers may be replaced by automatic bookkeeping and data-processing machines. In such instances, automation may reduce the share of white-collar labor in the work force of particular firms or industries.

In particular firms and industries mechanization may reduce the share of physical labor, while automation may reduce the share of mental (clerical, administrative) labor employed. This does not mean that automation tends to reduce the share of brain workers in the labor force of the economy as a whole. The design of automatic devices and their introduction and operation require brain workers of a higher calibre. This suggests that the distinction between physical and mental labor is really not adequate for the description of the consequences of labor replacement by machines. What we would need is a stratification of both physical and mental labor: physical labor of various degrees of manual skill, and mental labor of various degrees of analytical skill. On balance, the end effects of both mechanization and automation may then be found to lie in the demand for more highly skilled labor, manual and mental.

It would go too far beyond the scope of this volume to test this hypothesis on the basis of the statistical data at our disposal, though the census data on the occupational distribution of the labor force would be detailed enough to attempt a stratification of the sort proposed. At this juncture, we shall confine ourselves to two tasks: first, to observe what changes have occurred over the last 60 years in the relative distribution between "white-collar," "manual and service," and "farm" labor; and, secondly, to view the changing picture, over the same period, involving two groups, "knowledge-producing" and "not-knowledge-producing" or "primarily manual" labor. (These findings will be interesting enough, but I do intend in the near future to study the changing distribution of the labor force over *several* strata of skill in both knowledge-producing and manual occupations.)

THE CHANGES IN THE OCCUPATIONAL STRUCTURE

The U.S. Bureau of the Census publishes occupation statistics for all "employed" and for all "economically active" persons. "Employed" includes "self-employed"; "economically active" includes unemployed with previous work experience (who are listed in the occupation in which they were last employed). The labor force is divided into almost 400 occupations within eleven "major occupation groups." These eleven groups are: (1) Professional, technical, and kindred workers, (2) farmers and farm managers, (3) managers, officials, and proprietors, except farm, (4) clerical and kindred workers, (5) sales workers, (6) craftsmen, foremen, and kindred workers, (7) operatives and kindred workers, (8) private household workers, (9) service workers, except private household, (10) farm laborers and foremen, and (11) laborers, except farm and mine. The data are obtained from the decennial population-census *enumerations* and from quarterly *sample surveys*. In the tables used in the following discussion, the figures for 1900, 1910, 1920, 1930, 1940, and 1950 come from the decennial population census, the figures for 1959 from the current population survey.

White-Collar, Manual and Service, and Farm Workers

The eleven "major occupation groups" can be regrouped into three categories: (A) "white-collar workers," consisting of groups (1) professional, technical, etc. (3) managers, officials, and proprietors (except farm), (4) clerical, etc., and (5) sales workers; (B) "manual and service workers," consisting of (6) craftsmen, foremen, etc., (7) operatives, etc., (8) private household workers, (9) service workers (except household), and (11) laborers; and (C) "farm workers," consisting of (2) farmers and farm managers, and (10) farm laborers and foremen. Table 6.1 shows the number of persons in each of these three categories for given years from 1900 to 1959. This table shows that the number of white-collar workers increased steadily from 5 million in 1900 to 27 million in 1959, the number of manual and service workers increased from 13 million to 31 million, and the number of farm workers decreased from 11 million to 6 million. Thus, in 1959, white-collar workers were 540 percent, manual and service workers 238 percent, and farm workers 59 percent of their respective numbers in 1900. In the 19 years between 1940 and 1959 the number of white-collar workers increased by 69 percent, and the number of manual and service workers by only 16 percent, while the number of farm workers decreased by almost 29 percent.

The distribution of the labor force among the three categories is brought out in stronger relief if it is shown as a percentage of the total. This is done in Table 6.2. Farm workers, 37.5 percent of the labor force in 1900, were only 9.9 percent in 1959. Despite this decline in the percentage of farm workers, other physical workers, manual and service, increased only from 45 to 48 percent of the total labor force.

If all manual workers, industrial and agricultural, are taken together, their combined share in the labor force decreased from 82.4 percent in 1900 to 57.9 percent in 1959. White-collar workers, conversely, increased from 17.6 percent of

TABLE 6.1 Labor Force, or Economically Active Civilian Population, by Broad Occupation Categories, 1900–1959 (millions of persons)

Category	1900	1910	1920	1930	1940	1950	1959
White-collar	5	8	11	14	16	22	27
Manual and service	13	18	20	24	27	30	31
Farm	11	12	11	10	9	7	6
Total	29	37	42	49	52	59	65

Sources: For 1900 to 1950: U.S. Bureau of the Census, *Working Paper No. 5,* "Occupational Trends in the United States, 1900–1950." For 1959: *Current Population Reports,* Series P-60, No. 33, pp. 40–41.

Note: Figures do not always add up to total because of rounding. The 1959 data contain almost 4 million unemployed not distributed among occupation groups. In order to make the series comparable, these unemployed are here distributed among the three categories in the proportion in which the figures for "economically active" for 1950 exceeded those for "employed" in 1950, according to the *Current Population Reports,* Series P-60, No. 9 (April 1951), p. 36.

TABLE 6.2   Labor Force: Percentage Distribution Over Broad Occupation Categories, 1900–1959

Category	1900	1910	1920	1930	1940	1950	1959
White-collar	17.6	21.3	24.9	29.4	31.1	36.6	42.1
Manual and service	44.9	47.7	48.1	49.4	51.5	51.6	48.0
Farm	37.5	30.9	27.0	21.2	17.4	11.8	9.9
Total	100.0	100.0	100.0	100.0	100.0	100.0	100.0

Sources: Same as Table 6-1.

the labor force in 1900 to 42.1 percent in 1959. This trend, uninterrupted for 60 years and probably longer, is most impressive.

Knowledge-Producing and Not-Knowledge-Producing Workers

The "major occupation groups" distinguished by the Census Bureau, and the three occupation categories into which they were regrouped, are rather rough classifications for tests of the kinds of hypotheses that have suggested themselves in the course of the discussions in this survey of knowledge-production. Can all white-collar workers be regarded as knowledge-producing workers? Surely not without several qualifications or adjustments. In order to obtain a distribution of the labor force more suitable for our purposes, we must examine all occupations in the major groups distinguished by the Census Bureau, and make appropriate exclusions and inclusions.

In these adjustments we shall be guided by the definition and characterizations of knowledge-producing activities. Transporters, transformers, processors, interpreters, analyzers, and original creators of communications of all sorts will be regarded as knowledge-*producing* workers. (A narrower definition might well have been more appropriate, but we shall not change it at this point.) On the other hand, knowledge-*using* workers, however knowledgeable, will not be included if their product is not a communication or a service contributing to knowledge-transmission. If their product is a message, a piece of information, anything primarily designed to create an impression on someone's mind, they will be included among knowledge-producers, even if their own mental equipment is relatively poor. (This is emphasized as a reminder and a warning, not as a contention that this is necessarily the best thing to do.) Under this set of rules, the insurance salesman and the mail clerk are in the class of knowledge-producers, but dentists and veterinarians are not.

The following adjustments are made to carry out these resolutions. From the group of "professional, technical, and kindred workers," the first in the white-collar category, the following occupations are excluded as not knowledge-producing: chiropractors, dentists, funeral directors and embalmers, all nurses, pharmacists, 50 percent of physicians and surgeons (on the assumption that only half of their work is diagnostic and therapeutic advice and prescription), all technicians (medical, dental, testing, etc.), therapists and healers, and veterinarians. From the group "managers, officials, and proprietors (except farm)," railroad conductors, and all salaried or self-employed managers in retail trades, automobile repair services and garages, and miscellaneous repair services are excluded on the ground that they usually do not confine their activities to managerial tasks but participate in the physical work carried on in their shops. From the group "sales workers," hucksters, peddlers, and all persons in retail trade are excluded because they are less specialized in "sales talk" than in handling the merchandise sold. Finally, from the group "craftsmen, foremen, and kindred workers," the first in the blue-collar category, the members of the printing trades, particularly the electrotypers and stereotypers, engravers, photoengravers and lithographers, compositors and typesetters, pressmen and plate printers are shifted into the class of knowledge-producing workers.

These adjustments cause no difficulties in the census years. For 1959, however, the absence of detailed breakdowns necessitates some auxiliary manipulation. Assuming that the various detailed occupations had in 1959 the same relative membership, in percent of the "major occupation group" to which they belong, as in 1950, we use the 1950 shares of group totals to find the 1959 numbers of workers to be "transferred" from the knowledge-producing class to the not knowledge-producing class, or *vice versa*. Another makeshift is necessary for all census years because the numbers of retail sales workers are not separately stated. (They are given for 1959.) To make an educated guess of the numbers of retail sales workers, let us assume that they are equal to the numbers of managers or proprietors in the retail trades, an assumption suggested by the fact that they seem to consist chiefly of small-scale establishments with one hired worker helping the owner. The available figure for 1959 indicates that this procedure involves only a slight underestimation of the numbers of sales workers in retail trade in the preceding census years, say 1940 and 1950.

Table 6.3 presents the results of all these adjustments and estimates in the form of a total (for each year) of persons in knowledge-producing occupations ("Class I") and a total of persons in not knowledge-producing occupations ("Class II"), adding up to the Total Civilian Labor Force. Added to this is the number of full-time students in grades 9 and higher ("Class III") because students of working age should be considered as engaged in the production of knowledge in their own minds. They are members of a "potential" civilian labor force if labor force refers to "gainful" employment; alternatively, they may be regarded as members of the "actual" labor force, employed in their own education and presumably producing a value (embodied in human capital) at least equal to, and probably exceeding, the earnings foregone by their going to school.

The division of the civilian labor force into classes I and II shows a steady increase of Class I and steady decline of Class II. Class I, the knowledge-producing occupations, increased from 10.7 percent of the labor force in 1900 to 31.6 percent of the labor force in 1959. Class III, the potential members of the labor force who worked on producing knowledge in their own heads by going to school, in-

TABLE 6.3 Occupations of the Economically Active Populations, by Participation in Knowledge-Producing Activities, 1900–1959

	1900		1910		1920		1930		1940		1950		1959	
	(thousand)	per cent	(thousand)	per cent	(thousand)	per cent	(thousand)	per cent	(thousand)	per cent	(thousand)	per cent	(thousand)	per cent
Class I														
Professional, technical, and kindred workers	1,234		1,758		2,283		3,311		3,879		5,081		7,264	
Not knowledge-producing workers of this group	177		285		380		619		799		1,033		1,477	
Knowledge-producing workers of this group	1,057	3.64	1,473	3.95	1,903	4.51	2,692	5.53	3,080	5.95	4,048	6.86	5,787	8.42
Managers, officials, and proprietors, excl. farm	1,697		2,462		2,803		3,614		3,770		5,155		7,025	
Not knowledge-producing workers of this group	973		1,197		1,359		1,767		1,748		2,150		2,929	
Knowledge-producing workers of this group	724	2.49	1,265	3.39	1,444	3.42	1,847	3.79	2,022	3.91	3,005	5.26	4,096	5.96
Clerical and kindred workers	877	3.02	1,987	5.33	3,385	8.02	4,336	8.91	4,982	9.65	7,232	12.25	9,671	14.06
Sales workers	1,307		1,750		2,058		3,059		3,450		4,133		4,557	
Not knowledge-producing workers of this group	1,007		1,199		1,270		1,649		1,675		1,996		2,674	
Knowledge-producing workers of this group	300	1.03	551	1.48	788	1.87	1,410	2.90	1,775	3.43	2,137	3.62	1,883	2.74
Knowledge-producing craftsmen, foremen, and kindred workers	139	0.48	174	0.47	187	0.44	251	0.51	257	0.50	284	0.48	317	0.46
All knowledge-producing occupations	3,097	10.7	5,450	14.6	7,707	18.3	10,536	21.6	12,116	23.4	16,706	28.3	21,754	31.6

Class II

Craftsmen, foremen, and kindred workers (not knowledge-producing)	2,923		4,141		5,295		5,995		5,946		8,066		8,698	
Operatives and kindred workers	3,720		5,441		6,587		7,691		9,518		12,030		12,759	
Private household workers	1,579		1,851		1,411		1,998		2,412		1,539		2,302	
Service workers, except private household	1,047		1,711		1,901		2,774		3,657		4,641		6,217	
Laborers, except farm and mine	3,620		4,478		4,905		5,335		4,875		3,885		4,207	
Farmers and farm managers	5,763		6,163		6,442		6,032		5,362		4,375		3,028	
Farm laborers and foremen	5,125		5,370		4,948		4,290		3,632		2,578		2,694	
Occupations excluded from Class I	2,157		2,681		3,009		4,035		4,222		5,179		7,080	
All not-knowledge-producing occupations	25,934	89.3	31,836	85.4	34,498	81.7	38,150	78.4	39,624	76.6	42,293	71.7	46,985	68.4
Total civilian labor force	29,029	100	37,286	100	42,205	100	48,686	100	51,740	100	58,999	100	68,739	100

Class III

Full-time students in grades 9 and higher	937	3.2	1,470	3.9	3,098	7.3	5,905	12.1	8,617	16.7	9,068	15.4	13,340	19.4
A. Potential civilian labor force	29,966		38,756		45,303		54,581		60,357		68,067		82,079	
B. Potential civilian labor force in knowledge-producing occupations (Groups I + III)	4,034		6,920		10,805		16,441		20,733		25,774		35,094	
B as a percentage of A	13.5		17.9		23.9		30.1		34.4		37.9		42.8	

Sources: 1900–1950: Historical Statistics of the United States, pp. 75–78, based on David L. Kaplan and M. Claire Casey, Occupational Trends in the United States, 1900–1950, Bureau of the Census, Working Paper No. 5, 1958. 1959: Bureau of Labor Statistics, Special Labor Force Report No. 4, Washington, 1960, Tables C-6 and F-3; and U.S. Office of Education, Advance release. Explanations of transfers between Classes I and II are given in the discussion.

creased from 3.2 percent in 1900 to 19.4 percent in 1959. These are percentages of the sums of Classes I and II. Expressed as percentages of the sums of all three classes—that is, of the potential civilian labor force—the combined membership in both kinds of knowledge-producing occupations, Classes I and III, increased from 13.5 percent in 1900 to 42.8 percent in 1959. The decision to combine Classes I and III makes good sense or not, depending on the purposes of the analysis. If the purpose is to show how society has changed its allocation of human resources among alternative activities, one will want to see the knowledge-transmitters and the full-time knowledge-receivers combined. If the purpose is to show how the active labor force has changed its composition, largely in response to technological progress and economic growth, one will confine his attention to the relative role of the knowledge-transmitters.

Different Growth Rates within the Class

Since the class of knowledge-producing occupations consists of five major occupation groups, we ought to examine whether the large increase is equally distributed among the groups or whether one or another of these groups is chiefly responsible for it. We shall find that over different periods different occupation groups contributed most to the growth of the class.

Looking first at the change in composition over the entire 60-year period, we find that the clerical occupations grew most remarkably, from three percent of the labor force in 1900 to fourteen percent in 1959. But the other occupations in the class of knowledge-producers also assumed enlarged shares in the labor force, except the printers, who barely maintained theirs. Professional and technical workers grew from 3.6 percent in 1900 to 8.4 percent in 1959; managers, officials, and proprietors from 2.5 percent to almost six percent; sales workers (outside the retail field) from one percent to 2.7 percent.

Taking only the most recent decade into account, the improvement in the relative position of the professional-technical group is the most outstanding: from 6.8 percent in 1950 to 8.4 percent in 1959. This may indicate a strong impact of the technological "revolution" of which engineers and operations researchers have been telling us. On the other hand, the decline shown in the share of the sales workers (except retail) must not yet be accepted as a fact, because it may be merely the reflection of the probable underestimation of the retail sales force in 1940 and 1950 that was mentioned above.

Table 6.4 presents the same body of data in the form of growth rates over periods of different length. Over the period from 1900 to 1959, when the total civilian labor force increased by 137 percent, all knowledge-producing occupations increased by 602 percent, with the clerical workers showing the fastest growth rate: 1,002 percent. Over the 19 years from 1940 to 1959, the labor force increased by 23 percent, all knowledge-producing occupations by 80 percent, while the group of managers, officials, and proprietors led with a growth of 103 percent. Over the last nine years, from 1950 to 1959, the increase in the labor force

TABLE 6.4 Growth Rates of Knowledge-Producing Occupations over the Last 9, 19, and 59 Years

	Percentage Change in Number of Persons		
Occupation Group	*1900–1959*	*1940–1959*	*1950–1959*
Professional and techinical (excl. not-knowledge-producing occupations)	448	88	43
Managers, officials, and proprietors (excl. farm and other partly physically working occupations)	466	103	33
Clerical	1,002	94	34
Sales workers (excl. retail trade)	527	6	–12
Craftsmen and foremen in printing trades	128	23	12
All knowledge-producing occupations	602	80	30
Total civilian labor force	137	23	17

Source: Table 6.3.

was 17 percent, the increase in all knowledge-producing occupations 30 percent, and the group of professional and technical workers grew at the fastest rate, 43 percent.

THE INCOME SHARES OF KNOWLEDGE-PRODUCING OCCUPATIONS

If the remarkable rise of knowledge-producing occupations in the total labor force is interpreted as an "adjustment" to other economic changes and as a "response" to economic incentives, it would be interesting to see whether the change in the occupational structure was associated with an equal or greater change in income distribution between the two broad occupation classes. If the income share of the knowledge-producers has increased at a faster rate than their share in the employed labor force, one might interpret this as supporting the hypothesis that earnings differentials played a significant role in the change in the occupational structure. If, on the other hand, the income share increased only at the same rate or more slowly, or not at all, other hypotheses would be suggested; for example, that the mere availability of job opportunities accomplished the relative reallocation usually attributed to differentials in the rates of earnings; or that the supply of knowledge-producing labor had increased faster than the demand, causing the relative earnings of such labor to decline and its income share to lag behind its increased share in employment. In any case, we should like to see what happened.

The Incomes in Knowledge-Producing Occupations

In order to be able to assign income data to occupational groups, we shall have to use (1) the "gainfully employed" labor force rather than the "economically active" labor force (which includes unemployed); and (2) separate figures for male and female workers, since their earnings differ substantially (not so much for "equal work" as because they are given different kinds of jobs).

Census data are available for median wage-or-salary incomes for both sexes in each major occupation group. To estimate aggregate incomes we should appropriately have arithmetic means rather than medians, but the means have been estimated only for two years, 1939 and 1949, which is not sufficient for our purposes. In using the medians as a basis for computing the total incomes earned by various occupation groups, we shall have to bear in mind the likelihood of substantial underestimations, and in computing the relative income shares, the possibility of distortions because of different deviations of the medians from the arithmetic means. On the other hand, since we are interested only in changes over time, it is not at all certain that the arithmetic means, if they were available, would give us more relevant information. For the relative attractiveness of different occupations the median incomes may surely be pertinent; and while it may not be sensible to multiply the number of persons by their median income in order to obtain total group incomes, it is sensible to do this multiplication in order to get weighted averages of the medians for aggregations of occupation groups.

In Table 6.5 the occupational data are presented for the years 1940, 1950, and 1958, and the matching income data for 1939, 1949, and 1958. From each occupation group the same exclusions are made that were described previously in connection with Table 6.3, so that all not-knowledge-producing occupations are eliminated. [Herman P. Miller, *Income of the American People* (New York: Wiley, 1955), pp. 173–193.]

Since the numbers of employed sales workers in retail trades are given in the population census of 1940 and 1950, they can be eliminated without questionable estimation procedures; for 1958 the retail sales workers have to be estimated (by applying the 1950 ratios to the 1958 data of all sales workers) because they are not separately available in the same form as for 1940 and 1950.

It is not appropriate after these exclusions still to use the median incomes of the entire groups for the computations of the total incomes of the "expurgated" groups. But this is the best that can be done since income data for the detailed occupations are not available. As a consequence of such crude procedures, the "findings" may easily be vitiated, but we shall examine them none the less.

We find that in 1940 a total of 10,573,000 knowledge-producing workers were employed and earned a total of $15,120 million. In 1950 the number of this type of worker employed was 15,341,000 and their income $44,783 million. In 1958 there were 20,497,000 employed, earning $89,960 million. Their average annual incomes were $1,430 in 1940, $2,919 in 1950, and $4,389 in 1958—increases reflecting in a large part the inflation of the period. To interpret the changes in the total incomes of knowledge-producing workers we may compare these incomes (1) with total "employee compensation," (2) with the sum of employees' and proprietors' incomes, or (3) with national income. Since proprietors are included in one of the occupation groups, their incomes ought to be included too, though these incomes probably contain some returns other than labor income. To look into the ratios to national income will be pertinent because this will later afford us certain comparisons with some of the ratios developed from the industry approach.

The Shares in Total Income

The results of our calculations, reproduced in Table 6.6, conform with our expectations regarding the changes from 1950 to 1959, but are unexpected so far as 1940-1950 is concerned. Despite the large increase in the share of knowledge-producing workers in the total labor force (See Table 6.3) and the similar increase in their share in total employment (line 3, Table 6.6), their share in total income was the same in 1950 as in 1940. The absence of any growth in their income share is apparent in all three ratios, as percent of total employee compensation (line 5), as percent of employees' and proprietors' incomes (line 6), and as percent of national income (line 7). We must remember, of course, that these "findings" may be only statistical illusions, created by clumsy or crafty juggling of data; and that these data in turn are more or less reliable estimates by economic statisticians who have learned that poor figures are preferable to none. But assuming that the findings conform to actual fact, that is, assuming that between 1940 and 1950 the average salary or wage of knowledge-producing workers has actually declined relative to other wages, how can this fact be explained?

In order to exclude the possibility that the unexpected findings are not the result of our use of median incomes in lieu of arithmetic means, the computations made in connection with Table 6.5 were repeated using the means estimated for 1939 and 1949 by Herman P. Miller. Since these estimates are not available for all occupation groups which we have included among knowledge-producing labor, the tabulation resulted in smaller numbers of workers and smaller income totals, but the comparison between the two years, 1939 and 1949, was still possible. It showed that the income share of the workers in knowledge-producing occupations had even *declined*—not remained constant, as had the shares computed by the use of the median incomes. In other words, their relative incomes had fallen even more, on the basis of the arithmetic means, than on the basis of the medians.

The explanation may lie in the narrowing of wage differentials during the period of inflation, both between and within occupations, and in the fact that the spread between median and average income is usually much wider for high-level white-collar workers than for manual labor. For example, in 1939, before the distortion of the income structure through inflation, the arithmetic means exceeded the median incomes in knowledge-producing occupations by 17.2 percent on the average (and by as much as 36.4 percent in the group of managers, officials, and proprietors, and 21.0 percent in the group of professional and technical workers)

TABLE 6.5 Incomes From Employment In Knowledge-Producing Occupation Groups, 1940, 1950, and 1958

		1940			1950			1958		
		Number Employed (thousand)	Median Wage & Salary Income in Dollars 1939	Total Income (million dollars)	Number Employed (thousand)	Median Wage & Salary Income in Dollars 1949	Total Income (million dollars)	Number Employed (thousand)	Median Wage & Salary Income in Dollars 1958	Total Income (million dollars)
Professional, technical, and kindred workers	Male	1,875	1,809		2,911	3,699		4,420	5,956	
	Female	1,470	1,023		1,947	2,271		2,541	3,501	
Not-knowledge-producing workers of this group[a]	Male	346			422			641		
	Female	391			566			739		
Knowledge-producing workers of this group	Male	1,529		2,766	2,489		9,207	3,779		22,508
	Female	1,079		1,104	1,381		3,136	1,802		6,309
Managers, officials, and proprietors (excl. farm)	Male	3,326	2,136		4,211	4,172		5,751	6,034	
	Female	424	1,107		673	2,296		1,034	3,313	
Not-knowledge-producing workers of this group[a]	Male	1,508			1,684			2,300		
	Female	228			318			489		
Knowledge-producing workers of this group	Male	1,818		3,883	2,527		10,543	3,451		20,823
	Female	196		217	355		815	545		1,806
Clerical and kindred workers	Male	2,237	1,421	3,179	2,592	2,926	7,584	2,919	4,398	12,838
	Female	2,376	966	2,295	4,273	2,028	8,666	6,218	2,943	18,300
Sales workers	Male	2,124	1,277		2,570	2,916		2,580	4,291	
	Female	781	636		1,324	1,210		1,592	1,604	
Not-knowledge-producing workers of this group[a]	Male	1,069			1,257			1,262		
	Female	726			1,185			1,425		
Knowledge-producing workers of this group	Male	1,055		1,347	1,313		3,829	1,318		5,656
	Female	55		35	139		168	167		268

Category							
Craftsmen, foremen, and kindred workers	Male	4,949	1,309	7,464	3,137	8,244	4,970
	Female	107	827	237	2,001	225	3,000[b]
Not-knowledge-producing workers of this group[a]	Male	4,730		7,208		7,961	
	Female	98		221		210	
Knowledge-producing workers of this group	Male	219	287	256	803	283	1,407
	Female	9	7	16	32	15	45
All knowledge-producing workers		10,573	15,120	15,341	44,783	20,497	89,960
			Average income 1,430		Average income 2,919		Average income 4,389

Sources: 1940–50: U.S. Bureau of the Census, *Census of the United States, 1940 and 1950,* and *Current Population Reports,* Series P-60, No. 33. 1959: U.S. Bureau of Labor Statistics, *Special Labor Force Report* No. 4, 1960, and U.S. Bureau of the Census, *Current Population Reports,* Series P-60, No. 33.

[a]Explanations of exclusions of "not-knowledge-producing workers" are given in the discussion.

[b]This median wage income is not given in the Census Bureau reports. The round figure is an estimate not supported by evidence.

TABLE 6.6   Relative Employment and Relative Incomes from Employment
in Knowledge-Producing Occupation Groups, 1940, 1950, and 1958

	1940 (incomes for 1939)	1950 (incomes for 1949)	1958 (incomes for 1958)
(1) Total employed persons	44.9 million	56.2 million	65.6 million
(2) Knowledge-producing persons employed	10.6 million	15.3 million	20.5 million
(3) Share in total employment $\left[\dfrac{(2)}{(1)} \times 100\right]$	23.6%	27.3%	31.3%
(4) Income of all knowledge-producing occupations	$15,120 million	$ 44,783 million	$ 89,960 million
(5) Income of all employees	$52,129 million	$154,190 million	$277,400 million
(6) Income of all employees and proprietors	$65,139 million	$191,731 million	$303,386 million
(7) National income	$81,634 million	$241,876 million	$336,183 million
(8) Share in employees' income $\left[\dfrac{(4)}{(5)} \times 100\right]$	29.0%	29.0%	32.4%
(9) Share in income of employees and proprietors $\left[\dfrac{(4)}{(6)} \times 100\right]$	23.2%	23.4%	29.7%
(10) Share in national income $\left[\dfrac{(4)}{(7)} \times 100\right]$	18.5%	18.5%	26.8%

Sources: (1): *Census of Population.* (2), (4); Table 6.5. (5), (6), (7); U.S. Bureau of Economic Analysis, *Survey of Current Business* (Washington, D.C.: Government Printing Office, monthly eds.).

but only by 9.9 percent in not-knowledge-producing occupations. The spreads were much smaller in 1949. Hence, on the basis of mean incomes the knowledge-producing labor had suffered an even worse decline, relative to manual labor, than on the basis of median incomes.

Two hypotheses were advanced for such an event in the introduction to this section. One posits an increase in job opportunities for members of knowledge-producing occupations at a time when job opportunities for other types of labor are limited. In such a situation there can be an influx into the occupations favored by better chances of employment even if they do not promise chances for higher earnings than in other occupations. An alternative hypothesis posits an autonomous increase in the supply of workers in knowledge-producing occupations which is not matched by an autonomous increase in demand. A third hypothesis can be based on a peculiarity of periods of inflation, namely, differences in the speed with which incomes in different occupations are adjusted to expansions of effective demand. It is quite likely that wages and salaries in knowledge-producing occupations are less flexible than wages of manual labor, and, thus, rise more slowly during an inflationary period such as that between 1940 and 1950. Closer inspection of Table 6.5, however, reveals a fact which is almost sufficient to explain the relative decline of the earnings rates of knowledge-producing labor from 1940 to 1950: the number of women in clerical work increased by almost 80 percent and this group commands the lowest pay of all workers in knowledge-producing occupations. (The wage of female sales workers is still lower, but they were largely excluded from Class I.)

From 1950 to 1958 the share of knowledge-producing occupations in total income increased substantially; the income of this class of worker rose from 29 to 32.4 percent of total employee compensation; from 23.4 to 29.7 percent of the sum of employees' and proprietors' incomes; and from 18.5 to 26.8 percent of national income. These increases match or exceed the relative increase in employment in knowledge-producing occupations, which suggests that the demand for labor in these occupations increased more than the demand for other types of labor.

Different Changes of Income Shares within the Class

We strongly suspect that our broad classification involves aggregations of occupation groups so heterogeneous that the most significant structural changes remain hidden. Although professional, technical, clerical, and sales workers all earn their living chiefly by talking and writing—and are for this reason thrown together as members of knowledge-producing occupations—the kinds of talk and the kinds of pen-pushing and paper-shuffling are sufficiently different to merit separate treatment in many respects, particularly with regard to their employment and earnings opportunities. As a matter of fact, the statistical data of Table 6.5, however crude, do show that the income shares of particular occupation groups within the class of knowledge-producers have not all changed the same way as the share of the entire class.

Confining ourselves to one of the three ratios, that of the occupational-group income to the sum of all employees' and proprietors' incomes, we find that during the war-and-inflation decade, 1940–1950, the "managers, officials, and proprietors" and the clerical workers lost some ground. The income share of the former fell from 6.1 to 5.9 percent, the share of the latter from 8.7 to 8.5 percent. The sales workers barely held their ground, as did the printers, despite their strong trade union. On the other hand, the group of professional and technical workers—although it includes the teachers, who were notorious losers in this respect—improved its income share from 5.9 to 6.5 percent. Thus, the high-level-knowledge-producers—if we may assume that this group contains more knowledge interpreters, analysts, and creators than the others—gained both from 1940 to 1950 and from 1950 to 1958. The percentages are summarized in Table 6.7.

TABLE 6.7 Ratios of Incomes of Certain Occupation Groups to the Sums of All Employees' and Proprietors' Incomes, 1940, 1950, and 1958

Occupational Group	1940	1950	1958
Professional and technical workers (excl. not-knowledge-producing occupations)	5.9	6.5	9.5
Managers, officials, and proprietors (excl. farm and other partly physically working occupations)	6.1	5.9	7.5
Clerical	8.7	8.5	10.2
Sales workers (excl. retail trade)	2.1	2.1	2.0
Craftsmen and foremen in printing trades	0.45	0.43	0.47
All knowledge-producing occupations	23.2	23.4	29.7

Source: Table 6.5.

SOME IMPLICATIONS

Despite the poverty of the statistical series they do appear to establish certain facts and strong trends that are significant for our discussion.

The Facts and the Trends

Before we formulate what can be said about trends exhibited by our data, we should refer to one or two facts in addition to those already cited, for they throw a sharp light upon the employment situation of manual and white-collar workers.

From 1950 to 1959, while the total number employed increased, employment of "production workers" in manufacturing declined both relatively and absolutely; the employment of nonproduction workers increased by over 48 percent. This rise in employment of nonmanual labor and fall in employment of manual labor are also reflected in the incidence of unemployment: the ratio of unemployed to employed is now twice as high among blue-collar workers as among white-collar workers.

These are the trends read from the statistical series: (1) The knowledge-producing occupations have grown over the last 60 years much faster than occupations requiring manual labor. (2) The share of knowledge-producing occupations in the total labor force tripled between 1900 and 1959. (3) The share of these occupations in total employment has increased even more. (4) While in the first part of this century growth was fastest in clerical occupations, the lead was then taken by managerial and executive occupations, and more recently by professional and technical personnel. (5) The share of knowledge-producing occupations in total income has increased during the last decade. (6) The share of professional and technical personnel in total income has increased during the last two decades.

Interpretation

From these trends one may safely conclude that both the supply of and the demand for knowledge-producing personnel have been increasing. In particular it seems safe to conclude that technological progress has been such as to favor the employment of knowledge-producing labor; that shifts of demand for final products have been such as to increase the demand for such labor over the demand for unskilled manual labor, and that the supply of labor suitable for knowledge-producing occupations has increased, presumably as a result of more widespread school attendance.

Heavy emphasis, I submit, should be placed upon the fourth of the trend-propositions formulated above. It asserts a trend within a trend: while the ascendancy of knowledge-producing occupations has been an uninterrupted process, there has been a succession of occupations leading this movement, first clerical, then administrative and managerial, and now professional and technical personnel. Thus, the changing employment pattern indicates a continuing movement from manual to mental, and from less to more highly trained labor.

Implications

If employment opportunities continue to improve for high-level-knowledge-producing labor and to worsen for unskilled manual labor, the danger of increasing unemployment among the latter becomes more serious. To speak of absolute unemployability of people of low intelligence and little training may be going too far, because employability is partly a matter of the price at which labor is offered. But since society no longer tolerates "cheap" labor, and unskilled physical labor may find uses only if it is cheap, the combination of our social ideas with the continuing technological and economic trends may in fact spell unemployability for certain low-level types of labor. At socially acceptable wage rates, workers of very low economic productivity may remain permanently unemployed; and this unemployment is apt to persist even in the face of attempts to create "effective demand" if wage rates are promptly adjusted to inflated price levels.

A cogent exposition of this "Theory of Creeping Unemployment and Labor Force Displacement" has been presented by Clarence D. Long. [Delivered before the Catholic Economic Association at its annual meeting in St. Louis, December 27, 1960. An abstract appeared, under the title "The Challenge of the 1960's," in *Review of Social Economy,* Vol. xix (1961), pp. 14-17.]

The continuing upward creep of the unemployment rate in prosperity periods is, according to this theory, the result of a widening productivity spread and a constant relative-wage spread. Productivity of above-average workers increases faster than productivity of below-average workers: thus, productivity differentials among different types of labor become greater. If average wage rates rise at the rate at which average productivity increases, and if the lowest wage rates rise at the same rate as the average—so that the percentage spread between minimum and average wages does not increase—it follows that the minimum wage rates rise faster than the productivity of low-level labor, with the result that such labor can no longer be employed with profit. It is difficult to adduce empirical evidence for productivity differentials if money earnings cannot be used (since in the present case productivity differentials are compared with "inadequate" earnings differentials). Long does show widening differentials of intelligence scores and of the amount of schooling. (The minimum wage in this context need not be that prescribed by law; custom or employer ethics may forbid paying less.)

Long's theory is sufficiently general to apply to any kind of labor offered by workers of different ability and training. It applies, however, with special relevance to the situation described here, in which employment opportunities for low-skilled physical labor have been declining, and the economic productivity of high-level-knowledge-producing labor increasing. The implications, then, of the trends observed with regard to the occupational composition of the employed labor force are rather dismal. They seem to leave us with an unpleasant choice: either to resign ourselves to larger wage differentials, increasing spreads between minimum and average earnings, or to face a continuing upward creep of the rate of unemployment, not only in bad times, but also in prosperity. Perhaps this dilemma can be avoided by a third possibility, namely, through a drastic improvement of school programs that raises the lazy and unambitious to higher levels of accomplishment. But even if this is a possibility, it can be realized only years after the school reform, a reform which probably is not much less unpopular than low wages or unemployment.

INDUSTRIES AND OCCUPATIONS: RATIOS AND GROWTH RATES

One more promissory note remains to be redeemed. We have promised to compare the findings of the occupation approach with those of the industry approach. In particular, we want to compare (1) the total product of, or rather expenditures in, knowledge-producing *industries,* relative to the total product of the economy, with the total income of knowledge-producing *occupations,* relative to the total income of the economy; and (2) the growth of the output of or expenditures in knowledge-producing *industries* in the recent past with the growth of income of knowledge-producing *occupations* during approximately the same period.

Ratios to Total Product

The first of these comparisons requires only that we set side by side ratios computed earlier in this chapter. The 1958 expenditures in all branches of knowledge-production and obtained a total of $136,436 million, of which $109,204 million were regarded as "final product." Since this contained several items not included in the official Gross National Product, we added these items to the GNP and obtained approximately $478,000 million as the adjusted GNP for 1958. The expenditures for knowledge-production were almost 29 percent of the adjusted GNP. The expenditures for knowledge as final product were 23 percent of the adjusted GNP. In Table 6.5 we tabulated estimates of the incomes of workers in knowledge-producing occupations and obtained for 1958 a total of $89,960 million. The national income of the same year was $336,183 million. As shown in Table 6.6, the income of knowledge-producing workers was 26.8 percent of the national income in 1958. Neither the knowledge-workers' income nor the national income contained the earnings foregone by persons engaged in education. If these potential earnings, which we had included among the cost of education—$13,519 million for high-school students, $7,189 million for students in higher education, and $4,432 million for mothers staying home to educate their pre-school children, together $25,140 million—are added, we obtain $115,100 million as the total of actual and foregone incomes of knowledge-producing workers, and $361,323 million as the national income adjusted for the incomes foregone by potential workers giving or receiving education. The former figure is 32 percent of the latter.

This, then, is the set of ratios: 29 and 23 percent by the industry approach, and 27 and 32 percent by the occupation approach. These ratios refer to different things and, naturally, must not be expected to be the same. The discrepancies are certainly not greater than one should expect from an understanding of the concepts involved. As a matter of fact, there is no reason why the various approaches should yield ratios as similar as the above ones. When we first considered the possibility of the two approaches, we pictured an imaginary economy so organized that the results of the two approaches would be almost the same; and we concluded that the economies of the real world were quite different from the imaginary one.

Growth Rates

There is some reason for expecting that "growth rates" derived from the two approaches are similar, though any optimism in this respect should be tempered by a realization of the roughness of many of the estimates by which our statistical data were obtained.

The industry approach yielded "growth rates" for the four-year period 1954–1958 and for the eleven-year period 1947–1958. The occupation approach furnished growth figures for the eight-year period 1950–1958, for the 18-year period 1940–1958, and for even longer intervals. The only comparisons that can reasonably be made are between annual growth rates computed from the eleven-year period of industry growth and from the eight-year period of growth of workers' incomes.

The weighted average of the approximately eleven-year growth rates of 36 different knowledge industries tabulated in Table 6.2 was 10.6 percent per year.

Table 6.5 showed that for all workers in knowledge-producing occupations the incomes from employment rose from $44,783 million in 1950 to $89,960 mil-

lion in 1958, or by 100.88 percent. This growth over eight years constitutes a
growth rate of 9.1 percent per year.

The similarity of these results, 10.6 and 9.1 percent, is close. No attempt has
been made to reconsider or revise any of the estimates in the hope of achieving
greater correspondence in the results from the two approaches. All preceding
pages of my book, from which this excerpt is from, had been completed before the
consistency of the results was established at this point. This consistency should
not make us overly confident. The reliability of the data with which we worked
must not be overestimated, and the legitimacy of several of the uses we made of
them may be questioned. Indeed some of the statistical procedures were accepted
only as make-shifts and in the hope that others may improve upon our most imperfect effort.

STATISTICAL ACCURACY AND GENERAL CONCLUSIONS

Our attitude of caution regarding the accuracy of statistical data and the reliability of ratios between them should not be misread to imply serious reserva-
tions concerning the validity of the generalizations developed in this chapter.
Many things can be said about general trends and interrelated developments even
if the illustrative or supporting data are less than accurate. What has been said
about changes in the occupational structure remains valid even if the basic statistics are somewhat off the mark. And what has been said about the cost and efficiency of education, or research and development, is not vitiated by flaws that can
be detected in the statistical data. Thus, I hope no one will discard the proposal
for educational reform just on the ground that some of the estimates of the expenditures or implicit costs may be questionable. While statistical tables have
crowded the pages of this chapter, concern about their adequacy should not
crowd out the message it conveys.

7
Knowledge Production and Occupational Structure (2)

Michael Rogers Rubin and Mary Taylor Huber

It was inevitable that after Machlup's novel view of American economics that others would also examine the data, refine it, and offer additional descriptions of the modern knowledge worker. Two excellent scholars looked at the production of knowledge in the era 1960 to 1980, a shorter and more contemporary period than Machlup had. In this selection they examine the problem of data—who and how many knowledge workers there are—suggesting that the problem is an important one to address. Given the fact that at the end of the 1990s one uses the phrase "knowledge worker" as if it were well understood, we come to a harsher reality here.

KNOWLEDGE PRODUCTION AND OCCUPATIONAL STRUCTURE

Machlup offered the labor analyst a new perspective on the labor force. He proposed that "knowledge-producing" occupations have exceeded all other groups of occupations in growth since the turn of the century. In table and text, Machlup showed that growth of employment in knowledge production had proceeded more rapidly than growth in employment within the economy at large.

"Knowledge-producing" occupations were defined by Machlup as those that create new knowledge and those that communicate existing knowledge to others. Among those who create new knowledge are creators of original knowledge, like research scientists, and also those who, like doctors, apply existing knowledge to new situations. The second group, knowledge communicators, includes not only teachers, aircraft controllers, and others who communicate knowledge directly, but corporate chairmen, and middle managers who transmit

From, *The Knowledge Industry in the United States, 1960–1980* (Princeton, NJ: Princeton University Press, 1986): 192–201. Reprinted with permission. Materials for this chapter were prepared by Edward Wintraub.

information indirectly, through a large supporting cast of knowledge-producing employees. Of course, Machlup recognized that some occupational groups could fall easily in both the knowledge-producing and non-knowledge-producing categories. Thus, a physician examines a patient and takes certain actions based upon the examination, but whereas the cure is not considered to be "knowledge," the diagnosis is. For this reason, Machlup proposed that physicians' work be counted as half knowledge-producing and half not.

In *The Production and Distribution of Knowledge in the United States,* Machlup examined trends in the growth of knowledge occupations for the years from 1900 to 1958. Our task is to carry Machlup's analysis forward to 1980 and to compare the trends of the past twenty years with those of the preceding six decades.

DATA PROBLEMS

A variety of problems makes it difficult to compare data on occupations and employment over time. Among these are (1) different concepts of what constitutes the "labor force"; (2) the continual appearance of new jobs and a corresponding disappearance of old jobs; and (3) different systems for classifying occupations into major groups. Each of these difficulties is explained in more detail below, along with our approach to solving the problems.

Different Definitions of the Labor Force

There are at least four definitions of the "labor force" in common use. The first is simply those people who are actually employed on the day of a particular survey or census. This labor force, however, is only a subset of the second, which includes all "experienced" workers who are currently employed or who are actively seeking a new job in their old occupation. The third definition of the labor force is an even larger grouping constituted by all "economically active" men and women, including persons who are seeking employment in occupations for which they have no prior work experience. A student graduating from high school or college in search of a particular type of employment is an example of the inexperienced person included in this third group. The most expansive definition of the labor force encompasses the entire "non-institutional" population of working age, that is, all persons old enough to work who are not in prison, mental hospitals, and so on. Naturally, the concept of "working age" presents its own difficulties. Prior to 1970, fourteen-year-olds were included in most labor force statistics. Since the 1970 census, however, "working age" has typically been construed as sixteen years of age and above.

We have worked exclusively with the "economically active" as our definition of the labor force. Thus, in all of our tables we report on a comparable and consistently defined population for various years. The only exception to this rule is in Table 7.4, where we use the "employed" labor force to compute income in knowledge-producing occupations. The use of a more expansive definition of the labor force would have been inappropriate here, since it would overvalue the total actual earnings of this group. On working age, we are simply forced to accept the inclusion of fourteen-year-olds in earlier years and their exclusion later, since no other data sources are available.

Changes in Classification Systems

In 1977 a system was developed by the Office of Federal Statistical Policy Standards that was intended to make it easier in the future to compare the occupational data provided by future decennial censuses. Such official recognition of the problems inherent in the shifting classification schemes will be very helpful to future researchers, but offers little assistance to us. The three different classification schemes used in the 1960, 1970, and 1980 censuses present the researcher with the frequent appearance of new types of jobs and the disappearance of old jobs. Moreover, in different years the occupations were rearranged into different major groupings. For example, funeral directors were sometimes listed as "professional and technical workers" and other times as "managers." For our research we have carefully sought to bridge the various classification schemes and wherever possible, have arranged our results so that a valid comparison among years can be made.

ANALYSIS OF KNOWLEDGE-PRODUCING OCCUPATIONS

Composition of the Knowlege-Producing Occupations

The federal statistical agencies have long divided occupations into five general categories: (1) professional and technical workers; (2) managers, officials, and proprietors; (3) clerical workers; (4) sales workers; and (5) craftsmen and foremen. These categories vary to some degree from one source to another. In some tabulations professional and technical workers along with nonfarm managers and administrators and sales and clerical employees are classed under the broader heading of white-collar workers. The blue-collar classification includes craftsmen, operatives, and laborers except farm workers. Service workers and farm employees are independently listed.

Table 7.1 presents a broad picture of the occupational distribution of all economically active individuals in the United States for several years between 1958 and 1980. Using the broad categories—white-collar, manual and service, and farm, we see the substantial effects of the rise of technology upon the overall labor force. The number of white-collar workers has increased from 27.1 million workers in 1958 to 51.9 million workers in 1980. That is, the white-collar labor force nearly doubled in the past 22 years. In contrast, the manual and service sector has witnessed a somewhat lesser increase in employment from 30.3 million workers in 1958 to 44.7 million workers in 1980. In the farm area the trend is the

TABLE 7.1   Labor Force, or Economically Active Civilian Population, by Broad
Occupation Categories (thousands of persons)

Category	1958	1963	1967	1972	1977	1980
White-collar	27,056	32,378	34,232	39,092	45,187	51,887
Manual and service	30,319	34,014	36,586	39,542	42,603	44,680
Farm	5,591	4,615	3,554	3,069	2,756	2,714
Total	62,966	71,007	74,372	81,703	90,546	99,308

Sources: U.S. Bureau of the Census, *Statistical Abstract of the United States* (Washington, DC: Government Printing Office, annual ed.). Data are derived from Bureau of Labor Statistics data reported for the years cited.

reverse. Between 1958 and 1980 our economically active farm population actually dropped from 5.6 million to 2.7 million workers. Thus, the number of active farmers, including all categories of farm labor, decreased by 2.9 million workers, or over half of the farm working population in 1958.

Table 7.2 describes the composition of the economically active labor force in percentage terms. It indicates that white-collar workers increased from 43.0 percent of the work force as a whole in 1958 to 52.2 percent in 1980.

In the manual and service areas of employment, there was first a rise and then a decline in the percent of the work force included during the period 1958 through 1972: The figures are 48.2 percent in 1958; 47.9 percent in 1963; 49.2 percent in 1967; and 48.4 percent in 1972. From 1977 to 1980 manual and service employment began to decline more sharply, going from 47.1 percent to 45.0 percent. The net effect over those 22 years is that manual and service employment had declined as a percent of the entire labor force by 3.2 percent. The farm category declined steadily in the years 1958 through 1980. Constituting 8.8 percent of the active labor force in 1958, it fell to 2.8 percent in 1980. Over the 22-year period, there was a decrease of 6.0 percent.

Overall Growth in the Knowledge Occupations

Table 7.3 portrays the overall growth of knowledge-producing and non-knowledge occupations for the period of 1960–1980.

TABLE 7.2   Percentage Distribution of Labor Force, or Economically Active Civilian
Population, by Broad Occupation Categories

Category	1958	1963	1967	1972	1977	1980
White-collar	43.0	45.6	46.0	47.8	49.9	52.2
Manual and service	48.2	47.9	49.2	48.4	47.1	45.0
Farm	8.8	6.5	4.8	3.8	3.0	2.8
Total	100.0	100.0	100.0	100.0	100.0	100.0

Source: Table 7.1 in this book.

TABLE 7.3 Occupations of the Economically Active Populations by Participation in Knowledge-Producing Activities

	1960		1970		1980	
	(thou-sand)	per-cent	(thou-sand)	per-cent	(thou-sand)	per-cent
Class I						
Professional, technical, and kin-dred workers	7,090		11,561		15,337	
Not-knowledge-producing work-ers	1,844		2,610		5,370	
Knowledge-producing workers	5,246	7.72	8,951	11.22	9,967	9.54
Managers, officials, proprietors ex-cept farm	5,708		6,463		10,379	
Not-knowledge-producing work-ers	1,577		1,358		42	
Knowledge-producing workers	4,131	6.08	5,105	6.40	10,337	9.90
Clerical and kindred workers	9,431	13.87	14,208	17.80	17,564	16.82
Sales workers	4,799		5,625		10,257	
Not-knowledge-producing work-ers	2,731		2,967		5,500	
Knowledge-producing workers	2,068	3.04	2,658	3.33	4,757	4.55
Craftsmen, foremen, and kindred workers	9,465		11,082		13,555	
Not knowledge-producing work-ers	9,138		10,710		13,113	
Knowledge-producing workers	327	0.48	372	0.47	442	0.42
All knowledge-producing workers	21,203	31.19	31,294	39.21	43,067	41.23
Class II						
Operatives and kindred workers	12,254		14,335		14,902	
Private household workers	1,817		1,204		627	
Service workers, except household	6,086		9,047		12,979	
Laborers, except farm and mine	3,755		3,751		5,086	
Farmers and farm managers	2,528		1,428		1,315	
Farm laborers and foremen	1,604		1,022		1,717	
Excluded from Class I	15,290		17,645		24,025	
Others, and long-term unemployed	3,453		76		732	
All not-knowledge-producing	46,787	68.81	48,508	60.79	61,383	58.77
Total civilian labor force	67,990	100.0	79,802	100.0	104,450	100.0
Class III						
Full-time students in grades 9 and higher	12,816		21,554		26,871	
(A) Potential civilian labor force	80,806		101,356		131,321	
(B) Potential civilian labor force in knowledge-producing occupa-tions (Groups I + III)	34,019		52,848		69,938	
(B) as a percentage of (A)		42.10		52.14		53.26

Sources: (1960–1980): U.S. Bureau of the Census, *Census of Population* (Washington, DC: Government Printing Office, decennial eds.).

Note: Because of changes in classification systems and in age groups covered, the year-to-year groupings of occupations are not directly comparable. See the text for a fuller discussion of this problem.

Class I in the table contains five of the basic Census Bureau occupational classifications for each of the three decennial periods and shows the number of workers employed in knowledge-producing occupations for each classification and year. No knowledge-producing occupations occur in the remaining six basic Census Bureau classifications, which are listed for each year in Class II.

Class III shows the number of full-time students attending grades nine and higher on the secondary school level. Our objective in this latter class is to show the potential knowledge-producing labor force. Machlup argued that students of working age should be considered "as engaged in the production of knowledge in their own minds," and presumably, "producing a value (human capital) equal or exceeding earnings," except for their academic endeavors (*The Production and Distribution of Knowledge in the United States,* p. 386). Therefore, the role of potential knowledge-producing labor should be included in any analysis of knowledge-producing occupations.

We observe that there were 21.2 million knowledge-producing employees in 1960 constituting 31.19 percent of the total labor force; the number had increased by 1970 to 31.3 million or 39.21 percent of the labor force and increased further by 1980 to 43.1 million or 41.23 percent of the labor force. Consequently, the data indicated that the knowledge-producing labor force doubled from 21.2 million to 43.1 million during the 20-year period, thereby increasing from 31.19 percent to 41.23 percent of the total work force.

There were 5.2 million knowledge-producing employees in the professional category in 1960 constituting 7.72 percent of the total labor force; by 1970 this number increased to 8.95 million employees or 11.22 percent of the total labor force. By 1980 this group experienced a smaller increase to 9.97 million but decreased as a share of the overall labor force to 9.54 percent. Over the twenty years of our study this represents a net increase of 4. 7 million workers, or 1.82 percent. Growth in the clerical classification was increasing similarly from 9.43 million in 1960 to 14.21 million in 1970 and 17.56 million in 1980. The overall percentages again fell, however, between 1970 and 1980: the figures are 13.87 percent in 1960, 17.80 percent in 1970, and 16.82 percent in 1980.

The manager and sales workers classifications experienced a slow growth as a percent of the total labor force but accelerated sharply in absolute numbers. Knowledge-producing managers numbered 4.13 million in 1960 or 6.08 percent, grew slightly to 5.11 million in 1970 or 6.40 percent, but more than doubled in 1980 to 10.34 million or 9.9 percent. An overall addition of 6. 21 million managerial employees joined the knowledge-producing ranks, an increase of 3.82 percent. Knowledge-producing salesworkers underwent similar growth from 2.07 million or 3.04 percent in 1960; and 2.66 million or 3.33 percent in 1970; to 4.76 million in 1980, or 4.55 percent of the total population. Thus, there was a net 20-year increase of 2.69 million employees or 1.51 percent.

The knowledge-producing craftsmen underwent a steady decline on a percentage basis. In 1960 there were 327 thousand employees, constituting 0.48 percent of the total that increased slightly in 1970 to 372 thousand but fell on a percentage basis to 0.47 percent. The year 1980 shows a rise to 442 thousand workers but drops in percentage to 0.42. As a net result, during the period 1960-

1980, knowledge-producing craftsmen increased by 115 thousand but declined in the total labor force by 0.06 percent.

Class II, the non-knowledge-producing labor force, includes all occupational classifications not included in Class I. It is sufficient for our purposes to note that 46.8 million employees or 68.81 percent of the total labor force in 1960 were not knowledge-producing employees. There was a slight increase to 48.5 million employees in 1970, but a decrease on a percentage basis to 60.79. In 1980 there was a substantial increase in number of employees to 61.4 million, but a drop to 58.77 percent of the total labor force. Over the two decades of our study, non-knowledge-producing employees increased by 14.6 million workers, but lost ground in the total labor force by 10.04 percent.

Class III constitutes the future labor force that is involved in knowledge production by attending school. Taking the secondary academic level from the ninth grade through the twelfth grade, we find that there were 12.82 million students in 1960, increasing to 21.55 million in 1970 and to 26.87 million in 1980. The potential labor force comprises the economically active labor force for the decennial year plus the number of full-time students for that year. In 1960 on that basis it follows that there was a potential labor force of 80.81 million, an increase in 1970 to 101.36 million, and for 1980 a sharply increased total of 131.32 million. Since our objective is to determine the number of potential knowledge-producing employees, the addition of the number of knowledge-producing occupations in Class I to the number of full-time students for the same year gives us the potential civilian labor force in knowledge-producing occupations (Group I plus Group III). Thus, in 1960 there were potentially 34.02 million knowledge-producing workers, which increased to 52.85 million workers in 1970, and 69.94 million workers in 1980. Using the percentage of potential civilian labor force in knowledge-producing occupations of the potential labor force, that is, III.B of III. A, we obtain 42.10 percent for 1960, 52.14 percent for 1970, and 53.26 percent in 1980.

The reader should understand that the word "potential" is the critical concept for Class III. As an example, consider the statement that there were 131.52 million potential knowledge-producing employees in 1980. Because some students will not in fact become knowledge-producing employees, the term "potential" indicates that the figure is the maximum number that may become knowledge-producing employees and not the (unknown) number of those who actually will do so. The Class I data provide the actual number of knowledge-producing employees.

Income in Knowledge-Producing Occupations

Table 7.4 extends the analysis of knowledge-producing occupations to the income earned by the workers within that group. The table shows the number of workers actually employed in knowledge-producing occupations, their median income, and total income as a group for the years 1960, 1970, and 1980. It also reflects the differences of income by sex during those years.

TABLE 7.4 Income from Employment in Knowledge-Producing Occupation Groups

		1960			1970			1980		
		Number Employed (thousands)	Median Earnings (in dollars)	Total Income (million dollars)	Number Employed (thousands)	Median Earnings (in dollars)	Total Income (million dollars)	Number Employed (thousands)	Median earnings (in dollars)	Total Income (million dollars)
Professional, technical, and kindred workers	Male	4,303			6,517			8,904		
	Female	2,683			4,314			7,073		
Not-knowledge-producing workers	Male	1,003			1,352			873		
	Female	807			1,212			2,025		
Knowledge-producing workers	Male	3,300	6,848	22,598	5,165	11,806	60,978	8,031	23,026	184,922
	Female	1,876	4,384	8,224	3,102	7,878	24,438	5,038	15,285	77,006
Total, knowledge-producing workers		5,176	11,232	30,822	8,267	19,684	85,416	13,069	38,311	261,928
Managers, officials, proprietors except farm	Male	4,797			5,126			8,219		
	Female	829			1,014			2,920		
Not-knowledge-producing workers	Male	1,610			1,163			955		
	Female	306			210			458		
Knowledge-producing workers	Male	3,187	7,241	23,077	3,963	12,117	48,020	7,264	23,558	171,125
	Female	523	4,173	2,182	804	6,834	5,495	2,462	12,936	31,848
Total, knowledge-producing workers		3,710	11,414	25,259	4,767	18,951	53,515	9,726	36,494	202,973
Clerical and kindred workers	Male	2,922	5,247	15,332	3,452	8,617	29,746	3,687	18,247	67,277
	Female	6,204	3,586	22,248	9,582	5,551	53,190	14,787	10,997	162,613
Total, knowledge-producing workers		9,126	8,833	37,580	13,034	14,168	83,936	18,474	29,244	229,890
Sales workers	Male	2,986			3,268			3,450		
	Female	1,652			2,000			2,853		
Not-knowledge-producing workers	Male	1,271			1,437			1,185		
	Female	1,386			1,616			2,040		
Knowledge-producing workers	Male	1,715	5,755	9,870	1,831	9,790	17,925	2,265	19,910	45,096
	Female	266	2,428	646	384	4,188	1,608	813	9,748	7,925
Total, knowledge-producing workers		1,981	8,183	10,516	2,215	13,978	19,533	3,078	29,658	53,021

Craftsmen, foremen, and kindred workers	Male	8,668			9,502			12,018	
	Female	277			495			769	
Not-knowledge-producing workers	Male	8,374			9,181			11,697	
	Female	251			451			675	
Knowledge-producing workers	Male	294	5,868	1,725	321	9,254	2,971	321	18,671	5,993
	Female	26	2,934	76	44	5,089	224	94	11,701	1,100
Total, knowledge-producing workers		320	8,802	1,801	365	14,343	3,195	415	29,372	7,093
Total, all knowledge-producing workers		20,313	5,217	105,978	28,648	8,538	244,595	44,762	16,865	754,905
Total employed		64,639			77,309			99,303	

Sources: (1960, 1970): U.S. Bureau of the Census, *Census of Population*, 1960 and 1970, (1980): U.S. Bureau of Labor Statistics, unpublished tables.

Notes: Total employed figures are derived from the Bureau of Labor Statistics that are slightly lower than the previously used Bureau of the Census Total Employment figures. This has been done to remain consistent for the table as a whole and would have little or no effect upon the illustrated trends. Table 7.5 also necessarily utilizes the Bureau of Labor Statistics data for Total Employment.

The table shows that for 1960, 20.31 million knowledge-producing workers were employed with median earnings for both sexes of $5,217, or a total income of $105.98 billion. The 1970 figure rose substantially to 28.65 million workers employed with median earnings of $8,538, or a total income of $244.6 billion. In 1980 the number employed was slightly more than double the 1960 figure, or 44.76 million, but with the median income more than triple that of 1960 at $16,865 and a total income of $754.91 billion.

Table 7.5 compares the aggregate earnings of all workers in knowledge-producing occupations with the income earned by all workers. The table compares the relative employment and incomes from knowledge-producing employment with total employment and incomes between 1960 and 1980. Knowledge-producing employees in 1960 numbered 20.31 million and were 31.43 percent of the total employed work force with a group income of $105.98 billion. By 1980 they underwent an increase of approximately 14 percent to 45.08 percent of the work force and increased their income sevenfold over the 20-year period, to $754.91 billion. Knowledge-producing workers' share of all employee compensation economy-wide rose to 47.28 percent in 1980, from 35.93 percent in 1960. When compared to all employees and proprietors, knowledge workers' income rose from 31.0 percent in 1960 to 43.71 percent in 1980.

TABLE 7.5   Relative Employment and Relative Incomes from Employment in Knowledge-Producing Occupation Groups (millions)

	1960	1970	1980
(1) Total employed persons (thousands)	64,639	77,309	99,303
(2) Knowledge-producing persons employed (thousands)	20,313	28,648	44,762
(3) Percent of total employment [(2) ÷ (1) × 100]	31.43%	37.06%	45.08%
(4) Income of all knowledge-producing occupations	105,978	244,595	754,905
(5) Income of all employees	294,932	609,150	1,596,500
(6) Income of all employees and proprietors	341,910	674,290	1,727,200
(7) National income	412,008	798,374	2,119,500
(8) Percent of employees' income [(4) ÷ (5) × 100]	35.93%	40.15%	47.28%
(9) Percent of employees' and proprietors income [(4) ÷ (6) × 100]	31.00%	36.27%	43.71%
(10) Percent of national income [(4) ÷ (7) × 100]	25.72%	31.64%	35.62%

Sources: (1), (2), (4): Table 7.4. Items (5), (6), (7): U.S. Bureau of Economic Analysis, Survey of Current Businesses (Washington, D.C.: Government Printing Office, monthly eds.).

Notes: For Item 5 data will vary in accord with income factors which are added to the basic income; for example, rental income, personal interest income, transfer income (social security and veterans benefits, etc.). Consequently, such additional income is variable and cited as loose estimates. The term "personal income" might also be used. In 1960, the Bureau of Economic Analysis estimated Employees Personal Income to be 399.7 million, 801.3 million in 1970, and 2.17 billion in 1980. These figures could have been used for Item 5 of Table 7.5 and in Table 7.4.

8

The Information Economy: Definition and Measurement

Marc Uri Porat

By the mid-1970s, a number of economists were doing rigorous work in the area of knowledge professions. Porat undertook one of the largest American studies of the subject and, in 1977, published a massive amount of material while working for the U.S. Department of Commerce. In this selection, he summarizes his findings about the nature of knowledge work, identifying the primary knowledge professions of the period. This study became a minor classic even though it was published as a technical government study with limited circulation.

INFORMATION OCCUPATIONS

Planning, in short, requires a great variety of information. It requires variously informed men and women who are suitably specialized in obtaining the requisite information . . . those who have knowledge to plan price strategies . . . those who, at a higher level of technology, are so informed that they can work effectively with the state to see that it is suitably guided; and those who can organize the flow of information. Finally, following from the need for this variety of specialized talent, is the need for its coordination . . . information must be extracted from the various specialists, tested for its reliability and relevance, and made to yield a decision.

—J. K. Galbraith, The New Industrial State,
Houghton-Mifflin, Boston, 1971 (Second Ed.)

From *The Information Economy: Definition and Measurement,* by Marc Uri Porat, OT Special Publication 77-12(1) (Washington, DC: US Department of Commerce, May 1977): 104–134.

Fritz Machlup and Daniel Bell focused early on the structure of the United States work force as a basic indicator of a "postindustrial" or a "knowledge" society. They developed summary statistics from the census of population, showing the growth in professional, technical, and clerical occupations relative to blue-collar or crafts occupations. Both authors couch their conclusions as tentative, calling for a much more detailed study of the U.S. labor force. Machlup states, "The reliability of the data with which we worked must not be overestimated, and the legitimacy of several of the uses we made of them must be questioned. Indeed some of the statistical procedures were accepted only as makeshifts in the hope that others may improve upon our most imperfect efforts." (p. 400)

This chapter is one effort to dissect at the most tedious level the labor statistics underlying the phenomenon of "the information sector." Employee compensation and proprietors' income are analyzed in detail for 1967. Time series of the information workers in the U.S. labor force are built spanning the agricultural age (1860) to the present. Hopefully, these summary figures will be somewhat more instructive than the backup statistics to any future researchers interested in continuing this line of investigation. Bell summarizes how a transition to a postindustrial economy affects the work force:

> "In preindustrial societies—still the condition of most of the world today— the labor force is engaged overwhelmingly in the extractive industries: mining, fishing, forestry, agriculture. Life is primarily a game against nature. . . . Industrial societies—principally those around the North Atlantic littoral plus the Soviet Union and Japan—are goods-producing societies. Life is a game against fabricated nature. The world has become technical and rationalized. The machine predominates, and the rhythms of life are mechanically paced. . . . A postindustrial society is based on services. What counts is not raw muscle power, or energy, but information." (pp. 126–127)

The relative size of the occupations engaged in agricultural manufacturing, and informational activities is an indicator of the economy which supports the work force. It shows how "specialized" the economy has become in the provision of things that make life possible, that make life pleasant, or that make life human. Knowledge or information can indeed be a primary "good."

In this chapter, I attempt to answer several questions. Who are the information workers and on what basis are they selected? What share of the U.S. wage bill is earned by information workers? How has the information sector of the labor force grown over time? What is the exact occupational structure of the labor force broken down by industry? What is the information labor component of noninformation industries?

THE INFORMATION WORKERS

Stating precisely who is an information worker and who is not is a risky proposition. Obviously, every human endeavor involves some measure of information processing and cognition; intellectual content is present in every task no matter how mundane. It is, after all, the critical difference between humans and animals that the former can process symbolic information quite readily while the latter cannot. There is nothing to be gained by saying that certain occupations have a zero informational content while others are purely informationl.

We are trying to get at a different question: Which occupations are *primarily* engaged in the production, processing, or distribution of information as the output, and which occupations perform information processing tasks as activities ancillary to the primary function? To make the question clear, is there a qualitative difference on the issue of information between a computer programmer and a carpenter? Both are skilled workers, earning roughly the same salary. Both require a certain amount of education before they can function productively. And both use attention, concentration, and applied knowledge in their respective tasks. However, the programmer's livelihood originates with the provision of an information service (a set of instructions to a computer), while the carpenter's livelihood originates with the construction of a building or a piece of furniture—noninformational goods. The former sells information as a commodity; the latter sells a tangible physical product.

I have developed a conceptual scheme for classifying information workers, presented as an overview in Table 8.1. The scheme was developed with a theoretical concern in mind and divides occupations into three major classes.

The first, "Markets for Information," includes those workers whose output or primary activity is an information product. Information is produced and sold as output and often assumes the form of a knowledge commodity. The second major class of workers provides "Information in Markets." Their output is not knowledge for sale, but rather they serve as information gatherers and disseminators. These workers move information within firms and within markets—they search, coordinate, plan, and process market information. The last class is the "Information Infrastructure" workers, whose occupations involve operating the information machines and technologies to support the previous two activities.

Knowledge Producers

Knowledge producers, shown in Table 8.2, fall into two classes of workers—scientific and technical, and producers of private information services. "Scientific and Technical Workers" are often engaged in inventive activity. A large portion of this marketplace for knowledge is part of the "grants economy," subsidized from the public or philanthropic purse. The scientific community generally shares new knowledge universally through the invisible college and through inter-

TABLE 8.1   Typology of Information Workers and 1967 Compensation[a]

	Employee Compensation ($ Millions)
MARKETS FOR INFORMATION	
KNOWLEDGE PRODUCERS	46,964
Scientific & Technical Workers	18,777
Private Information Services	28,187
KNOWLEDGE DISTRIBUTORS	28,265
Educators	23,680
Public Information Disseminators	1,264
Communication Workers	3,321
INFORMATION IN MARKETS	
MARKET SEARCH & COORDINATION SPECIALISTS	93,370
Information Gatherers	6,132
Search & Coordination Specialists	28,252
Planning and Control Workers	58,986
INFORMATION PROCESSORS	61,340
Non-Electronic Based	34,317
Electronic Based	27,023
INFORMATION INFRASTRUCTURE	
INFORMATION MACHINE WORKERS	13,167
Non-Electronic Machine Operators	4,219
Electronic Machine Operators	3,660
Telecommunication Workers	5,288
TOTAL INFORMATION	243,106
TOTAL EMPLOYEE COMPENSATION	454,259[b]
INFORMATION AS % OF TOTAL	53.52%

[a]Employee compensation includes wages and salaries and supplements.
[b]Excluding military workers.
Source: Computed using BLS Occupation by Industry matrix, Census of Population average wages.

national scientific publications. Even when research scientists work for private industry, their knowledge outputs eventually take on a "publicness" unlike any
other occupation. When a corporate research scientist invents something useful it
eventually becomes public knowledge either through academic channels or
through the disclosure requirements of filing a patent. This class of workers is at
the heart of Machlup's definition of a "knowledge sector" in our society. The relevant policy questions in this sector focus on appropriability of one's efforts (i.e.,
property rights and the "publicness" nature of intellectual output), social allocation of resources to invention, and the distribution or utilization patterns of technical and scientific knowledge once it has been produced.

TABLE 8.2   Knowledge Producers

	1967 Employee Compensation ($ Millions)	
Scientific & Technical Workers	18,777	
Natural & Physical Sciences	2,181	
Agricultural Scientists		108
Atmospheric, Space Scientists		71
Biological Scientists		260
Chemists		1141
Geologists		266
Marine Scientists		34
Physicists and Astronomers		275
Life, Physical Scientists		26
Mathematical Sciences	2,239	
Mathematicians		95
Statisticians		194
Operations, Systems Research		811
Research Workers		1139
Social Sciences	1,327	
Economists		805
Political Scientists		25
Psychologists		324
Sociologists		10
Urban & Regional Planners		96
Other Social Scientists		67
Engineering	13,030	
Engineers, Aero-Astronautic		804
Engineers, Chemical		640
Engineers, Civil		1923
Engineers, Electrical		3334
Engineers, Industrial		1766
Engineers, Mechanical		2233
Engineers, Metallurgical		180
Engineers, Mining		54
Engineers, Petroleum		146
Engineers, Sales		475
Engineers, Other		1475
Private Information Service Providers	28,187	
Counselors and Advisors	14,632	
Lawyers		2275
Farm Management Advisors		64
Foresters, Conservationists		324
Home Management Advisors		36
Vocational, Education Counselors		952
Judges		246
Personnel Labor Relations		2707

(Continued on next page)

TABLE 8.2   *(Continued)*

	1967 Employee Compensation ($ Millions)	
Architects		588
Therapists		515
Dietitians		156
Pysicians (50%)		1644
Designers		1055
Draftsmen		2464
Social Workers		1606
Computer Specialists	2,675	
Computer Programmers		1551
Other Computer Specialists		163
Computer Systems Analysis		936
Numerical Tool Programmers		25
Financial Specialists	10,880	
Accountants		5816
Bank, Financial Managers		4470
Creditmen		531
Actuaries		63
TOTAL KNOWLEDGE PRODUCERS	46,964	

The second class of knowledge workers produce a wide variety of "private information services." This class includes lawyers, architects, computer programmers, and accountants. These occupations do not produce *new* knowledge but rather they apply old knowledge in ways which are specific to a particular client or situation. They sell knowledge "packages"—repackaging old knowledge in unique applications. Such markets tend always to be private, and function very well without the publicness aspects discussed above.

One of the most difficult (and lucrative) problems in an information-rich world is developing skills to package information that is useful: in the right form, at the right place, and at the right time. This problem is true whether information is being sold as a commodity in a recognizable marketplace (e.g., legal services), or whether the information is strictly for internal use (e.g., management information system). Particularly in "markets for information," the value of the service resides precisely in the worker's ability to package information in a uniquely useful way. Where there is a massive repository of preexisting knowledge *plus* a codified scheme for bringing the knowledge to bear on a particular problem, private information markets will work very well. Legal and medical consulting are the most obvious examples. The specialist does not create new knowledge; but a layperson cannot apply the publicly available knowledge without an information intermediary. Where "packaging" of extant knowledge can be routinized, information machines can be expected to play an ever-increasing role as augmenters of human skill. Lawyers and doctors are already beginning to make use of computers in their analytic and diagnostic work. The cost of these two classes of knowledge production in 1967 was $47.0 billion. Around $18.8 billion was spent on scientists and technical workers, and about $28.2 billion on private information services.

Knowledge Distributors

Knowledge distributors fall into three occupational classes: (1) educators, (2) public information disseminators, and (3) communication workers. A detailed breakdown is shown in Table 8.3. "Educators," as opposed to the scientific community, are mainly considered as providing public distribution of already produced knowledge. University educators also produce knowledge, in the form of scholarly research. No attempt is made to allocate their time between the two activities.

"Public information disseminators" include librarians and archivists. Whether these people work in public libraries or in privately financed (corporate) libraries, their services are in the provision of a "free good" to the user community—distribution of knowledge. Whether society allocates sufficient resources for this public good is a matter of much debate. "Communications workers" include a number of occupations in the established news and entertainment media—newspapers, magazines, radio, film, and television. Although journalists engage in knowledge producing activities, such as investigative or analytic reporting, their instrument is a distributive medium.

In 1967, this group of occupations earned $28.3 billion, with over $23 billion earned by educators.

Market Search and Coordination Specialists

The requirements of organizing firms and markets involve several types of information. Information *about* the market environment is gathered by firms: prices, supply and demand conditions, the intentions of other firms, new technologies, and condition of other relevant markets (such as labor and capital markets). Also, firms engage in a tremendous amount of in-house information processing—such as planning, coordinating, and controlling the enterprise; meeting the informational needs of governments (forms and reports), of other firms (business communication), and of households (invoices, catalogs). Table 8.4 presents a breakdown of the market search and coordination specialists, whose knowledge production services are market specific. This group creates, supports, and maintains the market information system.

"Information gatherers" include a variety of occupations involved in the form of intelligence or simple investigatory work. Their job is to discover something about the state of the world—the extent of damage on an insurance claim, the value of a piece of property, the reading on a utility meter.

"Search and coordination specialists" operate entirely in the exchange marketplace. I have divided this class into three groups. On the "buy side" are buyers and purchasing agents whose job is to search the exchange market for the best

TABLE 8.3   Knowledge Distributors

	1967 Employee Compensation ($ Millions)	
Educators	23,680	
Adult Education Teachers		426
Agriculture Teachers		58
Art, Drama, Music Teachers		268
Atmospheric, Earth Marine Teachers		48
Biology Teachers		226
Business, Commerce Teachers		154
Chemistry Teachers		190
Economic Teachers		131
Education Teachers		86
Elementary School Teachers		8902
Engineering Teachers		219
English Teachers		365
Foreign Language Teachers		176
Health Specialties Teachers		386
History Teachers		170
Home Economics Teachers		31
Law Teachers		51
Mathematics Teachers		277
Physics Teachers		165
Preschool, Kindergarten Teachers		536
Psychology Teachers		156
Secondary School Teachers		7692
Sociology Teachers		72
Social Science Teachers		144
Miscellaneous College & University Teachers		195
College, University NEC		1426
Theology Teachers		38
Trade, Industrial Teachers		26
Teachers, Exc. College, University		567
Teachers Aides, Exc. Monitors		422
Coaches, Phys Ed Teachers (50%)		77
Public Information Disseminators	1,264	
Librarians		755
Archivists and Curators		44
Library Attendants, Assistant		465
Communication Workers	3,321	
Writers, Artists, Entertainers		528
Editors and Reporters		1288
Photographers		391
Authors		146
Public Relations People, Writers		802
Radio, TV Announcers		166
TOTAL KNOWLEDGE DISTRIBUTORS	28,265	

TABLE 8.4 Market Search and Coordination Specialists

	1967 Employee Compensation ($ Millions)	
Information Gatherers	6,132	
Enumerators and Interviewers		327
Estimators, Investigators		2470
Inspectors, Exc. Construction, Public		763
Assess, Control, Local Public Admin.		198
Construction Inspector, Public		170
Real Estate Appraisers		205
Insurance Adjusters, Exam.		778
Meter Readers, Utilities		220
Weighers		266
Surveyors		408
Bill Collectors		327
Search and Coordination Specialists	28,252	
Buy Side	2,967	
Buyers, Shippers, Farm Prod.		146
Buyers, Wholesale, Retail		1185
Purchasing Agents, Buyers		1636
Brokers	7,193	
Insurance Agents, Brokers, etc.		3494
Real Estate Agents, Brokers		2219
Stock and Bond Salesmen		1450
Auctioneers		30
Sell Side	18,092	
Advertising Agents, Salesmen		598
Sales Representatives, Manufacturing		4092
Sales Representatives, Wholesale Trade		5501
Sales Manager, Retail Trade		2287
Sales Manager, Exec. Retail Trade		3622
Demonstrators		143
Salesmen, Retail (50%)		1313
Salesmen, Service (50%)		536
Planning and Control Workers	58,986	
Administrators and Managers	53,057	
Officials, Administrators, Public		2667
School Administrators, College		475
School Admin., Elementary & Secondary		1801
Office Managers		2363
Other Managers, Administrators		39709
Foremen (50%)		5890
Officer, Ship (50%)		152
Process Control Workers	5929	
Clerical Supervisors		1600
Postmasters and Mail Superintendents		274
Health Administrators		912
Dispatcher, Starter, Vehicle		432
Expeditors, Production Controllers		1463
Air Traffic Controllers		283
Payroll, Time Keeping Clerks		965
TOTAL MARKET SEARCH AND CO-ORDINATION SPECIALISTS	93,370	

possible good or service available. On the "sell side" are all the occupations whose job is to distribute relevant market information—prices, product characteristics, delivery schedules, and so on. And operating as both buyers and sellers simultaneously are the "brokers," whose income is earned exclusively by performing search activities on behalf of both sides of the market. These three groups earned over $28 billion in 1967.

"Planning and control workers" include all occupations which serve in administrative or managerial roles. Under administrators are public and private bureaucrats, school administrators, and office managers. Also included in this category are a variety of process-control supervisors, such as expediters and air-traffic controllers.

The administrative and managerial work force is the main engine of any organization. In public bureaucracies its job is to implement programs legislated by Congress, to regulate markets, to carry out all income distribution programs which fit into some political plan. Its members might be inspired public servants, or they may be fugitives from the "productive sector"—the accounts do not tell. But their job titles imply some organizational or administrative duty which is purely informational in nature: they receive commands from the top of the hierarchy, process them in some routine or creative fashion, and issue commands towards the bottom of the hierarchy. All that passes through their domain are information flows—memos, conferences, decisions, reports—and all that they do during the workday is talk, think, and write. Their counterparts in the private bureaucracies are similarly placed. Operating in a market context, their job is to plan the firm's actions, to design, carry out, and evaluate the firm's movement into marketplaces, to plan and implement technical changes in the firm's production processes, to investigate and analyze their competitors' behavior. They are successful when the firm's market share increases—when the firm is relatively shielded from competitive pressures. The larger and more entrenched the firm, the larger its bureaucracy. In 1967, the administrators and managers earned close to $59 billion dollars, or 7.4 percent of GNP.

The "process control workers" include seven occupations which are of a coordinating or supervisory nature. Three occupations—dispatchers, expediters and air traffic controllers—are heavy users of information technology in their daily tasks. A layer of management that is of a purely control nature (e.g., quality, schedule, inventory) will increasingly take on the artifacts of an information economy—computer terminals, distributed information networks, remote sensing instruments and communication hardware.

Information Processors

The information processing occupations are divided into two groups—nonelectronic based and electronic based. Table 8.5 shows a detailed breakdown of the occupations. "Nonelectronic based" processors include proofreaders, secretaries, file clerks, telegraph messengers, and statistical clerks. Many of these occupations are subject to rapid change with the introduction of new information

TABLE 8.5   Information Processors

	1967 Employee Compensation ($ Millions)	
Non-Electronic Based*	34,317	
Proofreaders		145
Secretaries, Legal		520
Secretaries, Medical		349
Secretaries, Other		12312
File Clerks		1166
Postal Clerks		2076
Motion Picture Projectionists		113
Newsboys		139
Mail Carriers, Post Office		1829
Mail Handler, Exc. Post Office		632
Messengers and Office Boys		234
Telegraph Messengers		9
Shipping, Receiving Clerks		2481
Statistical Clerks		1651
Health Record Technologist		71
Clerical Asst., Soc Welfare		6
Inspectors, Log and Lumber		93
Inspectors, Other		920
Checkers, Examiners, etc.		3957
Receptionists (50%)		789
Miscellaneous Clerical		5953
Railroad Conductors (50%)		32
Electronic Based*	27,023	
Bank Tellers		1201
Billing Clerks		556
Bookkeepers		6896
Cashiers		3347
Typists		4117
Ticket Station, Express Agents		642
Sales Clerks, Retail Trade (50%)		8239
Registered Nurses (50%)		1876
Radiology Technical (50%)		149
TOTAL INFORMATION PROCESSORS	61,340	

*The last Census *Handbook of Occupational Titles* describes which occupations are electronic-based. This table reflects the expected changes in classifications based on 1980 technology.

technologies. For example, the job of proofreading book galleys is now handled by a computer-driven dictionary; file clerks now manage computer files rather than paper files; telegraph messengers are being replaced by inexpensive on-site teletype and facsimile machines. In all, some $34.3 billion was earned by this class of workers in 1967.

"Electronic based" processors include bank tellers, bookkeepers, cashiers, typists, and sales clerks. A significant component of these workers' information handling is already machine based. Tellers operate real-time computers; bookkeepers supply data entry into automated accounting systems; sales clerks operate point-of-purchase terminals. About half of registered nurses' incomes is also allocated to this group. This allocation is made on the basis of observations by a research team at a California hospital of how a nurse allocates time to different activities. A significant portion of the time was spent filling out computer forms, checking computerized log books and entering patient information into a computer file. As hospitals adopt sophisticated information systems, registered nurses will increasingly interact with machines as well as with patients. Whether patients fare better or worse is still a matter of debate within the medical community.

Some occupations have undergone a most remarkable transformation in the past ten years. These machine-based occupations are now the "sensors" of an information creature that is endowed with unlimited processing power, but, without human help, is blind and deaf to the environment. The entire banking system and airline system would be crippled without the constant interaction between machine-using clerks and the computer.

The development of very good real-time sensors allows a host of planning and control activities that were impossible before. As the grocery clerk checks out food by scanning it with a light pen, inventory files are being altered, ordering schedules are being updated, and a financial statement on the day's events is being prepared. This intensity of coordination will require a variety of occupations to become machine based if they are not already so. It is unlikely that typists 20 years from now will still be using stand-alone mechanical typewriters. It costs too much money to type a letter, correct it, transmit it, and file it. Letters will probably be composed on a machine, transmitted, and filed all in one execution—not only business letters, but invoices and receipts. In tandem with a developed funds transfer system, today's typist may be tomorrow's bank clerk, postman, and file clerk, all wrapped up in one. In 1967, the electronic based information processors earned $27 billion. Together with the nonelectronic based processors, this group accounts for $61.3 billion, or 7.7% of GNP.

Information Machine Workers

The last group of workers maintains and operates the information infrastructure—the computers, telecommunication networks, printing presses, and the like. The occupations displayed in Table 8.6 earned over $13 billion in 1967.

"Nonelectronic machine operators" work on duplicating machines, typesetting machines, and printing presses. Although these machines are currently nonelectronic, the picture may change drastically in the next 20 years. Newsrooms are already automated, from the journalist's input via a terminal through computer-controlled photocomposition, layout, and platemaking. The big printing presses are almost the last nonelectronic pieces of a highly electronic production line. Plans for electronic newspapers, delivered via cable lines, will further

TABLE 8.6 Information Machine Workers

	1967 Employee Compensation ($ Millions)	
Non-Electronic Machine Operators	4,219	
Stenographers		663
Duplicating Machines Operators		92
Other Office Machine Operators		240
Bookbinders		171
Compositors and Typesetters		1138
Electrotypers, Stereotypers		60
Engravers, Exc. Photoengravers		67
Photoengravers, Lithographers		266
Pressmen and Plate Printers		1010
Pressmen Apprentices		19
Printing Apprentices, Exc. Press		31
Photographic Process Workers		379
Sign Painters		83
Electronic Machine Operators	3,660	
Bookkeeping, Billing Operators		310
Calculating Machine Operators		162
Computer, Peripheral Equipment Operators		970
Keypunch Operators		1423
Tabulating Machine Operators		48
Data Processing Machine Repair		315
Office Machine Repairmen		432
Telecommunication Workers	5,288	
Telegraph Operators		82
Telephone Operators		1738
Telephone Installers, Repairmen		2204
Telephone Linemen, Splicers		375
Radio Operators		190
Radio, Television Repairmen		699
TOTAL INFORMATION MACHINE WORKERS	13,167	

reduce the requirements for nonelectronic information machine occupations. This reality has already touched off some serious strikes against national newspapers.

"Electronic machine operators" include computer operators, keypunch operators, and office machine repairmen. This category includes the new "blue-collar" component of the information sector—workers who might have worked in factories 50 years ago, but who are now working in air-conditioned office buildings tending to computer-oriented machinery. Their pay, if not their sense of alienation, is commensurately higher.

"Telecommunications workers" operate, repair, and install telephone and telegraph equipment. They support the telecommunications network at the "assembly" level. Conceptually, this group of workers is indistinguishable from any machine-based blue-collar or crafts occupation. They are accounted separately, however, because without their help the information machines would not be as-sembled and repaired. By analogy, if one were writing a thesis on "The Transpor-tation Economy," repair mechanics and automobile-assembly workers would surely be included. This group of workers earned some $13 billion in 1967. It is conceivable that demand for mechanical and repair skills of information machines will increase quite quickly in the near future, although the jobs are likely to be re-defined as white-collar (e.g., "electrical engineer").

THE NON-INFORMATION WORKERS

The rest of the United States work force was divided into three conventional sectors—agriculture, industry, and services. In 1967, this group accounted for about 55 percent of the work force and about 45 percent of total compensation. The following classification scheme follows in the convention of Clark, who first defined the primary, secondary, and tertiary sectors of the economy as stages of economic growth.

Agriculture

The agriculture sector includes farm owners, managers, foremen, and labor-ers. Some owners and managers may be information workers, but they were in-cluded in the agriculture sector. Farmers actually spend a great deal of their time in a variety of informational activities. The morning weather reports and com-modity exchange prices are ritual sources of information gathering. Farmers also spend considerable time with information "pushers" such as salesmen for seed and fertilizer companies (who often supply very detailed data on how to apply and use their products), and government advisers (such as the Agricultural Exten-sion Service). In addition, the agriculture sector hires information workers who are specialized in the various skills necessary to run a modern agribusiness—sales-men, accountants, lawyers, secretaries, and the like. This last group is not in-cluded as agriculture workers *per se*, but will be accounted later in this chapter.

Industry

Industrial workers include the bulk of blue-collar manufacturing occupa-tions, skilled and unskilled crafts, operatives, and laborers. A variety of service-type jobs are included in industry, such as plumbers and glazers, since these occupations engage in manipulating physical objects rather than providing per-sonal or informational services. The industry category conceptually includes all skilled crafts whether they are based in factories or not.

Several transportation occupations have been included in this sector. For ex-ample, railroad brakemen and truck drivers are in the transportation sector, hence included as a "service." But transportation of bulk commodities is an essential feature of an industrial economy, as distinct from the transportation of people. Taxicab drivers and bus drivers have been defined as part of the service sector; truck drivers and barge captains are part of industry.

Services

The service sector includes mostly personal and repair-service occupations, such as hairdressers, waiters, airplane pilots, auto repairmen, and counter clerks. In addition, half the wages of selected managers is included as services rather than information. Managers at the retail level, whether self-employed or salaried, perform both informational and noninformational roles depending on the type of business. For example, managers of gas stations usually perform the same duties as mechanics and station attendants—repairing automobiles, pumping gas—and are classified in "services." Managers of retail grocery stores may stock shelves and bag food for customers—noninformational activities—or they may specialize in purchasing, financial control, and personnel types of activities. This distinction depends entirely on the size of the establishment, the preferences of the manager, and the legal form of organization. One might expect salaried managers to be more like information workers than small "ma and pa" retail proprietorships. Salesmen at the retail and service level also perform both an informational service and a personal service. For example, a salesman at a clothing store might be there only to counsel a customer as to the price and quality features of a garment and to ring up a sale, or he may actually help the customer try on garments. Many sales-clerks only operate information machines—credit verification and point-of-purchase terminals. Without a detailed time budget study, it is impossible to determine which portion of a salesman's time is informational, and which should be allocated to service. Half the income was allocated to each.

Physicians' incomes were also prorated equally between services and information. Time budget studies of physicians' offices revealed that over 70 percent of a physician's time is spent in receiving patient histories, performing diagnoses, and dispensing medical or self-care patient education—all information tasks. A relatively small part of the time is spent in the skilled-craft aspect, such as office surgery, cleaning wounds, and setting broken bones. Dentists, by contrast, were entirely allocated to services since most of their time is spent in the skilled-craft aspect attending to a personal service.

Summary of Ambiguous Occupations

About 28 occupations were judged to be sufficiently "mixed" in nature that they were allocated into two sectors. This ambiguous class was specifically carried through the time-series charts that follow. Table 8.7 shows the occupations which

TABLE 8.7   Occupations Allocated Fifty Percent to Service and Fifty Percent to Information

Physicians	Hucksters
Registered Nurses	Sales Clerks, Retail Trades
Dietitians	Misc. Clerical Workers
Clinical Lab Technologists	Managers, Retail Trade, Salary
Health Record Technologists	Managers, Retail Trade, Self-Emp.
Radiological Technologists	Managers, Personal Services, Salaried
Designers	Managers, Personal Services, Self-Employed
Counter Clerks, Exc. Food	Managers, Business Services, Salaried
Officers, Pilots, Pursers on Ships	Managers, Business and Repair Services,
Officials of Lodges, Societies, Unions	Self-Employed
Railroad Conductors	Receptionists
Demonstrators	

were split equally between information and services under the "inclusive" definition, and allocated entirely to services under the "restrictive" definition.

Table 8.8 shows the occupations that were split equally between industry and information under the inclusive definition, and allocated entirely to industry under the restrictive definition.

Foremen used to work on machines alongside craftsmen. However, with the advent of unions, foremen were increasingly relegated to nonproduction jobs such as scheduling, inventory control, and on-the-job training. They are now a "buffer" between the productive workers and the managers, and are often specifically barred from working on machines for fear of breaking union rules. Similarly, inspectors, checkers, and the like often work in industrial settings but most of their time is spent gathering information about a production process.

Change in the Work Force over Time

The change in the labor force toward a predominance of information workers has been persistent since the 1940s. Figure 8.1 shows a two-sector aggrega-

TABLE 8.8   Occupations Allocated Fifty Percent to Industry and Fifty Percent to Information

Foreman, NEC
Inspectors, Scalers, Graders, Lumber
Inspectors, NEC
Chainmen, Rodmen (Surveying)
Checkers, Examiners, Inspectors (Manufacturing)
Graders and Sorters (Manufacturing)

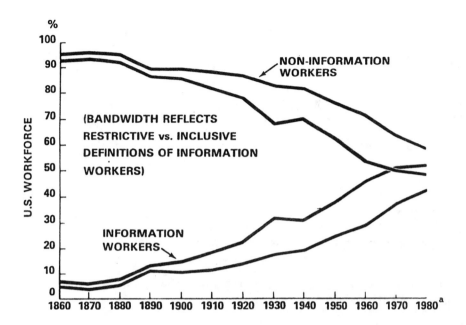

a 1980 projections supplied by the Bureau of Labor Statistics (unpublished).

FIGURE 8-1 Time Series of U.S. Labor Force (1860–1980): Two Sector Aggregate by Percent

tion, using the restrictive and inclusive definitions discussed above. The information work force in 1860 comprised less than 10 percent of the total. By 1975, the information workers (under the inclusive definition) surpassed the noninformation group. The crossover in employee compensation occurred much sooner, since information occupations tend to earn a higher average income. By 1967, some 53 percent of total compensation was paid to information workers.

In Stage I (1860–1906) of Figure 8.2, the largest single group in the labor force was *agriculture*. By the turn of the century, *industrial* occupations began to grow rapidly and became predominant during Stage II (1906–1954). In the current period, Stage III, *information* occupations comprise the largest group.

The charts also reveal several events worthy of further research. The detailed data show a decline in information occupations' growth during the Depression, attributable to layoffs of nonessential personnel. A hypothesis emerges: that layoffs in information occupations lag recessions by one or two years. Since the output of an information worker is not easily measurable, and since informational skills generalize more easily than physical skills, the group as a whole seems quite vulnerable to layoffs. When a factory is faced with declining demand for its goods, the rate of production slowdown precisely determines how many production workers lose their jobs. Machines and manpower are locked by virtue of fixed

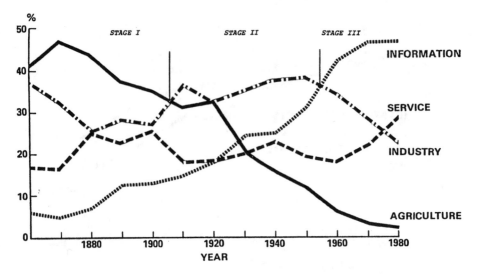

FIGURE 8-2   Four Sector Aggregation of the U.S. Work Force by Percent 1860–1980
(Using Median Estimates of Information Workers)

capital/labor ratios. Hence, a reduction in machine utilization determines a proportionate reduction in labor. To a certain extent, even this reduction of production workers can be cushioned by inventory accumulation. By contrast, information workers are not locked into capacity utilization. They can be hired and fired at a rate that is relatively decoupled from the production line. The managerial "slack"—such as extra secretaries, a heavy line of middle management, and a large sales force—can be trimmed quite quickly.

Note also the rapid rise of information occupations immediately following World War II. As the soldiers came home, they apparently joined the private and public bureaucracies in droves. They did not return to manufacturing jobs or service work (as was the trend immediately before the war). This postwar period is associated with the emergence of the modern corporation: far-flung, national or multinational in scope, bureaucratic. And it is also associated with the development of new information machines—computers, xerographic copiers, telecommunication networks.

New information applications were found, and the labor force adjusted to fill the new demand. In part, the rapid growth of information occupations is explained by increased division of labor and specialization. Simple one-person information tasks split into two jobs. Information machines required highly specialized labor. Job titles and duties became narrower. However, calling a job by a different name does not change the basic function. Governments expanded very rapidly at the State and local level (less so at the Federal level), and these, too, required a huge information work force. Science and technology enjoyed a sizable growth in activity, both within the university and within private industry. The education system concurrently began receiving massive Federal grants and transfers, further increasing both the demand for teachers and the supply of information workers (managers, scientists, engineers, computer programmers).

Note also that the industrial work force reached a peak of around 40 percent of the work force in 1950, and has been declining precipitously since then. It plunged from a position of predominance in 1940, when the information work force was less than half the size of the industrial work force, to the present, with the industrial work force only half the size of the information work force. This reversal was extremely rapid, and from all indications the trend has only recently been abated.

Note lastly that service occupations, which held a steady 15–20 percent of the work force for 100 years (1860–1960) suddenly took off again in 1965. This is due to two phenomena. First, I believe that we have temporarily saturated the work force with information workers—no more can be easily absorbed into industry and government. Hence, the growth of new occupations is mostly in the personal services. The second phenomenon is the increase in the medical professions, such as physicians, surgeons, nurses, medical technologists, and therapists. Part of this increase is due to the demand for new medical services, buoyed by rising expectations, rising income, and financed by insurance programs which stack the incentives in favor of surgery and hospitalization instead of preventative care. Partly, the rise in medical occupations has reflected the fact that people are living longer and requiring more medical attention. The growth rate of the service occupations is now almost equal to that of information workers.

INFORMATION WORKERS IN INDUSTRY AND GOVERNMENT

The previous sections discussed only one dimension of the U.S. work force—who the workers are and how much they receive in employee compensation. In this section, we shall look at the second dimension—where they work.

The following results are based on the Occupation by Industry matrix, prepared by the Bureau of the Census and the Bureau of Labor Statistics. The matrix shows the location of the 422 occupations in 201 major industries. We converted the matrix to show the employee compensation paid to each type of worker in each industry.

Information Workers in Industry

Table 8.9 shows the labor income earned in the primary information industries. Wages paid to information workers hired by private corporations amounted to $69 billion. In addition, the information industries spent $26 billion on noninformation workers (e.g., assemblers in a computer manufacturing firm). Proprietors working as information workers, in pure management roles, earned $7 billion in 1967. An additional $2 billion was earned by "blue-collar" partnerships in the primary information sector (e.g., self-employed TV repairmen). "Unpaid family workers" are spouses and children who are assigned a salary if they perform informational types of jobs (e.g., bookkeeper or typist). In all, the primary information industries accounted for nearly $29 billion in labor income in 1967.

Table 8.10 shows the wage bill for information workers employed in the bureaucracies of non-information firms; and partners who are essentially specialized in informational duties but are located in non-information enterprises. Together

TABLE 8.9   Labor Income in the Primary Information Industries

	($ Millions, 1967)			
Primary Info Industry	Em- ployee Comp- ensation	Prop- rietor's Comp- ensation	Unpaid Family Comp- ensation	Total Income
INFORMATION WORKERS				
11* Info buildings: office, education, comm	1232	222	10	1464
12* Maintenance & repair on info buildings	1280	230	10	1520
23* Office furniture & equipment	117	8	1	126
24* Paper: printing (exc boxes)	403	2	0	405
26* Printing & publishing	6340	304	44	6688
27* Ink	36	0	0	36
48* Printing & paper machinery	153	4	0	157
51* Computers, calculators, office equip.	1517	7	1	1525
53* Electronic measuring instruments	267	2	0	269
56* Radio, TV, comm'n equipment	4131	11	1	4143
57* Electronic components	1651	13	1	1665
58* Misc electronic instruments	40	0	0	40
62* Mechanical measuring & control instruments	842	7	1	850
63* Photographic & related equipment	765	8	1	774
64* Advertising signs & displays	226	19	1	246
66* Telecommunications, exc. radio & TV	6091	10	2	6103
67* Radio, TV, CATV	939	23	5	967
69* Trade margin on info goods	5576	1169	117	6862
70* Finance & insurance: components	18505	1144	48	19697
71* Real estate: fees, royalties, office rentals	341	225	9	575
72* Repair: radio & TV equipment	141	123	11	275
73* Misc business info services	10114	2320	88	12522
76* Motion pictures	842	125	8	975
77* Medical, educational, nonprofit	7401	553	49	8003
TOTAL INCOME OF INFO WORKERS	68950	6529	408	75887

(Continued)

with Table 8.11 which shows the non-information workers in non-information firms, the entire wage bill is fully apportioned.

The last two tables show the intensity of information resources used in each industry. For example, the ratio of information to non-information labor in the livestock industry (#l) is 1:128, whereas in the ordnance industry (#13) the ratio runs nearly 2:1 in the *opposite* direction. For all industries, every production worker on average carries an information "overhead" of about 74 cents per dollar earned.

TABLE 8.9   *(Continued)*

	($ Millions, 1967)			
Primary Info Industry	*Em- ployee Comp- ensation*	*Prop- rietor's Comp- ensation*	*Unpaid Family Comp- ensation*	*Total Income*
NON-INFORMATION WORKERS				
11* Info buildings: office, education, comm	2487	358	7	2852
12* Maintenance & repair on info buildings	2584	372	8	2964
23* Office furniture & equipment	247	5	0	252
24* Paper: printing (exc boxes)	595	1	0	596
26* Printing & publishing	1267	18	5	1290
27* Ink	34	0	0	34
48* Printing & paper machinery	174	3	0	177
51* Computers, calculators, office equip.	483	2	0	485
53* Electronic measuring instruments	237	0	0	237
56* Radio, TV, comm'n equipment	2183	4	1	2188
57* Electronic components	1468	3	1	1472
58* Misc electronic instruments	36	0	0	36
62* Mechanical measuring & control instruments	550	2	0	552
63* Photographic & related equipment	515	3	0	518
64* Advertising signs & displays	261	11	1	273
66* Telecommunications, exc. radio & TV	407	2	0	409
67* Radio, TV, CATV	121	3	0	124
69* Trade margin on info goods	3925	437	62	4424
70* Finance & insurance: components	483	12	1	496
71* Real estate: fees, royalties, office rentals	12	28	4	44
72* Repair: radio & TV equipment	351	93	9	453
73* Misc business info services	2566	387	11	2964
76* Motion pictures	624	110	2	736
77* Medical, educational, nonprofit	4820	259	25	5104
TOTAL INCOME OF NON-INFO WORKERS	26430	2113	137	28955

TABLE 8.10   Labor Income in the Secondary Information Industries

IO Industry	Employee Compensation	Proprietor's Compensation	Unpaid Family Compensation	Total Income
	($ Millions, 1967)			
1) Livestock & products	24	10	4	38
2) Other agricultural products	43	17	7	67
3) Forestry and fishery products	23	25	6	54
4) Agr., forest, fish services	166	88	32	286
5) Iron & ferroalloy ores mining	69	2	0	71
6) Nonferrous metal ores mining	116	3	0	119
7) Coal mining	179	9	1	189
8) Crude petroleum and natural gas	481	94	6	581
9) Stone, clay mining, & quarrying	217	14	2	233
10) Chemical & fertilizer mineral min.	55	4	1	60
11) New construction, Net	7084	1273	55	8412
12) Maintenance & repair construction	2618	471	20	3109
13) Ordnance and accessories	2651	3	0	2654
14) Food & kindred products	4569	101	15	4685
15) Tobacco manufactures	247	1	0	248
16) Fabrics, yarn, & thread mills	1016	17	1	1034
17) Misc. textile goods & floor cover.	312	5	0	317
18) Apparel	2182	71	6	2259
19) Misc. fabricated textile products	345	26	2	373
20) Lumber, wood prod. exc. containers	826	168	4	998
21) Wooden containers	50	5	0	55
22) Household furniture	538	36	2	576
23) Other furniture, fixtures, Net	180	12	1	193
24) Paper, allied prod. exc containers, Net	1145	6	1	1152
25) Paperboard containers, boxes	726	7	0	733
26) Printing & publishing, Net	514	25	4	543
27) Chemicals, sel Chem products, Net	2213	11	1	2225
28) Plastics, synthetic materials	855	4	0	859
29) Drugs, cleaning, toilet preparations	1579	14	3	1596
30) Paints & allied products	380	4	2	386
31) Petroleum refining & related ind's.	1274	5	0	1279
32) Rubber & misc plastics products	1651	21	3	1675
33) Leather tanning, ind. leather prods.	60	2	0	62
34) Footwear & other leather products	436	15	1	452
35) Glass & glass products	554	10	1	565
36) Stone & clay products	1345	61	5	1411
37) Primary iron & steel manufacturing	2842	14	1	2857

(Continued)

TABLE 8.10 *(Continued)*

IO Industry	Employee Compensation	Proprietor's Compensation	Unpaid Family Compensation	Total Income
	($ Millions, 1967)			
38) Primary nonferrous metal manufacturing	1312	12	1	1325
39) Metal containers	315	6	0	321
40) Heating, plumbing, & struc metal prods.	1475	50	4	1529
41) Stamping, screw mach. prods, & bolts	1183	13	1	1197
42) Other fabricated metal products	1535	28	2	1565
43) Engines and turbines	467	1	0	468
44) Farm machinery & equipment	550	6	1	557
45) Const., mining, & oil field machs.	823	7	0	830
46) Materials handling mach & equipment	376	3	0	379
47) Metalworking mach & equipment	1436	43	3	1482
48) Spec ind mach & equipment, Net	733	21	1	755
49) General ind mach & equipment	1203	35	2	1240
50) Machine shop products	766	22	2	790
52) Service industry machines	539	16	1	556
53) Elec ind equip & apparatus, Net	1497	12	1	1510
54) Household appliances	540	7	1	548
55) Electric lighting & wiring equip.	635	5	0	640
58) Misc elec machinery, Net	478	4	0	482
59) Motor vehicles & equipment	2969	17	3	2989
60) Aircraft and parts	5077	11	1	5089
61) Other transportation equipment	887	26	2	915
62) Scientific and controlling instru.	267	8	1	276
63) Optical, ophthalmic, & photo equip, Net	70	3	0	73
64) Misc manufacturing, Net	1035	85	6	1126
65) Transportation & warehousing	7272	460	62	7794
68) Electric, gas, water, & sanitary svcs	2467	30	4	2501
69) Wholesale & retail trade, Net	32279	8673	915	41867
70) Finance & insurance, Net	469	71	2	542
71) Real estate & rental, Net	1474	970	41	2485
72) Hotels: personal & rep svcs exc auto, Net	1779	1728	154	3661
73) Business services, Net	2837	3503	33	6373
75) Automobile repair & services	1072	257	31	1360
76) Amusements, Net	504	206	14	724
77) Medical, educ svcs, & non-profit org, Net	4331	2265	53	6649
85) Rest of the world industry	32	0	0	32
86) Household industry	421	64	4	486
TOTAL INCOME	120,670	21,322	1,526	143,518

TABLE 8.11   Labor Income in the Non-Information Industries

Industry	Employee Compensation	Proprietor's Compensation	Unpaid Family Compensation	Total Income
	($ Millions, 1967)			
1) Livestock & products	1187	3332	336	4855
2) Other agricultural products	2126	5967	602	8695
3) Forestry and fishery products	89	101	11	201
4) Agr., forest, fish services	552	704	56	1312
5) Iron & ferroalloy ores mining	183	1	0	184
6) Nonferrous metal ores mining	307	2	0	309
7) Coal mining	1058	8	1	1067
8) Crude petroleum and natural gas	401	30	2	433
9) Stone, clay mining, & quarrying	516	9	1	526
10) Chemical & fertilizer mineral min.	131	2	0	133
11) New construction, Net	14293	2060	42	16395
12) Maintenance & repair construction	5281	761	16	6058
13) Ordnance and accessories	1446	2	0	1448
14) Food & kindred products	8613	72	15	8700
15) Tobacco manufactures	356	1	0	357
16) Fabrics, yarn, & thread mills	2369	8	2	2379
17) Misc. textile goods & floor cover.	480	2	0	482
18) Apparel	4624	16	4	4644
19) Misc. fabricated textile products	557	13	2	572
20) Lumber, wood prod. exc. containers	2258	223	12	2493
21) Wooden containers	103	3	0	106
22) Household furniture	1136	22	2	1160
23) Other furniture, fixtures, Net	381	7	1	389
24) Paper, allied prod. exc containers, Net	1688	4	1	1693
25) Paperboard containers, boxes	951	2	1	954
26) Printing & publishing, Net	103	1	0	104
27) Chemicals, sel Chem products, Net	1977	3	1	1981
28) Plastics, synthetic materials	1171	1	0	1132
29) Drugs, cleaning, toilet preparations	882	2	1	885
30) Paints & allied products	263	1	0	264
31) Petroleum refining & related ind's.	992	3	0	995
32) Rubber & misc plastics products	2355	7	3	2365
33) Leather tanning, ind. leather prods.	174	1	0	175
34) Footwear & other leather products	1043	5	1	1049
35) Glass & glass products	860	5	1	866
36) Stone & clay products	2036	21	3	2060
37) Primary iron & steel manufacturing	6334	12	1	6347

(Continued)

TABLE 8.11   *(Continued)*

| | *($ Millions, 1967)* | | | |
Industry	Em- ployee Comp- ensation	Prop- rietor's Comp- ensation	Unpaid Family Comp- ensation	Total Income
38) Primary nonferrous metal manufacturing	2141	6	0	2147
39) Metal containers	438	3	0	441
40) Heating, plumbing, & struc metal prods.	1961	22	1	1984
41) Stamping, screw mach. prods, & bolts	1896	4	1	1901
42) Other fabricated metal products	2091	12	1	2104
43) Engines and turbines	537	1	1	539
44) Farm machinery & equipment	699	2	0	701
45) Const., mining, & oil field machs.	904	3	0	907
46) Materials handling mach & equipment	413	2	0	415
47) Metalworking mach & equipment	1855	24	1	1880
48) Spec ind mach & equipment, Net	832	15	1	848
49) General ind mach & equipment	1367	24	1	1392
50) Machine shop products	870	16	1	887
52) Service industry machines	612	11	0	623
53) Elec ind equip & apparatus, Net	1331	3	1	1335
54) Household appliances	805	2	1	808
55) Electric lighting & wiring equip.	565	1	0	566
58) Misc elec machinery, Net	425	1	0	426
59) Motor vehicles & equipment	5484	14	3	5501
60) Aircraft and parts	3498	8	0	3506
61) Other transportation equipment	1603	21	2	1626
62) Scientific and controlling instru.	300	5	0	305
63) Optical, ophthalmic, & photo equip, Net	69	1	0	70
64) Misc manufacturing, Net	1197	49	3	1249
65) Transportation & warehousing	13657	901	44	14602
68) Electric, gas, water, & sanitary svcs	2437	46	3	2486
69) Wholesale & retail trade, Net	28032	3696	541	32269
70) Finance & insurance, Net	12	0	0	12
71) Real estate & rental, Net	53	122	17	192
72) Hotels: personal & rep svcs exc auto, Net	4804	2996	96	7896
73) Business services, Net	519	37	2	558
75) Automobile repair & services	2713	801	24	3538
76) Amusements, Net	905	64	7	976
77) Medical, educ svcs, & non-profit org, Net	6985	4297	45	11327
85) Rest of the world industry	13	0	0	13
86) Househeld industry	4280	38	4	4322
TOTAL INCOME	165,539	26,662	1,919	194,120

Definition of Proprietors' Income

One methodological note on the meaning of labor income is in order. Employee compensation totalled $471,090 million in 1967 and included wages, salaries, and supplements paid to employees of firms (incorporated and unincorporated), plus governments and nonprofit organizations. All proprietors' income is usually not counted as employee compensation, but appears as a property-type income. Proprietorships' income is in the form of retained earnings of unincorporated businesses, and represents a return to both capital (invested in the business and owned by the proprietor) *and* labor. The problem is how to separate the returns to labor from returns to capital, and three approaches are available: (1) Denison defined labor earnings in the economy as the sum of employee compensation plus 60 percent of proprietors' income, the other 40 percent representing returns to capital holding. (2) The National Income Accounts define *all* of proprietors' income as profit or property-type income. (3) Jorgenson and Griliches chose the opposite tack—that all of proprietors' income should be allocated to labor.

We adopted a method to test these three approaches. Proprietors are allocated an average wage (as if they were salaried) based on empirical observation of similar occupations. The distinction between a proprietor and a salaried worker hinges entirely on the firm's legal form of organization—if a proprietor incorporated the business, his earnings would be accounted as a salary. The difference between the "wages" earned by proprietors and total proprietors' income is counted as returns to capital. In this procedure, all unpaid family workers are assigned "wages" based on what they would earn if they were in fact salaried. Using this empirical approach, we discovered that about $60.6 billion was earned as "wages" by proprietors and unpaid family workers, while about $2 billion represents a return to capital. These figures are summarized in Table 8.12 below.

TABLE 8.12   Summary of Proprietors' Income

	1967 ($ Millions)	
TOTAL PROPRIETORS' INCOME (labor & capital)	62,147	
"Compensation" to proprietors' labor	56,626	
In primary information industries		8,642
In secondary information, industries		21,322
In non-information industries		26,662
Proprietors' comp/total income		91.1%
"Compensation" to unpaid family workers	3,990	
In primary information industries		545
In secondary information industries		1,526
In non-information industries		1,919
Unpaid family/total income		6.41%
Imputed return on capital	1,531	
Capital/total income		2.6%
Capital/income (exc. unpaid family)		8.9%

The share of proprietors' income earned as wages (on a par with salaried managers) amounted to some 91 percent of total income. If we supplement that income with par wages earned by their unpaid family workers, the total share of income attributed to labor rises to 97 percent. Using the proprietors' "compensation" only (and excluding unpaid family), we see that around 8.9 percent of total income represents a return to capital.

The 8.9 percent, as an imputed return to capital, compares with the corporate sector's capital share of 17.4 percent shown in Table 8.13. Proprietors earn less "profits" on average than do corporations. This statistic probably confounds the capital shares experienced in the two sectors since partnerships are significantly smaller than most active corporations. The difference between the 8.9 percent and the 17.4 percent could be explained by dividing the sample into similar firms (in revenue terms), and comparing the capital share in each. Also, proprietorships tend to be found in businesses which are *not* capital intensive, such as retail and service establishments, hence their portion of total income accruing from capital ownership is likely to be smaller than the average corporation.

We conclude from these data that the Jorgenson and Griliches approach—allocating proprietors' income to labor—is more correct than either Denison's or the NIA's approach.

Information Workers in Government

Governments, by habit and tradition, tend to spawn into permanent bureaucracies. The Federal, State and local governments are filled with administrators and clerks whose job is to know, to deliberate, and to decide. All this thinking, talking, and writing requires human labor, and Table 8.14 shows the price tag paid for all government workers. Some things that governments do are also done in the primary information sector. For example, data processing shops are found both inside government and in the private economy.

TABLE 8.13 Labor and Capital Shares in the Corporate Sector

	1967 ($ Millions)	
TOTAL CORPORATE INCOME (labor & capital)	451,221	
Compensation to employees	372,535	
Wages and salaries (private)		337,322
Supplements		35,213
Corporate profits and inventory valuation adjustment	78,686	
Profits before taxes		79,815
Inventory valuation adjustments		–1,129
Capital income/total income		17.4%
Labor income/total income		82.6%

TABLE 8.14   Employee Compensation in Governments

	($ Millions, 1967)				
	Primary Info Activities	*Secondary Info Activities*	*Total Info Activities*	*Non-Info Activities*	*Total Labor Income*
ALL GOVERNMENTS	40,699	18,735	59,434	30,073	89,507
Total General Government	37,160	15,958	53,118	28,536	81,654
Total Federal Government	10,232	6,357	16,589	18,616	35,205
Civilian	5,800	3,009	8,809	7,554	16,363
Military	4,432	3,348	7,780	11,062	18,842
Total State and Local	26,928	9,601	36,529	9,920	46,449
Education	26,928	0	26,928	0	26,928
Other	0	9,601	9,601	9,920	19,521
Total Enterprises	3,539	2,777	6,316	1,537	7,853
Total Federal Enterprises	3,539	1,336	4,875	908	5,783
Postal Service	3,539	0	3,539	0	3,539
Other	0	1,336	1,336	908	2,244
Total State & Local Enterprises	0	1,441	1,441	629	2,070

Table 8.14 reveals that around $59 billion—or 7.5 percent of GNP in 1967—is generated by the primary and secondary informational activities of Federal, State, and local governments and their enterprises. Of this sum, nearly $27 billion is paid by State and local governments for education workers; $9 billion pays for the Federal information bureaucracy; $8 billion pays for the purely informational portion of the military establishment; and slightly more than $1 billion pays for moving the U.S. mail. Note that the Federal bureaucracy is less than half the size of the state and local bureaucracies. It has the cosmetic disadvantage, however, of being concentrated in a nine square mile area on the banks of the Potomac. The noninformational aspects of government, activities such as protecting bald eagles and polishing brass on nuclear submarines, account for $30 billion. The combined wage bill for all blue-collar workers in State and local enterprises is less than $11 billion.

Labor Income Summary

The information wage bill in 1967 amounted to $307.5 billion—$145 billion for all primary information activities, and $162 billion for the secondary activities. About 58 percent of all labor income—or 38.7 percent of the 1967 GNP—was earned in some informationally related occupation. These figures are summarized in Table 8.15.

TABLE 8.15 Labor Income Summary

	($ Millions, 1967)				
	(1) Primary Info Industries	*(2)* Secondary Info Industries	*(1+2)* Total Info Industries	*(3)* Non-Info Industries	*(1+2+3)* Total Labor Income
I. TOTAL LABOR INCOME	145,266	162,253	307,519	224,187	531,706
Employee Compensation	136,079	139,405	275,484	195,606	471,090
Private Sector	95,380	120,670	216,050	165,533	381,583
Public Sector	40,699	18,735	59,434	30,073	89,507
Proprietors' Income[a]	9,187	22,848	32,035	28,581	60,616
II. INFORMATION WORKERS' INCOME	116,311	162,253	278,564	0	278,564
Employee Compensation	109,374	139,405	248,779	0	248,779
Private Sector	68,950	120,670	189,620	0	189,620
Public Sector	40,424	18,735	59,159	0	59,159
Proprietors' Income[a]	6,937	22,848	29,785	0	29,785
III. NON-INFORMATION WORKERS' INCOME	28,955	0	28,955	224,187	253,142
Employee Compensation	26,705	0	26,705	195,606	222,311
Private Sector	26,430	0	26,430	165,533	191,963
Public Sector	275	0	275	30,073	30,348
Proprietors' Income[a]	2,250	0	2,250	28,581	30,831

[a]Includes self-employed and unpaid family.

GROWTH RATES OF THE INFORMATION WORK FORCE

The information work force expanded at a compound (annual) rate of 3.85% during the period 1860–1980, doubling every 18.7 years on the average. During the same period, the total work force increased at 2.06% per year; hence, information workers experienced a net annual average growth of 1.79%.

This astonishing growth rate was far from monotonic, as Table 8.16 and Figure 8.3 clearly show. The growth of the information work force (r^i) is compared to the growth of the whole work force ($\bar{r}$),

$$r^i - \bar{r} = \left(\frac{t^i_1}{t^i_2}\right)^{\frac{1}{n}} - \left(\frac{t_{\bar{1}}}{t_{\bar{2}}}\right)^{\frac{1}{n}}$$

where, t^i_1, $t_{\bar{1}}$ = the size of the information and the whole workforce at time 1.

t^i_2, $t_{\bar{2}}$ = the same at time 2.

n = time period between the measurements.

TABLE 8.16   Compound Annual Growth Rates of the Labor Force

| | (By Percents) | | |
Period	Information Workers	Total Labor Force	Net Information Growth[a]
TEN-YEAR PERIODS			
1860–1870	2.26	4.21	−1.95
1870–1880	6.53	3.35	3.18
1880–1890	9.57	2.72	6.85
1890–1900	2.84	2.51	0.33
1900–1910	4.74	3.16	1.58
1910–1920	3.06	1.30	1.76
1920–1930	4.55	1.21	3.34
1930–1940	0.64	0.48	0.16
1940–1950	2.94	0.77	2.17
1950–1960	4.80	1.60	3.20
1960–1970	2.69	1.68	1.01
1970–1980	1.85	1.81	0.04
TWENTY-YEAR PERIODS			
1940–1960	3.87	1.18	2.69
1960–1980	2.27	1.74	0.53
FORTY-YEAR PERIODS			
1860–1980	3.85	2.06	1.79
1860–1900	5.26	3.20	2.06
1900–1940	3.24	1.53	1.71
1940–1980	3.07	1.46	1.61

[a]Growth rate of information workers minus the growth rate of the total labor force.

In the most recent period, the information workers expanded at almost the same rate as the overall work force (net rates of 1.01 percent for 1960–1970, and 0.04 percent projected for 1970–1980). New entrants to the labor force simply could not be absorbed into information occupations, and had to move into the service sector, including a large contingency into the medical service sector.

The decade immediately following World War II showed the fastest net growth rates of information occupations, posting 2.2 percent between 1940–1950, and 3.2 percent between 1950–1960. This confirms the trend in both the public and the private sectors towards increased bureaucratization. New information machines and management techniques were introduced around this time, and the work force rapidly expanded to fill the need.

The Depression years, extending into the mid 1930's, saw a slow down in the growth of information jobs. While the total work force increased at a snail's pace of 0.48 percent per year, information occupations grew only 0.64 percent—a net difference of only 0.16 percent. Unfortunately, the census data do not appear at more frequent intervals so we lose the trend in the late 30's.

The first 30 years of this century are associated with the industrial age; however, information workers consistently expanded faster than the overall labor

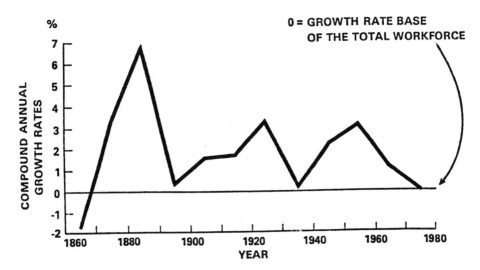

FIGURE 8-3 Net Growth Rates of Information Occupations (Relative to the Overall Workforce)

force, increasing in net terms at over 3 percent between 1920 and 1930 alone. This growth corresponds to the "secondary information sector"—information services performed within non-information firms. At no point have the information occupations lagged behind the overall work force, although the net rates dip twice to the zero line (between 1930–1940, and between 1970–1980). The data in Table 8.16 shows extremely rapid growth rates between 1870 and 1890. In part, the growth is a definitional artifact: as family farms and businesses dissolved in the face of industrialization and urbanization, jobs assumed a formality that was measured by the Census. The son and daughter vanished, and an employee took their place. Also, this period marked the beginning of the national corporations. The railroads, the marketing chains, and the steel firms set up national headquarters in New York and Chicago, and established the first fledgling private bureaucracies.

It remains to be seen whether the information work force increases at the pace of the 1940s and 1950s ever again. I rather doubt it. Resurgence in the information occupations is likely only if new types of information industries are launched by entrepreneurs—information utilities, search services, storage and retrieval, computer-based diagnostics of everything from cars to hearts, facsimile and electronic mail transmission services, specialized microcomputer programming, and so on. But as of this decade, the private and public bureaucracies are glutted with information workers. No more can be easily absorbed. The school systems are shrinking as the baby boom rumbles away; "lifelong education" has yet to become a reality; and the primary information service industries such as finance, law, and advertising are increasing at roughly the same rate as GNP.

9

The New Industrial Society

Jorge Reina Schement and Terry Curtis

The debate continued about who and how many knowledge workers there were. Two professors of communications, Schement at Rutgers University and Curtis at California State University at Chico, provide the most recent analysis of the problems originally laid out by Machlup. This selection could just as easily qualified as the first for this book, because it provides an overview of many of the debates that have been underway for nearly a half century over the nature of knowledge work, its role in modern economic thinking, and in the structure of society.

Behind the Thomson and Homestead and Keystone plants were the famous Lucy and Carrie furnaces for making pig iron; and behind them was the enormous Henry Clay Frick Coke Company with its 40,000 acres of coal land, its 2,688 railway cars, and its 13,252 coking ovens; and behind this, in turn, were 244 miles of railways (organized into three main companies) to ship materials to and from the coking ovens; and then at a still more distant remove were a shipping company and a dock company with a fleet of Great Lakes ore-carrying steamers; and then at the very point of origin of the steel-making process, was the Oliver Mining Company with its great mines in Michigan and Wisconsin.

—Robert Heilbroner

World satellite systems now make distance and time irrelevant. We witness and react to crises simultaneously with their happening. Networks of tele-phones, telex, radio, and television have exponentially increased the density of human contact. More people can be in touch with one another during any single day in the new communications environment than many did in a life-

From *Tendencies and Tensions of the Information Age: The Production and Distribution of Informa-tion in the United States* (New Brunswick, NJ: Transaction Publisher, 1995): 21–39. Reprinted with permission.

time in the fourteenth century. The convergence of telecommunications and
computing technologies distribute information automation to the limits of
the world's communication networks. We are well past the point of having
the capability to transform most of human knowledge into electronic form
for access at any point on the earth's surface.

—Frederick Williams

Heilbroner's panorama evokes a familiar image of industrial America because it links America's present to its past. The second image has gained familiarity more recently and associates the present with the future. It portrays America as
an information society. The idea that a society can organize itself around the production and consumption of information comes from the theories of two social
scientists and the reinterpretations of a third. Fritz Machlup, an economist, first
introduced the theory of a knowledge economy from his analysis of the contribution of information activities to the 1958 U.S. Gross National Product. Daniel
Bell, a sociologist, identified the decline of the industrial sector and the expansion
of the service sector as leading indicators of the advance of "post-industrial society." While a doctoral student in communication studies, Marc Porat described a
new information sector within the 1967 U.S. economy by breaking down the traditional sectors of agriculture, industry, and service. As a result, he found the information sector to be the largest of the four, and on that basis declared the
United States an information economy. More than anyone else, Porat contributed
to the popularization of the idea of an information society built on an information
economy.

The information society is a powerful idea precisely because it provokes the
imagination. To Americans concerned about the direction of their society, it proposes an exotic but increasingly familiar future. To economists, sociologists, communications researchers, and information scientists, it provides a framework for
interpreting patterns of culture and behavior. The notion of an information economy, for example, encouraged economists to consider information as a good exchanged in the marketplace, and to ponder its contribution to the GNP. Likewise,
the growing importance of information work led sociologists and communications researchers to reconsider the roles of information technologies in everyday
life. Across the social sciences, the idea of an information society opened conceptual territory and sparked a great deal of fruitful speculation and theorizing.

But if recognition of the existence of the information society has lately
spread across the social sciences, pieces to the puzzle have been lying around
much longer. Shortly after the end of World War II, social observers began noting
the importance of various informational activities. Derek J. de Solla Price surveyed the growth of "big science" in the 1950s and discovered that the size of
scientific literatures doubled every ten to fifteen years. At the end of his administration, president Eisenhower recognized the economy's increased dependence on
the products of scientific research and warned the nation against the alliance of
science with industry and the military. Already in the 1950s, a few social scientists
found evidence of the commercial exchange of information and of the presence of

information work, and suggested the importance of these activities. Machlup thought so in 1962, when he noted the 1958 U.S. economy.

As an economy develops and as a society becomes more complex, efficient organization of production, trade, and government seems to require an increasing degree of division of labor between knowledge production and physical production. A quite remarkable increase in the division of labor between "brain work" and largely physical performance has occurred in all sectors of our economic and social organization. To others, these emerging patterns implied new social relations. From his observations of changes in the workforce, Bell suggested that the post-war growth of informational activities offered conclusive evidence that industrial society was giving way to a "post-industrial" society. The growth of the information economy, the increase in numbers of information workers, the drop in numbers of factory workers, and the proliferation of computer based technologies led numerous social scientists to infer the passing of the industrial era and to describe the information society as post-industrial. Feeling the momentum, scholars who support a post-industrial interpretation have at times seemed ready to close the book on industrial society. But they would be hasty.

Attractive though the evidence might be, it leaves important questions unanswered. What gave rise to an information society? Has the industrial framework of society given way to some other form of social organization? If so, what are the characteristics of this post-industrial form? Can an information society also be industrial? If the information society is post-industrial, as claimed by Bell and others, then is it also post-capitalist? The answers to these questions are important because a theory of the information society must account for the historical forces that generated the tendencies and tensions of the information society. A theory that cannot answer these questions is a theory out of time, since it cannot place the information society in a historical context. Thus, if we fail to resolve the question of origins, we lack the historical perspective necessary to build a theory that accounts for the pervasiveness and diversity of information and communication patterns in modern society.

A logical resolution to the question of origins depends on the following premises:

1. Since capitalism played an indispensable role in the kindling of the industrial revolution, capitalism's role in the ascent of the information society must be explained as well.
2. If the information society is to be considered a post-industrial society, then it must be shown that the primary social forces driving industrial society—that is, the framework within which change occurs—have given way to a different set of social forces.

To argue, for example, that the expansion of the information workforce constitutes sufficient evidence for the passing of industrial society is to assume that the growth of information work results from a different set of social forces than those that formed the industrial workforce. If there are new social forces whose existence has prompted the growth of information work, or the information economy, or changes in private media environments, then there is indeed a basis for proposing that the information society is post-industrial. On the other hand, evidence for the continuing influence of industrial capitalism would indicate a strong connection between industrial work and the information work. Therefore, in order to understand the origins of the information society, its relationship to industrial society must be clarified.

CONTENDING VIEWS ON THE ORIGINS OF THE INFORMATION SOCIETY

Breaking with the past is a popular image in the literature that explores changes in the twentieth century. By choosing *The Age of Discontinuity* as his title, Peter Drucker took change as his basic premise. Daniel Bell resolved the question of continuity by forecasting *The Coming of Post-Industrial Society*. Fred Williams chose the disjunctive phrase communications revolution, and others have similarly described recent changes in society. Wilson Dizard paid homage to Bell's *The Coming of Post-Industrial Society*, by titling his book, *The Coming Information Age,* and by identifying a new stage of socio-economic development.

The resources are so pervasive and influential that it is now becoming clear the United States is moving into a new era—the information age. Ours is the first nation to complete the three-stage shift from an agricultural society to an industrial one and to a society whose new patterns are only now emerging. At its briefest, this is the gist of the post-industrial position. The prevalence of information related activities seems to prove that a revolutionary social change has taken place. In *The Coming of Post-Industrial Society,* Bell identified eleven transformations occurring in the 1950s and 1960s, and proposed that their interplay was reweaving the American social fabric into a post-industrial society.

The shape of the new society: (1) *The centrality of theoretical knowledge*—will become the primary source for inventions, as big science institutionalized the process of innovation; (2) *The creation of a new intellectual technology*—experts can now exploit computers to make use of mathematical techniques to construct algorithms, models, and simulations, for the purpose of engineering more efficient and rational solutions to economic, material, and even social problems; (3) *The spread of a knowledge class*—will emerge from the ranks of the rapidly growing technical and professional workforce; (4) *The change from goods to services*—by 1970, the U.S. had evolved into an economy where 6.5 out of every 10 workers were engaged in the provision of services; (5) *A change in the character of work*—in post-industrial society, work will primarily be a game against people, human behavior, and facing completely new and unparalleled circumstances; (6) *The role of women*—in post-industrial society the nature of service work will expand their employment opportunities, providing women with the basis for economic independence; (7) *Science as imago*—the practice of science will become more bureaucratized and tied to the payoffs derived from its applications; (8) *Situses as political units*—political and social conflicts of the future will arise amidst the new social groupings created from within the service sector, possibly even preventing class formation among the new technocrats; (9) *Meritocracy*—a more efficient and rational society will reward education and skill at the expense of inheritance and property; (10) *The end of scarcity*—post-industrial society will place new scarcities of information and time alongside the old scarcities of material resources, causing even more complex problems of efficient allocation; and (11) *The economics of information*—there will be a growing need for cooperative strategies to insure the optimal distribution of knowledge in society.

Bell's extrapolations helped establish the idea that a new information society has replaced industrial society. Although he initially resisted the idea of an information society, by the early 1980s he had adopted the concept. According to this view, the *rate* of technological and social change has increased to the point where a genuine discontinuity has occurred. Consequently, the United States, as the second industrial nation, becomes the first information society.

To arrive at their version of the information society, post-industrialists depend on five basic assumptions. The first principle holds that industrial society, and its forms of social organization are believed to have largely passed; proponents describe new products, industries, and social classes. Secondly, the sheer volume of information-related activities seems to validate the idea of a post-industrial information society, though not all scholars pay equal attention to all information-related activities; nevertheless, they have amassed much empirical evidence to document the existence of these activities. In a third assumption, post-industrial interpretations assume sequential development, where all the world's nations presumably travel a single evolutionary path, from hunting and gathering to informational; and, in so doing, the post-industrial view draws a parallel with evolutionary social theories, such as Walt Rostow's stages of economic growth. From this perspective, we may imagine a post-industrial information society as the most advanced stage of economic growth, or as Nora and Minc exult, the ultimate civilization. Fourth, only Bell reviews the period of industrialization, and his critics have accused him of being a selective historian. The rest of the post-industrial literature accepts his proposition that great discontinuities suit from periods of high rates of change, concluding, like Dizard, that rapid changes in information retrieval and distribution mean fundamental societal transformations. As a result, Bell's followers focus on the future—his book is subtitled, "A Venture in Social Forecasting"—while neglecting the influence of the past. Fifth, none of these writers acknowledge an effect on capitalism from the withering away of industrialism. They assume that post-industrial society replaces the industrial era while capitalism remains undisturbed. Bell alone foresaw a new capitalist society where technocratic efficiency would dominate policy and economics, though Michael Harrington has pointed out that any society where social goals supersede the economic function is also post-capitalist. But, Bell wavers, while other authors seem to treat capitalism as mere background noise to the information revolution. Considerable research on the production, distribution, and use of information has followed Bell's initial premise. What we know of the specific patterns comes mostly from researchers who built on the post-industrial theme. But they have not substantially added to Bell's theory, so that his original interpretation remains the dominant context for thinking about information and society—though not without critics.

Herbert I. Schiller first criticized the post-industrial view in *Who Knows: Information in the Age of the Fortune 500*. In the first pages, he rejects any attribution of uniqueness to the patterns of change identified by Bell, especially those changes involving information technology and work. He further charges that the entire information society idea can be understood within the framework of the processes that have characterized American capitalism. He documents the motivating role played by capitalist values in the transfer of information from the public sector to the private sector. Resulting privatization of information, he maintains, leads to a greater concentration of ownership among large American corporations, developing along the same lines experienced in non-informational industries. Moreover, this trend does not result from the computer revolution. Instead, the information society operates within the "long prevailing imperatives of a market economy."

In his analysis of teletext, Vincent Mosco continues Schiller's argument and points out that the characteristics associated with a post-industrial information society permit increased control of the labor process, a relationship closely associated with the evolution of capitalism. He criticizes enthusiasts for selling "tinny visions of utopia" while ignoring the negative consequences of capitalist development. Like Schiller, he concludes that much of what goes under the rubric of the information society can be explained as part of the progress of capitalism. Sarah Douglas and Thomas Guback, in their review of the same literature, question one of its basic assumptions, the idea that information society is revolutionary. They argue that the term "revolution" is poorly understood in the literature where it often appears as a buzz word. They find no evidence that historically significantly social relationships, such as the class struggle, have disappeared. In addition, they challenged the claim that information may replace capital as a primary resource. Douglas and Guback further criticize information economists for focusing on information as output, rather than as part of the social process, thereby confusing imaginary revolutionary change with the effects of capitalism. Like Schiller and Mosco, they explain all information activities as resulting from the forces of capitalism, implying that the idea of an informationally oriented society lacks validity.

In Eileen Meehan's *Towards a Third Vision of an Information Society*, she presents a less extreme perspective, criticizing both optimistic and pessimistic visions of the information society. She criticizes those who predict a computerized utopia of electronic cottages as well as those who envision an Orwellian dystopia of masses of information poor watched over by Big Brother. Meehan disagrees with the excessive negativism of Schiller and Mosco, but she accepts their view of unmodified capitalism. She, therefore, predicts that life in a future information society will be just as boring and tedious as it is now, "an ordinary dystopia of material relationships driven by the momentum of traditional capitalist values."

Bell's theory of post-industrial society (and his implicit assumptions) constitutes the foundation for most studies that focus on the information society. In the meantime, his critics have laid out the territory of the debate by introducing competing visions. As each side's strengths provide the basis for verifying the existence of an information oriented society, their weaknesses point to the need for a synthesis. Writers who adopt Bell's point of view show little concern for proposing a fundamental social shift so soon after the previous one. The industrial revolution was in full swing only in the last decades of the nineteenth century. Yet just a century later, another equally momentous revolution is hypothesized. Aside from the problems created by positing a social model based on ever increasing rates of change, taking this position also requires an overly narrow view of industrial society. In the post-industrial literature, the industrial revolution is usually defined by its earliest technology, for example, the steam engine. Consequently, inventions of the twentieth century (computers, satellites) seem "post-industrial." That is, by arguing that an increase in the *rate* of change constitutes a societal revolution, those who assume the post-industrial position confound change with the context in which it takes place. For a social revolution to occur, the basis for social organization—the very context of change—must shift. For example, the overthrow of the king's government in the American revolution established the basis for a new political framework. Similarly, the invention and diffusion of the alphabet changed the rules of communication and altered human modes of thought. What Bell and others overlook, by holding that a post-industrial revolution emerged from an increase in the rate of change, is that capitalism is a context that encourages certain kinds of change. Entrepreneurs of the industrial revolution pursued profits by encouraging social change. Industrial entrepreneurs sought wealth through the growth of firms, economies of scale in production, increased productivity, deskilled labor, and mechanization, that is, by concentrating on the processes of industrialization. These same tendencies appear today in the "new" information industries, in virtually all of the same recognizable forms. The logic of the post-industrial point of view, therefore, rests on a tenuous foundation.

If the logic of post-industrialism is weak, then why is its appeal so strong? Post-industrialism is popular because it conforms to our general belief that we live in times of rapid and revolutionary change—that we late twentieth century Americans are somehow exempt from the course of history. Certainly academics and professionals, in such fields as information science, computer science, systems analysis, communication, engineering, and management—especially those who have led the way in computer applications—seem willing to assume that technological advances in information retrieval constitute the whole of a fundamental revolution altering the social fabric. The products or outcomes of change have been mistaken for the process or context of change.

Led by Schiller, the critics have introduced questions concerning the processes and effects of capitalism to a literature largely focused on scenarios of the future. By establishing capitalism as a cause of the changes Bell identified, they warn against accepting these changes as the dawn of a new era, and challenge those explanations that see the information society as primarily determined by technological innovations. By demonstrating that capitalism continues to operate within the same framework, they venture an interpretation that stresses continuity and undermines visions of the information society as an era breaking with the past. By applying theories of capitalism such as those of Karl Marx, they connect the information society literature with an older richer literature offering insights into the essence of the tendencies and tensions. By introducing capitalism as a cause of change, Schiller, Mosco, and others address a glaring omission; and, in so doing, they draw attention to changes in the quality of life brought on by the information society, as well as provide a basis for testing the assertions made by supporters of post-industrial theory. They have broadened the scope of analysis by recognizing the role played by capitalism; thus, acknowledging the importance of other social influences like the idea of information. However, they overlook the primary theme, that is, industrialization giving way to post-industrialization. They explain the role of capitalism in the formation of the information society, but they do not distinguish the influence of industrialization from that of capitalism. To be fair, they may not believe the distinction carries validity. Oscar Gandy is one who argues that it is not possible to distinguish between the impact of industrialization and the constraints of capitalist relations. Yet by focusing solely on the dynamics of capitalism, their critique remains incomplete and does not answer the question we have asked of Bell, "Does industrial society end where the information society begins?" As they stand, the two positions do not actually oppose each other. Rather, like ships in the night, their directions are skewed. Each addresses what the other ignores. The advocates of post-industrialism hold that new social relations emerge as the old ones of the industrial era fade, while the critics led by Schiller argue that social relations characteristic of capitalism continue to dominate society. To move the discussion beyond these poles, we must clarify how capitalism and industrialism interact, and how they affect the tendencies manifest within the information society.

HOW CAPITALISM AND THE COMMODITIZATION OF INFORMATION INTERACT

All parties to the debate acknowledge the purchase and sale of information as the most visible consequence of an information economy. Proponents of the post-industrial view have pondered the peculiarities of information commodities as compared to material commodities, while critics have expressed alarm at the adaptation of information to the requirements of advanced capitalism. The ease and inexpensiveness with which information can be replicated attracts the profit seeker. Yet that same ease of replication torments the entrepreneur who fails to control the dissemination of her/his property. For information to function as a commodity, it must fit into the order imposed by capitalism—an economic order based on the profit motive, and founded on the right of the individual to own private property. In capitalist societies, many individuals devote considerable energy trying to get rich. Moreover, they do not measure their wealth simply by the extent of their private property, as did feudal barons, but by the capital value, or worth, of that property. These two characteristics, private property and the pursuit of profit, are the driving forces behind the conversion of information into a commodity. Economically speaking, the history of the United States is the story of individuals who sought to exploit for profit the nation's many resources. The intensifying commoditization of information is the most recent part of this story. But the seeds of the information economy were sown early in the nation's history.

In Article I, Section 8, the writers of the Constitution gave the U.S. Congress the power, "To promote the Progress of Science and the useful Arts." Exercising this power in the passage of the first patent law in 1790, the Congress guaranteed inventors exclusive rights to the value of their discoveries. Both documents expressed the beliefs that there is a natural property right to ideas, that society should reward citizens for useful ideas, and that inventors will only refine and put their ideas to work when they know their property right has society's protection. The entire United States now conformed to a trend begun in 1641, when the Massachusetts General Court granted Samuel Winslow the first patent in North America to protect his invention of a new process for making salt. Yet even as they asserted their commitment to the supremacy of individual property, the founders recognized intrinsic contradictions. As followers of Adam Smith, they believed in the evil of monopolies. Nevertheless, they accepted "temporary monopolies" in order to reward inventors for their contributions and to compensate them for their risk and expense. They understood the essential meaning of information as well as its economic value, because they acknowledged complaints that something could not be stolen if the inventor still possessed it, but overruled striking down the patent laws on the basis of this argument.

The copyright statute of 1790 attempted to reconcile two opposing principles: (1) access—the freest possible dissemination of knowledge; versus, (2) protected profit—legal restrictions to secure intellectual property. The framers of the Constitution committed themselves to both views and, by laying a copyright statute alongside the First Amendment, laid the basis for the growth of publishing. Because the First Amendment to the Constitution guaranteed freedom of the press, nineteenth century newspaper publishers wrote without fear of government censorship. Their views were varied and impassioned, but their principal interest lay in the sale of their newspaper. In 1760, seventeen newspapers existed in the colonies. By 1850, 254 dailies circulated the news to approximately 758,000 readers. The New York Sun, whose masthead declared "It Shines for All," claimed a circulation of 50,000 by 1851. It shared New York, population 515,547, with four other penny dailies and ten six-penny papers. Ultimately, their success in the first half of the nineteenth century established foundations for the commercial dissemination of information in the twentieth.

The profit motive also encouraged the commercial implementation of information technology, though disapproving voices were hardly silent. In an 1844 letter to the U.S. House of Representatives, Samuel F. B. Morse, inventor of the telegraph, expressed his desire to avoid privatization, "For myself, I should prefer that the government should possess the invention, although pecuniary interests of

the proprietors induce them to lean towards arrangements with private companies." Accordingly, the government completed a line from Washington to Baltimore in 1844. But the commercial potential was obvious and Congress soon
leased the line to the Magnetic Telegraph Company. From then on, the pattern
was set. Thirty years later, Alexander Graham Bell sought commercial exploitation from the moment of his earliest tinkering. His machine worked for the first
time in 1876. ["Mr. Watson—come here—I want to see you."] In 1877, the Bell
Telephone Company issued its first 5,000 shares, with Bell receiving 10. It's not as
bad as it appears. Mabel Hubbard received 1,497 shares and she soon married
Bell. Similarly, David H. Houston invented the first practical roll film camera, his
1881 Kodak. His partner George Eastman bought most of the patents when he
formed the Eastman Dry Plate and Film Company in 1884, and by 1892 the Eastman Kodak Company owned all of the available patents.

Although Eadweard Muybridge did not exploit the commercial potential of
his motion picture camera, the Zoopraxiscope, others pursued business possibilities. William Dickson, an assistant to Thomas Edison, perfected the motion picture camera/projector and in 1889 Edison patented the essential components as
the Vitascope. However, the profit potential of motion pictures was so obvious
that tinkers and inventors jumped in with their copies, improvements, and creations. Dickson himself left Edison to go it alone with his Biograph projector. Soon
Edison found himself tangled in a melee of patent litigation for control of the medium's technology and its commercial opportunities. In the twentieth century, a
persistently receptive American market for information machines has encouraged
entrepreneurs to exploit each new invention for its money making potential, so
that a stream of inventions, often subsidized by the federal government, spews
from corporate research laboratories, each one aimed at securing a market advantage.

Beyond the invention of information devices, the desire for greater profits
has also encouraged entrepreneurs to exploit the media's power to urge consumers
to buy more goods. The New York Sun might shine for all, but it was only one of
many beacons beckoning consumers. In the early nineteenth century, handbills
and posters carried the weight of consumer ads, though the proliferation of the
penny press quickly eclipsed them in volume. After the Civil War, factory-made
goods began to pour into local markets replacing goods produced by cottage industries. Marketing initiatives centered on advertising to complement innovations
in organization and distribution. Capitalizing on the integration of factories and
managerial hierarchies, Montgomery Ward utilized an improving postal system to
mail a 540-page catalog in 1887. One by one, in each new industry, thousands
of small local and regional markets were welded into a national market for
consumer goods. Within the new integrated production-distribution structure nationwide advertising campaigns made sense. The National Biscuit Company promoted the Uneeda Biscuit with the first million dollar campaign in 1889, at a time
when the U.S. GNP barely topped 12.5 billion. As Michael Schudson explains,
"For nationally advertised, branded products that arose in continuous-process
production industries after 1880, advertising was one important element in a mar-

keting mix that included direct salesmanship, packaging, and the establishment of hierarchical, national marketing organizations."

When incorporated along with the direct sale of information machines, products, and services, advertising contributed to the formation of the complex and interdependent markets that permeate the American economy. In the nineteenth century, advertising emerged as the principal source of revenue for the modern mass media, and it encouraged their proliferation in the twentieth century. In step with demand for information goods as final products, advertising accelerated the momentum of the information economy, up from 25 percent of the 1967 GNP to 34 percent of the 1980 GNP. Moreover, the growth of these markets has also affected the distribution of labor.

Capitalism provided the incentive to convert information into a commodity. Commoditization, in turn, affects technology and labor. Though it never went unopposed, the tendency to commoditize information was apparent at the birth of the republic; and, by 1889, was clearly a vital part of American business. Yet, capitalism alone does not fully explain the scope of all of the activities associated with the information society. Managerial systems, white-collar workers, and bureaucracies have more to do with process than with product. Independent of the goods they contribute to the marketplace, these corporate structures are the result of industrialization.

INDUSTRIALIZATION, MANAGEMENT, AND THE INFORMATION ECONOMY

Industrialization is the path that capitalism took in the United States, where entrepreneurs brought capital, labor, and machines together in one place to recreate the industrial system from its English prototype. Aspiring industrialists had to amass and expend enormous amounts of capital, and invent new forms of organization in order to effectively coordinate the elements. Or, as Harry Braverman put it in his influential work, *Labor and Monopoly Capital,* holds that, "Industrial capitalism begins when a significant number of workers is employed by a single capitalist." Workers formerly laboring within the craft system increasingly found themselves at the receiving end of a strict division of labor similar to the one observed by Adam Smith in his famous visit to a British pin factory. Machines were introduced into the work process so extensively that eventually production could not occur without them. Then, with the introduction of machines, individual workers encountered a new relationship. They became one of several elements that might be substituted for each other in the total production process. In fact, the relationship between machines and human labor is so significant that for some sociologists like Anthony Giddens, the transformation of human labor via the application of inanimate sources of energy into productive activity constitutes the essential feature of industrialism. When Francis Cabot Lowell recruited farmers' daughters to work in his textile mill between 1813 and 1817, he introduced industrialism within a social context already committed to an established economic system. That is, the United States was already a capitalist society before entrepreneurs began adapting the industrial system to the pursuit of profit. Thus, capitalism, which spawned the industrial revolution, was channeled into the forms of organization required by industrialization.

The principal advantage of the industrial system is its ability to exploit the momentum of growth. When factories increase production, the numbers of units produced goes up but the cost per unit goes down. These economies of scale result from higher productive efficiency and offer greater profit margins, as well as competitive advantages in the marketplace. To early capitalists, the allure of growth proved so irresistible that they sought any means available to expand the size of their operations and create larger businesses. Soon, they discovered that the benefits of growth reached beyond the domain of commerce into the arena of politics. President Ulysses S. Grant enjoyed the company of Jay Cooke, Jim Fiske, and Jay Gould, all wealthy directors of large railroad companies. Leland Stanford, a partner in the Southern Pacific Railroad monopoly, later became governor of California and endowed a university with his profits. Larger business organizations wielded more influence with government. Moreover, their political weight could be coupled with their economic advantage to gain and protect large shares of the market.

Sheer size, however, also brought problems. Huge firms that dominated their industries also suffered growing pains. For example, in 1841, the Western Railroad's efforts to run three trains in each direction between Albany and Worcestor, thereby maximizing the productivity of the rail line, led to a head-on collision with fatalities. Western's size had outstripped management's ability to control scheduling and communications. Corporate growth created a crisis of control, whose solution was found in the development of a system of supervision. Not surprisingly, railroads, where the crisis first surfaced, contributed the first solutions. At the New York and Erie Railroad, a general superintendent named Daniel C. McCallum pioneered the system that evolved modern administrative management. He recognized that an organization's principal administrator should be the focus of both authority and communication. The key to controlling a complex organization such as a railroad rests in the continuous flow of information from the bottom to the top. He restructured the railroad and stimulated the flow of information through hourly, daily, weekly, and monthly reports on all matter of operations. He received many of these reports by telegraph and condensed them into statistical summaries; and, as part of the reorganization of 1855, he drew what was probably the first organization table. The chart itself is lost, but Alfred Chandler has preserved a description: The design of the chart was a tree whose roots represented the president and the board of directors; the branches were the five operating divisions and the service departments, engine repairs, car, bridge, telegraph, printing, and the treasurer's and the secretary's offices; while the leaves indicated the various local ticket, freight, and forwarding agents, subordinate superintendents, train crews, foremen, and so forth.

McCallum's innovation of technique was followed by communication breakthroughs, such as the memo, whereby executives learned to rationalize their own internal communications. These inventions and others became the basis for administrative management and the massive corporate bureaucracies that exist today. Once adopted, administrative management required two commitments from managers. First, they needed to believe in the superiority of rational decision making over intuitive decision-making. They could not allow themselves the excitement of wheeling and dealing in the manner of their predecessors. As McCallum wrote to the president of the New York and Erie, "It is very important, however, that principal officers should be in possession of all the information necessary to enable them to judge correctly as to the industry and efficiency of subordinates of every grade." Henry Varnum Poor, the influential editor of the *American Railroad Journal,* also noted this new attitude, "By the energies and genius of our superintendents, it [railroad management] is approaching the position of an accurate science; not limited to theoretical discussion, but developing reliable formulae for the practical estimates of the engineer." By contrast, Jay Gould wheeled and dealed himself into an enormous railroad empire by manipulating stocks and favors. But his machinations risked the entire enterprise more than once. With the new attitude in mind, his successors eschewed such intuitive behavior in favor of the security of systematic planning and organization. If decisions were to be made systematically, then the decision makers would need to make informed judgments. The new approach demanded more information.

Second, rational decision-making could not function without clear and easy access to whatever information managers deemed necessary. Like the New York and Erie, large firms began to sprout staff departments. More personal styles of management became inappropriate as proprietors found themselves unable to attend to every detail or to visit every factory owned by the company. Entrepreneurs who started these growing enterprises often did not have the personalities or skills to run complex organizations. When Alfred P. Sloan came to General Motors in 1918, he noted to his surprise that, " . . . no one knew how much was being contributed—plus or minus—by each division to the common good of the corporation." Staff departments were the solution. They, and the new middle managers that came with them, introduced new forms of administration and coordination. Sloan stood at the cusp of this transition within General Motors. "Mr. [William C.] Durant had been able to operate the corporation in his own way, as the saying goes, 'by the seat of his pants.' When Sloan took over, he led an administration made up of men with very different ideas about business administration, men who desired a highly rational and objective mode of operation."

Sloan's organization study of GM was the vehicle. He recommended broad changes, among them: (1) Determining the actual functioning of the various departments, not only in relation to one another, but in relation to the central organization; (2) Developing statistics to determine the relation between net return and the invested capital of each operating, division; (3) Centralizing the power of all executive functions in the president, as chief executive of the corporation; and, (4) Limiting to the practical minimum, the number of executives reporting directly to the president. The last two, in particular, required building an enormous infrastructure to funnel information from the distant corners of the corporation to the president through a series of progressive summaries. General Motors came to be administered by employees who were not owners but professionals. Similarly, the Gambles, Swifts, Armours, Eastmans, Bordens, Deerings, and McCormicks gradually removed themselves from operational control of the firms they had founded. They owned but no longer managed.

In the end, belief in rational decision-making, along with commitment to institutionalize it in an information system, resolved the crisis of control and laid the foundation for the "technostructure" observed in all corporations of the twentieth century. Corporations now devote a large proportion of their resources to maintaining their managerial bureaucracies by purchasing information from outside vendors as well as from internal sources. So successfully do managers apply these organizational techniques that they regularly seek to rationalize activities beyond the firm as well. Large corporations try to manage the marketplace itself by influencing prices and encouraging specific demand for their products, as John Kenneth Galbraith notes in *The New Industrial State:*

> *Although advertising will be thought the central feature of this management, and is certainly important, much more is involved. . . . The management of demand consists of devising a sales strategy for a particular product. It also consists in devising a product, around which a sales strategy can be built. Product design, model change, packaging, and even performance reflect the need to provide what are called strong selling points. They are, thus, as much a part of the process of demand management as an advertising campaign.*

The language of management refers to this as the "marketing mix." Its successful implementation requires the extension of the information infrastructure beyond the boundaries of the organization and into the affairs of all who come in contact with the market. Thus, corporate managers devise complex price, product, package, and promotion strategies to penetrate the media environments of consumers. Industrialization created the system that operationalized the profit motive within capitalism and transformed American values by introducing new ways to make decisions and accomplish goals. In this century, administrative management has been the dominant paradigm for decision-making and has diffused far beyond industrial enterprises, even to interpersonal services like health care and religious organizations. It has become *the* culturally approved way to make decisions in all organized settings, so that even if intuition is the actual basis for making a judgment, the form of administrative management is followed. Information replaced intuition and tradition as the currency for making decisions, first within the corporation and later beyond it. Even though the goals of government are different from those of the corporation, it too has modeled itself along these same lines. McCallum and Sloan, and all of those who contributed to the building of industrial enterprises, instituted a new system of organization in response to the powerful stimulus of capitalism. Administrative management, as one characteristic consequence of the industrial revolution, contributed heavily to the establishment of an information infrastructure and an information economy.

Within the theme of capitalism and the industrial origins of the information society, one book merits special attention. In his influential book, *The Control Revolution,* James Beniger presents the view that the information society emerged from within the industrial revolution. He maintains that changes in the collection, processing, and retrieval of information, developing during the last decades of the nineteenth century, led to increased dependence on formal and programmed decision-making and resulted in greater control over organizations and all manner of activities in society. Prior to the industrial revolution material processing operated at the pace of human motion, industrialization speeded up the pace of material processing so that direct human control became impossible. Starting with the railroads, industries encountered crises of control and each solved their particular dilemma by increased reliance on managerial techniques facilitated by information processing and communication technologies. In Beniger's words, "As the crisis of control spread through the material economy, it inspired a continuing stream of innovations in control technology." The resulting revolution in control allowed increased reliance on programmed decisions, the only possible way to control large scale operations.

For Beniger, control depends on information processing and reciprocal communication, so that advances in these two areas resolved the crisis. Beniger sees these changes constituting so profound a shift in the ways in which humans organize themselves that he perceives the control revolution to be as momentous as the industrial revolution itself. He, therefore, rejects the notion that the information society emerged out of recent social and technological changes. Instead, the information society emerged out of the control revolution and continues as changes in a control penetrate society.

Beniger amasses ample evidence to make the case that the forces set in motion by the industrial revolution required a subsequent control revolution, in order to prevent the new industrial economy from being overwhelmed by its own creations. By identifying the control revolution as a disjunctive shift in the rules for making decisions, he overcomes Bell's faulty definition of a revolution caused only by an increase in the rate of change. His analysis of the crisis and response within the railroads is superb and adds to Chandler's discussion in *The Visible Hand.* In addition, Beniger carefully documents, industry by industry, the growth of administrative management techniques and corporate bureaucracies. However, like Bell, he largely ignores Schiller's critique, so that capitalism is dealt with more as context than cause. Beniger does distinguish between commercial, or mercantile, capitalism and industrial capitalism, and demonstrates how industrial capitalism acted as a precondition for the industrial revolution. Furthermore, he recognizes the role played by capitalism in generating industrial markets for physical products and stimulating technological innovation. "If profit provided the incentive to process matter faster, then steam power provided the means." But he does not consider the role of capitalism in stimulating the growth of information markets. To be fair, when seen from within the framework of his theory of control, economic man seems less important since human behavior is explained by a series of control revolutions embodying culture, bureaucracy, and technology. Actually, Beniger's theory extends far beyond the industrial origins of the information society to encompass all living things, because as he says, "Life itself implies purposive activity and hence control. . . . " This broader theory, a general theory of life from an information, perspective, presents interesting conclusions about the prevalence of controlling behaviors in all living things, but falls outside the scope of our analysis here. Therefore, his analysis adds to our understanding of industrialization as a cause of the information society, but does not integrate it with an analysis of the dynamics of economic behavior. Capitalism and industrialization appear as distinct non-interactive phenomena. In this regard, he typifies most of the literature.

THE INFORMATION SOCIETY AS A SPECIES OF INDUSTRIAL CAPITALISM

Morse and McCallum traveled along the same lines. Morse took the first unwilling steps toward a technology that would facilitate the sale of information as a major commodity. McCallum laid the foundation for an organizational structure to exploit what Morse had wrought. From the 1850s, the growing demand for information to coordinate the production and distribution of all goods and services complemented the sale of information as a commodity. But if the roots of the information society are embedded in early American capitalism and industrialization, then what evidence exists to support the argument that the information society has grown gradually and continuously throughout the nineteenth and twentieth centuries? After all, those holding to the post-industrial view could easily accept the changes of the nineteenth century while still claiming great discontinuities in the decades of the 1950s and 1960s, the decades when post-industrial society supposedly began. The essential tendencies intensified throughout the 20th century. For our purposes here, patents, copyrights, and trademarks typify the uses of information as a commodity and represent gross measures of the exchange of certain kinds of information in the marketplace; similarly, the growth of the information workforce reflects the impetus of administrative management, as well as the labor demands of information markets. Taken together, they illustrate the interplay of capitalism and industrialization in forging the information society.

As the instrument by which Morse and Bell protected their ideas, the buying and selling of patents constitute the oldest information markets in the United States for which we have consistent data. Though patent registrations do not actually represent sales, they do indicate the growth of new ideas with commercial value. Moreover, as a function of population, they also offer a measure of the idea pool in society. Therefore, they present a good measure of the growth of a key resource of the information economy. When examined for rapid growth, the curve for patents issued per 100,000 population does show a dramatic increase, but that increase occurred during the 1850s and 1860s, and continued into the 1890s. The discontinuity that might be expected in the decades when post-industrial theorists locate the revolution that engendered the information society does not appear in the data. Instead, the data reflect the disjuncture of the industrial revolution and, by association, the control revolution. Copyrights and trademarks also represent a turn toward the commoditization of information and the rise of the information economy. In fact, copyright registrations do increase noticeably after 1970, in the years when the information economy became most visible. But the curve hardly demonstrates a disjuncture from the previous decades. The number of trademarks also rose rapidly between 1900 and 1930, the years when large scale consumer markets were established. And, as with copyrights, trademarks display significant growth during the decades associated with the information economy, all three reflecting the growing importance of information as a commodity. Still, industrial era interpretations suffice to explain the growth in each of the curves without having to resort to a break in history.

Growth of information workers in the labor force is another good measure, especially since it reflects managerial demands and the sale of information. A quick review of some findings supports the data for patents, copyrights, and trademarks. Information workers also increased as a percentage of the labor force throughout the century. With the exception of the Great Depression, the numbers and percentage of information workers shows no significant change in slope between 1900 and 1990. Contrary to post-industrial interpretations that focus on the workforce in the 1950s and 1960s, this data shows the information workforce becoming the largest of the four work sectors just prior to 1930. Thus, data on the information workforce conforms well to data on patents, copyrights, and trademarks, all indicating the emergence of an information economy in harmony with the industrial economy rather than in schism.

Desire for profits and for rational solutions to problems of production and distribution led to the present configuration of information workers, information technologies, messages, and channels. Capitalism *and* industrialism caused the expansion of those activities collectively defined as the information society. Nevertheless, we are just now getting a feel for the actual progression of the information society amidst a tidal wave of questions. For example, how does information become a public resource and how does information become a commodity? Though aspects of the conversion of information from a public resource into a commodity have been analyzed in specific cases, we know from studying the framing of the Constitution and the development of the telegraph that these are complex phenomena. After all, capitalism, which drives commoditization, acts amidst countervailing forces. Thinking of them as a tension provides greater understanding.

How do information occupations experience industrialization? Evidence indicates that some white-collar work bears striking similarities to factory work. The experience of the current recession indicates that information jobs are susceptible to mechanization and that they differ in levels of susceptibility. But categories for defining information work are still being worked out.

How does the movement toward the information society differ when capitalism is removed from the equation? Further study of those industrialized societies that did not develop under capitalism will almost certainly provide clues to the relative influence of industrialization in forming information economies, while comparative analyses of the former Soviet Union, the United States, the United Kingdom, Japan, France, and Korea, to name a few, will further our understanding of the variety of interactions between capitalism and industrialization, that is, of the different paths to the information society. The key to understanding the information society depends on recognizing elements of both change and continuity. American industry is no longer hog butcher to the world, because it has changed, or more properly, evolved away from its earlier form. Instead, it is now educator, banker, entertainer, and data processor to the world, and for the same reasons as before—because of the profit motive and the industrial character of these activities.

To view the information society as unique or historically unprecedented, reinforces a myth, albeit a powerful one. Because of it, researchers mistook the early forms of industrialization—the smokestacks and the factories—for the entire range of possibilities. Schiller and his colleagues pierced the myth by identifying capitalism as a cause, but did not push their analysis to include industrialization. However, we now see the United States producing and distributing information as its primary economic activity precisely because capitalism remains the motivator and industrialism remains the organizing principle. Thus, between the ore cars and smoke stacks of the nineteenth century, and the satellites and microchips of the twentieth century, lie changes that transformed the United States into an information society.

10

Is the United States Becoming an Information Economy?

William J. Baumol, Sue Anne Batey Blackman,
and Edward N. Wolff

Baumol and his team of economists have concerned themselves with the study of productivity in national economies. In the book in which the selection below is drawn, they look at the role of technology, service sector, and information as sources of insight in explaining why various national economies experience increases or flat levels of productivity. In the process of doing that, they had to concern themselves with the question of the role of information. They provide an explanation—linked to issues of productivity—as to how advanced economies are evolving and the effects on productivity. The first two authors—economists at Princeton—and the third, also an economist, but at New York University, continue the line of research begun by Machlup.

IS THE UNITED STATES BECOMING AN INFORMATION ECONOMY?

By virtue of this concatenation of processes the modern industrial system at large bears the character of a comprehensive, balanced mechanical process. . . . The higher the degree of development reached by a given industrial community, the more comprehensive and urgent becomes the requirement of interstitial adjustment.

—Veblen [1904]

From *Productivity and American Leadership: The Long View* (Cambridge, MA: The MIT Press, 1989): 143–159. Reprinted with permission.

To say that the advanced industrial world is rapidly becoming an Informa-
tion Society may already be a cliche. In the United States, Canada, Western
Europe, and Japan, the bulk of the labor force now works primarily at in-
formational tasks such as systems analysis and computer programming,
while wealth comes increasingly from informational goods such as micro-
processors and from informational services such as data processing.
                                                                —Beniger [1986]

The evidence does not support the popular view that the United States is rapidly
becoming a service economy. Indeed, the facts conflict directly with the assertion
that the services constitute an ever-growing share of the real output of the American economy. In this chapter we shall investigate another, parallel, premise about
the United States—that it is evolving into an "information economy," that is, that
the increasing complexity and technical sophistication of our economic activities,
coupled with the growth in the complexity of the interrelations among the country's business firms, makes it ever more necessary for them to engage in massive
accumulation and processing of information, and that this constitutes a major up-
heaval in our way of doing business. Since information gathering and processing
(because they are themselves largely service activities) may be as vulnerable to the
cost disease as are the services generally, this opens up the possibility that exactly
the same illusion generated in the service sector is also applicable to the information sector. In other words, the spectacular growth of this sector of the economy
may be due largely to the characteristic that the amount of labor it uses is not easily reduced. Exploration of this possibility for the nation's information activities is
no mere idle exercise. If the cost disease, rather than a growing demand for information, does account for the bulk of the growth of the information sector, then
the "information economy" view apparently must be deflated considerably by the
results of our study of the pertinent statistics. This is, in fact, what the data suggest, as will be reported in this chapter.

GROWTH OF THE INFORMATION ECONOMY:
OUR CLASSIFICATION SCHEME

Before turning to the statistics about the nature of the information economy,
we first describe the procedures we shall adopt. The central procedural problem
of all studies of the size and growth of the information sector is the absence of any
obvious boundary between the activities that should be included in that sector and
those that should be interpreted to be outside it. Any such boundary must inevitably be somewhat arbitrary at best. Where, for example, should one classify banking, insurance, and even book publication (with its double purpose: entertainment
and provision of information)? There is, of course, no one correct solution to this
classification problem. We shall adopt an arbitrary classification scheme whose
justification is that it is closely related to those used by previous writers on the
subject. More to the point is evidence that our qualitative conclusions remain ro-

bust under substantial changes in the classification. This should not be very surprising, first because the growth in the proportion of information workers must be evaluated via a comparison of that share at two different dates (so whatever classification one adopts must remain the same at both dates) and second because the evidence indicates that the upsurge in information-related employment has been so large that it will show up in the data, no matter what taxonomy is adopted.

Our basic data are from the U.S. Decennial Censuses of 1960, 1970, and 1980. In our calculations, the row figures in the Census tables of occupations-by-industry were first aggregated, in conformity with an internally consistent classification scheme, into 267 occupations and 64 industries (See Wolff and Baumol [1989] for details). The occupations were aggregated once more into six categories:

1. knowledge production,
2. data processing,
3. supply of services,
4. goods production,
5. a hybrid class including both knowledge and data activities, and
6. a second hybrid class including both data and service activities.

We then (somewhat arbitrarily) divided those that fell into the hybrid knowledge/data category, classing half of them as knowledge workers and half as data workers, and, in similar fashion, we have split the hybrid data/service category half into data and half into service workers. The resulting groups are referred to as the "total knowledge," "total data," and "total service" categories. Information workers were then defined as the sum of (total) knowledge and (total) data workers. The non-information category is composed of the residual, including (total) service and goods workers.

GROWTH OF THE INFORMATION SECTOR'S LABOR FORCE: THE EMPIRICAL DATA

The statistics that are usually presented to suggest the validity of the information economy hypothesis are similar to those cited by proponents of the service economy hypothesis. The standard evidence used for the purpose consists of figures indicating that there has been a striking increase in the share of the U.S. labor force that produces, acquires, or processes information. It may be noted that these figures are, if anything, considerably more shaky than the corresponding statistics pertaining to the services, since the boundaries of the service sector are at least tolerably well-defined, while, as has already been emphasized, no clear-cut boundaries for the economy's knowledge sector even seem possible, unless they are settled by arbitrary convention. Yet the data on the explosive growth of the information sector's share of the labor force are so striking that it seems reasonable to conjecture that the conclusion is highly robust—that any reasonable change in the boundary lines will not materially affect the conclusion.

Figure 10.1, derived from data reported by James R. Beniger [1986], is a good example of the sort of observations that emerge from such studies. The graph divides the American labor force into four sectors: agriculture, industry, (other) services, and information. We see that the information sector's share of the labor force toward the beginning of the nineteenth century was so close to zero as not to be discernible on the graph (at least before 1830). By 1980, according to Beniger, employment in this sector had expanded so dramatically that it accounted for some 45 percent of the total labor force and, in this respect, handily outdistanced any of the remaining three sectors. This is extraordinary growth indeed. One can easily understand why, from this observation alone, reasonable observers have been prepared to infer that there has been an explosion in the economy's information activity.

Our own data, taken from U.S. Census tables, permit us to provide similar supplementary statistics along with further details for the briefer period since the conclusion of World War II. Table 10.1 gives a breakdown of total employment by type of worker from 1960 to 1980 and the corresponding growth rates in each category, while Table 10.2 reports the pertinent percentages. Over the two decades, knowledge workers were the fastest growing of the group, increasing 3.5

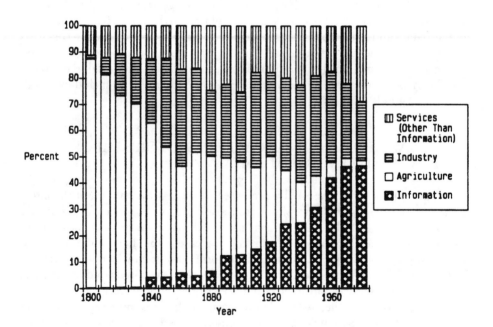

FIGURE 10-1 Sector Shares, U.S. Labor Force, 1800–1980. Source: Beniger (1986, p. 24).

TABLE 10.1 Growth in U.S. Employment: Information Workers and Others, 1960–1980

Type of worker	Total employment (thousands)			Annual rate of growth (percent)		
	1960	1970	1980	1960–1970	1970–1980	1960–1980
1. Knowledge	1,951	3,294	4,821	5.24	3.81	4.52
2. Data	19,399	26,214	35,861	3.01	3.13	3.07
3. Knowledge/data	4,893	5,216	8,044	0.64	4.33	2.49
4. Data/services	1,950	2,735	4,796	3.38	5.62	4.50
5. Services	8,266	9,830	13,250	1.73	2.99	2.36
6. Goods	28,056	27,010	30,596	−0.38	1.25	0.43
7. Totals	64,515	74,299	97,369	1.41	2.70	2.06
8. Total knowledge[a]	4,398	5,902	8,843	2.94	4.04	3.49
9. Total data[a]	22,821	30,189	42,282	2.80	3.37	3.08
10. Total information[a]	27,218	36,091	51,125	2.82	3.48	3.15
11. Total non-information[a]	37,297	38,208	46,244	0.24	1.91	1.08

[a]The total for knowledge workers (line 8) is defined as the sum of line 1 and half of line 3. The total for data workers (line 9) is defined as the sum of line 2, half of line 3, and half of line 4. The total for information workers (line 10) is defined as the sum of line 8 and line 9. The total for non-information workers (line 11) is the residual.

percent per year (line 8). They were followed by the data workers at 3.1 percent per year (line 9) and service workers (after inclusion of the allocated portion of the mixed data/service category), at 2.4 percent per year. In contrast, goods producers increased their number by only 0.4 percent per year (line 6). Altogether, employment of information workers grew 3.2 percent per year (about 1 percentage point above average), while noninformation workers increased 1.1 percent per year (a point below average). The developments can also be described by decade. Between 1960 and 1970, the total number of knowledge and data workers (line 10) increased by 2.8 percent per year, almost twice the overall rate of growth of employment, while the combined employment of service and goods employees remained almost unchanged in number. In the second decade, 1970 to 1980, total employment in the United States grew at 2.7 percent per year. Altogether information (knowledge and data) workers rose in number 3.5 percent per year, while the employment of noninformation workers increased by 1.9 percent per annum.

Table 10.2 provides another way of viewing the growth of the information sector. In 1960, 7 percent of total employment consisted of knowledge workers and 35 percent of data workers. Altogether, 42 percent of the employed labor force was made up of information workers and 58 percent of noninformation workers. By 1980, the proportion of information workers in total employment had increased to over half the total. The number of knowledge workers had risen to 9 percent and that of data workers to 43 percent of total employment.

TABLE 10.2   Percentage Composition of U.S. Employment by Type of Worker, 1960–1980

Type of worker	Percent of total			Percentage change		
	1960	1970	1980	1960–1970	1970–1980	1960–1980
1. Total knowledge	6.8	7.9	9.1	16.5	14.3	33.2
2. Total data	35.4	40.6	43.4	14.9	6.9	22.8
3. Total services	14.3	15.1	16.1	5.2	6.6	12.2
4. Goods	43.5	36.4	31.4	–16.4	–13.6	–27.7
5. Totals	100.0	100.0	100.0	0.0	0.0	0.0
6. Total information[a]	42.2	48.6	52.5	15.1	8.1	24.5
7. Total non-information[a]	57.8	51.4	47.5	–11.0	–7.6	–17.8

[a]See note to Table 10.1 for details.

GROWTH OF THE INFORMATION ECONOMY: BREAKDOWN BY INDUSTRY AND SECTOR

Since our subsequent analysis depends substantially on comparative shifts in the share of information workers among industries, we pause here to examine what the data show on this matter. Table 10.3 reports the percent of information workers in the labor force of each of the major industrial groups. It is instructive, first, to consider the relative information-intensity of the various sectors. The finance, insurance, and real estate sector is the most information-intensive—about 90 percent of its employees are knowledge or data workers. The trade, services, and government sectors are next in line, with between 45 percent and 70 percent of the employees in information occupations. In mining, construction, manufacturing, and transportation, information workers comprise between 19 percent and 47 percent of total employment. Agriculture is the least information-intensive, with under 10 percent of its employees in information jobs.

What about trends? In most sectors, the relative growth in employment of knowledge workers was maintained over the two decades. Between 1960 and 1980, data workers increased relative to total employment in all industries except trade and the government sectors, where they declined slightly in percentage terms. However, the relative gains were greater in the 1960s than in the 1970s. All told, information workers increased in number relative to noninformation workers in all sectors except trade over the two decades. One obvious explanation for these trends is that the increasing sophistication and complexity of our productive mechanism requires ever more information for its "interstitial" adjustments, or that an increasingly educated population demands products with ever greater information content. However, an alternative line of explanation is possible. According to our unbalanced growth hypothesis, *with constant output proportions,*

TABLE 10.3 Knowledge and Data Workers as a Percent of U.S. Employment by Major Industry, 1960–1980

	1960			1970			1980		
	Knowl-edge	Data	Infor-mation	Knowl-edge	Data	Infor-mation	Knowl-edge	Data	Infor-mation
1. Agriculture	0.8	1.4	2.3	2.2	4.1	6.3	3.2	6.4	9.6
2. Mining	6.4	18.4	24.8	8.7	24.8	33.4	10.6	28.3	38.9
3. Construction	6.9	12.6	19.4	7.0	17.3	24.3	7.1	20.3	27.4
4. Nondurable manufacturing	5.3	22.7	28.0	6.7	26.5	33.2	7.3	28.5	35.8
5. Durable manufacturing	7.2	24.8	32.0	9.9	27.0	36.8	10.1	28.0	38.2
6. Transportation	5.8	32.7	38.6	6.9	36.6	43.5	8.5	38.2	46.6
7. Trade	7.5	54.9	62.4	6.5	53.0	59.5	8.8	52.1	60.9
8. Finance, insurance, and real estate	8.7	81.0	89.6	8.5	82.4	90.9	8.4	83.0	91.4
9. Services	8.4	37.9	46.2	9.4	45.7	55.1	10.2	48.7	58.9
10. Government	8.7	57.2	65.9	10.7	56.1	66.8	11.7	55.0	66.7
Totals	6.8	35.4	42.2	7.9	40.6	48.6	9.1	43.4	52.5

employment in activities with relatively slower rates of productivity growth must increase relative to employment in high-productivity growth activities. Also, the cost disease affects (asymptotically stagnant) industrial activities that use in fixed proportions some inputs whose production is progressive and some that are stagnant in terms of labor productivity growth. If the progressive and stagnant inputs are used in fixed proportions in real terms, then it follows that labor employed in producing the stagnant component will increase relative to the employment in the progressive component. Thus, there will be a relative increase of employment of workers engaged in relatively stagnant activities if output or input proportions stay relatively fixed. Of the four classes of workers in our classification scheme, it seems plausible that the activity of knowledge workers is the most technologically stagnant, in the sense that the production of knowledge is itself an activity that is not readily amenable to technical change. The activity of data workers would seem to be more progressive, since part of their task involves the acquisition and transmission of information activities that *do* benefit from technological advance (through computers, new telecommunications equipment, and the like). However, the portion of their activity that involves the analysis and comprehension of information (reading, for example) seems much more difficult to change technologically. The activity of service workers is, perhaps, a bit more progressive than that of data workers, since new equipment can often increase their productivity (as in telecommunications). Finally, the activity of goods workers, as a group, is the most progressive, since goods production would appear to be the most amenable to the substitution of capital for labor.

The relative decline in the number of goods workers over the period and the corresponding increase in knowledge, data, and service workers can, thus, conceivably be attributed, at least in part, to unbalanced growth. The increase in the number of knowledge workers relative to service and goods workers during the 1960s and relative to the other three categories of labor during the 1970s is also consistent with that phenomenon. However, the explanation offered by the unbalanced growth hyphothesis is imperfect at best. For example, it does not account in any obvious way for the fact that the employment of knowledge workers and data workers both increased at about the same rate during the 1960s, while that of data and service workers grew proportionately during the 1970's. Obviously, the influence of unbalanced growth has to be tested with the aid of tools more powerful than just review of the statistics. This is a task to which we turn next.

IS THE INFORMATION EXPLOSION REAL?: THE TESTING PROCEDURE FOR OUR CENTRAL HYPOTHESIS

We now turn to the central issue of the chapter—whether the information explosion is a real phenomenon or is largely an illusion contributed by the cost disease. To examine this issue empirically we shall break down the changes in the information workers' share of the labor force into three parts:

1. The *input substitution* of information labor for labor of other types within the production process, that is, the change in the proportion of information workers in each industry's labor force,
2. the change in each industry's share of the economy's total *output,* and
3. the change associated with relative variations in *labor productivity* of the different industries.

The first of these three components can be interpreted to indicate the extent to which the composition of the labor force in a typical industry has become more information-intensive (assuming all other things remain the same). If all output proportions had remained unchanged and all industries had experienced the same rate of productivity growth, we would ascribe to this input substitution element the entire observed rise in the share of information workers in the overall labor force. The second element in our breakdown, output composition, relates to different industries' shares of the economy's total output and is pertinent in determining the extent to which the expansion in information-related employment is attributable to an increase in the economy's *demand* for products with a high information content. Finally, the productivity-growth component in our breakdown plays the critical part in testing the role of unbalanced growth in the information explosion. If *it* were the only one of our three elements to undergo a nonzero change, that would imply that the entire information explosion of the labor force could be attributed to relatively higher productivity growth in industries using less information, driving the labor force toward the remaining industries, where slow productivity growth kept demand for information-related labor (along with that for other types of labor) relatively high. For brevity, it is convenient to refer to these three elements, respectively, as (1) the input-substitution component, (2) the output-composition component, and (3) the productivity-lag component. Our analysis then proceeds by direct use of the available estimates of the input-output coefficients and the statistics on information workers, total employment, and outputs by industry, simply substituting these data into a mathematical equation that encompasses the breakdown of information employment growth into its three components. The proportions among the resulting terms, then, are taken to indicate the relative shares of the three components in the explosion of information employment in particular industries, in particular sectors, and in the economy as a whole.

The implication of two of these components about the source of the growing share of information labor is unambiguous. If the output-composition component turns out to be large, it must imply that consumers (or industry) shifted their preferences toward heavy information-using goods and services, as the term "information revolution" implies. A large productivity-lag component has the reverse implication—that a correspondingly substantial share of the shift in the labor force represents mere technical readjustment rather than a true rise in the share of information output. However, the remaining element, the input-substitution component, is rather ambiguous. True, it surely is, in part, a consequence of technical changes in the production processes, which require more information creation and use, and hence, also, constitute legitimate manifestations of an information revolution. However, there is also a second side to the substitution of inputs that is merely an unbalanced-growth response to uneven productivity growth in different processes. For example, consider an industry which engages in just two activities, A and B. Assume that A is much more information labor-intensive than B but that labor productivity in A grows far more slowly than that in B. Then even if the relative use of activities A and B by the industry is absolutely fixed, the share of the labor force devoted to A must grow as rising productivity reduces B's relative demand for labor. As a result, the use of labor by activity A must rise *in comparison with activity B* and so the share of information labor will also rise automatically, not because of an increase in sophistication of the total production process that requires more use of information labor, but because of the relative lag of productivity of information-intensive process A. If information-intensive activities are generally those whose productivity grows most slowly, such a scenario will not be rare.

Unfortunately, unavailability of the requisite data prevents us from subdividing the input-substitution component into its information-demand and the productivity-lag portions. In much of the following discussion we shall treat it as though it were made up entirely of the former. However, it must be recognized that this may substantially overestimate the share of the relative rise in informa-

tion employment legitimately attributable to growing complexity and sophistication of the production process.

THE GROWTH OF THE INFORMATION ECONOMY:
OVERALL RESULTS OF OUR STATISTICAL STUDY

Table 10.4 reports the results derived from our breakdown of information
employment growth. The table contains three panels: The first shows the growth
(in percentage points) of each type of employment and divides it into our three
components; the second translates these figures for the components into percentages of the total growth of employment in each labor category; and the third
panel shows what annual percentage growth rate of each occupational group
would have resulted from each component if total employment had been fixed. To
show how to interpret this table, let us consider as an example the change in the
share of the knowledge workers (the *producers* of information) in total employment during the first subperiod of our study. According to the first line in the left-
hand panel of Table 10.4, this share increased by 1.13 percentage points in that
1960–1970 decade. Of this, the input-substitution component accounted for 0.78
percentage points (first panel), or 70 percent of the total change (second panel). If
total employment had been fixed, knowledge workers would have grown at a rate
of 1.09 percent per year over this period because of the input-substitution component alone (third panel).

Before discussing the details, let us see what overall results are shown by
Table 10.4. The last line summarizes what happened to the share of all information workers (that is, knowledge plus data workers) over the entire 20-year period. We see that this share grew by 10.3 percentage points (panel 1). Some 53
percent of this change was made up of the input-substitution component, and 38
percent was due to the productivity-lag (unbalanced-growth) component (panel 2,
last line), while the shift in the composition of final output contributed only 9
percent.

In sum, on the production side of the economy, a large contribution was
made by technological change within each industry that substituted information
labor for other types of labor (our input-substitution component). The interindustry productivity-lag component was also quite strong. The absorption of workers
by industries whose productivity grew relatively slowly served to increase the
share of information workers by a significant amount (our productivity-lag component). The magnitude of these two components together implies that the so-
called "information explosion" is primarily a consequence of unbalanced growth,
and that the substitution of information labor within production and uneven productivity growth among industries together may have raised the share of information labor in the labor force by over 9 percentage points in two decades (panel 1,
last line). In contrast, the role of demand shifts toward heavily information-using
products (our output-composition component) was very modest. By itself it might
perhaps have raised the demand for information labor only 0.1% per year, com-

TABLE 10.4 Decomposition of the Change in U.S. Employment Composition into Input-Substitution, Productivity-Lag, and Output-Composition Effects, 1960–1980[a]

Type of Worker	Panel (1): Decomposition (in percentage points) of Change in Employment Composition				Panel (2): Change in Employment Composition (as percent of total)				Panel (3): Annual Rate of Growth of Employment in Percent (assuming total employment fixed)			
	Input-Substitution Effect	Productivity-Lag Effect	Output-Composition Effect	Total Change	Input-Substitution Effect	Productivity-Lag Effect	Output-Composition Effect	Total Change	Input-Substitution Effect	Productivity-Lag Effect	Output-Composition Effect	Total Change
I. 1960–1970 period												
1. Knowledge	0.78	0.36	-0.02	1.13	69.6	32.3	-1.9	100.0	1.09	0.42	0.02	1.53
2. Data	2.06	2.69	0.51	5.26	39.1	51.2	9.6	100.0	0.57	0.74	0.08	1.39
3. Services	0.06	0.73	-0.05	0.75	7.8	98.3	-6.1	100.0	0.04	0.48	-0.02	0.51
4. Goods	-2.94	-4.00	-0.19	-7.13	41.3	56.1	2.6	100.0	-0.70	-1.00	-0.09	-1.79
Information[b]	3.01	3.01	0.36	6.39	47.2	47.2	5.6	100.0	0.69	0.68	0.04	1.41
II. 1970–1980 period												
1. Knowledge	0.96	0.52	-0.34	1.14	84.1	45.3	-29.5	100.0	1.14	0.45	-0.25	1.34
2. Data	1.40	0.78	0.62	2.79	50.1	27.8	22.2	100.0	0.34	0.18	0.15	0.66
3. Services	-0.08	0.99	0.09	1.00	-7.8	99.2	8.7	100.0	-0.05	0.65	0.05	0.64
4. Goods	-2.42	-1.99	-0.52	-4.93	49.0	40.4	-10.6	100.0	-0.69	-0.61	-0.16	-1.46
Information[b]	2.40	1.04	0.49	3.93	61.0	26.6	12.4	100.0	0.48	0.19	0.11	0.78
III. 1960–1980 period												
1. Knowledge	1.74	0.67	-0.15	2.27	76.9	29.6	-6.5	100.0	1.14	0.18	0.12	1.43
2. Data	3.51	3.28	1.26	8.05	43.5	40.8	15.7	100.0	0.47	0.43	0.13	1.03
3. Services	0.02	1.65	-0.08	1.75	1.3	94.3	4.4	100.0	0.01	0.54	0.03	0.58
4. Goods	-5.41	-5.76	-0.90	-12.06	44.8	47.7	7.4	100.0	-0.66	-0.79	-0.17	-1.62
Information[b]	5.49	3.90	0.93	10.32	53.2	37.8	9.0	100.0	0.61	0.39	0.09	1.09

[a]Average period weights are used in all cases. The input-substitution, productivity-lag, and output-composition components are derived from equation (3) in the appendix.

[b]Sum of (1) and (2).

pounded, had total employment in the economy remained constant over the two decades (last panel of the table). In conclusion, the data indicate that, like the so-called "shift to the services," the autonomous growth in demand for information labor was quite minimal.

DETAILS OF THE STATISTICAL STUDY: CONCLUSIONS BY DECADE, AND BY KNOWLEDGE AND DATA WORKER CATEGORIES

Having examined the overall implications of the decomposition calculation, let us turn to some of its details. For this purpose we go back to our subclassification of information workers into knowledge workers (information producers) and data workers (knowledge users). We begin with the knowledge worker subgroup. As we saw in our introductory discussion of the top row of Table 10.4, the most important component in the relative growth of knowledge workers over the 1960s and 1970s was the substitution of knowledge workers for other classes of workers within industries. This component accounted for 70 percent of their relative growth over the 1960s and 84 percent over the 1970s. Productivity growth in knowledge-intensive industries was relatively low over the two decades and served to increase the employment of knowledge workers. During the 1960s, the relatively low productivity growth in this sector accounted for a 0.36 percentage point increase in the employment of knowledge workers, while during the 1970s it accounted for a 0.52 percentage point rise. The productivity-lag component was about half as strong as the input-substitution component in each of the two decades. The shift in output demand toward knowledge-intensive products was of negligible importance during the 1960s, while during the 1970s it actually served to depress the demand for knowledge workers. Over the two decades, the input-substitution component accounted for about three-fourths of relative employment growth of the knowledge workers, and the interindustry productivity-lag component the other quarter.

Next, consider data workers (second row in each section of Table 10.4). Almost 40 percent of the increase in their relative share during the 1960s is attributed by the calculation to the substitution of data workers for other workers within industries. As in the knowledge-intensive industries, productivity growth was slower than average in data-intensive industries, and about half of the growth in employment of data workers is attributable to the relatively slower productivity growth of these sectors. The shift in demand toward data-intensive output was of minor importance during this period. During the 1970s, the input-substitution component was the dominant element, accounting for half of the increase in the share of data workers, while the interindustry productivity-lag component accounted for 28 percent. During the 1970s, there was a significant shift in demand toward data-intensive output, and this accounted for 22 percent of the employment growth of this period.

Next, consider the share of service workers. For them, as shown in previous studies, the interindustry productivity-lag component was dominant, accounting for almost all of their employment growth during the two decades. The relatively slower productivity growth of service-intensive sectors served to increase service workers' employment share in the two decades by 1.7 percentage points. Both the substitution of industry employment away from service workers and shifts in final output composition had a negligible effect on their relative employment. Finally, turning to goods workers, the two unbalanced growth components together accounted for almost all of the relative decline in their employment share. During the 1960s, over 40 percent of the relative decline in the employment of goods workers was accounted for by the substitution of other workers for goods producers within industries and 56 percent by the relatively *higher* rate of productivity growth of the goods-producing sectors. During the 1970s, the combined magnitudes of the two components remained virtually unchanged. The shift in output demand was again of relatively minor importance in the two decades, accounting for only 3 percent of the relative decline in the employment of goods producers during the first decade and 11 percent during the second.

In summary, the two dominant elements in the composition of employment were the input-substitution and interindustry productivity-lag components. Shifts in the composition of output were a relatively minor element, though the output-composition component grew in importance over the two decades. For knowledge workers, the substitution of workers within industry production was twice as important as unbalanced growth between industries. For both data and goods workers, the two components were of almost equal magnitude. On the other hand, relative productivity movements between industries were by far the dominant element in explaining the relative growth of service workers.

Finally, the third panel of Table 10.4 exhibits another relationship that seems consistent with the expectations that might have been stimulated by unbalanced growth. To the extent that the logic of unbalanced growth underlies the behavior of the input-substitution component, we should expect, in terms of that component alone, that employment of knowledge workers would grow fastest, that of data workers second fastest, service workers third, and goods workers slowest (since in terms of their productivity growth they would be ranked in reverse order). This turns out to have been true in both the 1960s and the 1970s. Moreover, the number of service workers grew faster than total employment during the two decades, while goods workers grew less slowly than total employment, as unbalanced growth calls for. We would also expect the productivity-lag component to lead to these same employment growth rankings, and, indeed, this occurred over the two decades, with the important exception of knowledge workers. Finally, the output-composition component was positive for knowledge, data, and service workers, and negative for goods workers. The relative magnitude of this component varied over the two decades. However, over the 20-year period, the output-composition component was largest for knowledge and data workers, ranked second (and almost zero) for service workers, and ranked last (and negative) for goods workers. These results indicate a slight shift in demand toward information-intensive output.

CONCLUSION

This chapter documents once again the rapid growth of information workers in the U.S. economy, in both absolute and relative terms, over the period from 1960 to 1980. In terms of our classification, over these years knowledge workers (those who produce information) grew from 6.8 percent to 9.1 percent of total employment, data workers (those whose job is to use information) grew from 36 percent to 43 percent, and information workers as a body from 42 percent to 53 percent. These results are consistent with those of other studies.

The novel result of the work reported here is the evidence that the rising share of the labor force in information-related occupations is the result of two distinct forces, both of which may be considered the ingredients of unbalanced growth, leaving relatively little to be attributed to an autonomous explosion in demand for information. The first, and more important, of these is the substitution of information workers, particularly knowledge producers, for non-information workers within production. This accounted for over half of the increase in the share of information employees in total employment. The second is relative productivity growth movements among industries, which accounted for over a third of the relative growth of information workers and over 40 percent of the relative growth of data workers. The shift in demand toward information-intensive output, then, was of relatively minor importance, accounting for only 9 percent of the growth in information employment, though 16 percent of the growth in data workers.

The one apparent anomaly in our results is that, contrary to expectations, low productivity growth in knowledge-intensive sectors did not play a large role in the relative increase in knowledge workers over the two decades. Yet, on second thought, this result may not be too surprising, since productivity growth in a sector can be stimulated by the employment of a large number of knowledge workers. Indeed, research on the sources of productivity growth have consistently found a large positive effect of the number of knowledge workers on an industry's rate of technological progress. Thus, even though knowledge production may itself be a stagnant activity, it may nonetheless contribute strongly to productivity growth in sectors in which the activity is located.

Part Three

Social and Personal Consequences

11

Daniel Bell and the Post-industrial Society

Malcolm Waters

What Mills did in the 1950s to call attention to the rise of a modern middle class, Daniel Bell did in the 1970s with the notion that society and its economy was evolving out of industrialism into a new form. In the process he coined the term so widely used since then, "Post-industrial Society." This sociologist, more than any other scholar, stimulated new thinking about the nature of late twentieth-century society as service sector, heavily endowed with knowledge workers, and clearly evolving to new forms with novel mores and practices. Because he wrote so much, a biographical treatment is a good way to be introduced to his ideas. The selection below is from the first biography of Bell.

THE POST-INDUSTRIAL SOCIETY

The notion that ideology has been exhausted as a principle for the organization of political life. In this chapter we address perhaps the biggest of his ideas, the one that has become the most influential both inside sociology and in wider intellectual circles, the idea that society is becoming "post-industrial." The term "post-industrial society" has become common conceptual currency because of Bell's construction of it, even where that construction is not acknowledged, much as the concept of "charisma" is invoked without making reference to Weber. This alone is a tribute to the effectiveness of the conceptualization. The term "post-industrial society" is used to describe a series of contemporary macro-social changes. Bell had sensed that such changes were occurring as early as 1950. One of the histori-

From *Daniel Bell*, by Malcolm Waters (London: Routledge, 1996): 105–123. Reprinted with permission.

cal shifts that was contributing to the decomposition of Marxist ideology was the reconstruction of the techno-economic structure. Bell gropes for a term to describe it, "In the dimly-emerging social structure, new power sources are being created and new power sources are being formed. Whatever the character of that new social structure may be—whether state capitalism, managerial society, or corporative capitalism—by 1950 American socialism as a political and social fact had become simply a notation in the archives of history."

By the late 1950s he had the terminology within his grasp. In 1959 he gave lectures using the term "post-industrial society" at the Salzburg Seminar in Austria and in 1962 he wrote a long paper on the topic under the title "The Post-industrial Society: A Speculative View of the United States and Beyond." This must be one of the most influential unpublished papers ever written because it circulated widely in academic and public policy circles. It was pirated both in *Current* and in *Dun's Review* and it moved the journal *Science* (12/6/64) to comment, "One of the prophets most honoured by quotation and imitation is Daniel Bell, Columbia University sociologist and a former labor editor of *Fortune* who drew a convincing and intimidating picture of what is coming, barring war, in a paper called 'The Post-industrial Society'" (in Bell 1971a: 167n).

Bell decided not to publish at the time, however, "because I felt that the idea was unfinished" (1971: 167n). However, the temptations of public exposure could not be resisted for long and several papers incorporating the original idea appeared in the mid- to late 1960s. One such that must be close to original appeared in a volume on scientific progress (1967a) and a set of more developed "notes" on the concept appeared in *The Public Interest* at about the same time (1967b; 1967c). The "notes" had a widespread, international impact. The various essays that Bell wrote on the topic were collected and published as *The Coming of Post-Industrial Society: a Venture in Social Forecasting* (COPIS) in 1973.

Bell is hesitant about taking credit for the invention of the term. He developed it originally, self-consciously to debate Dahrendorf's claims about changes in the class structure of contemporary industrial society (1959). However, it had been used by Riesman in an essay called "Leisure and Work in Post-industrial Society" published in 1958. Bell admits: "I had, quite likely, read Riesman's essay at the time and the phrase undoubtedly came from him, though I have developed it in various writings in a vastly different way" (1971a: 167n). Certainly, Bell does not intend the term to mean a post-work society as Riesman did. In any event, the issue of terminological originality is redundant because it was first used by a now obscure British socialist theorist, Arthur Penty, as early as 1917 (COPIS: 37n).

Curiously, Bell received little credit among his immediate contemporaries for his development of the idea. Kuhns' *The Post-industrial Prophets* (1971) does not include or even reference Bell. Kleinberg gives large coverage to Bell's end-of-ideology thesis and even makes reference to the "notes," but for him the concept of "post-industrial society" is evanescent, having "become widely ad[o]pted as a basic term of reference for discussions of the new society" (1973: 1). Touraine's book entitled *The Post-industrial Society* (1971), originally published in French in 1969, makes no reference to Bell.

Bell outlines four intellectual influences on the formulation (1971a: 165–7):

- his own analysis of the break-up of family capitalism in which he proposes that societies are no longer ruled by business managers but by a technical-intellectual elite (EI: 39–46; see Chapter 3)—"the perennial interest of a sociologist in scanning the historical skies for a 'new class' was the starting point of the argument" (1971a: 165–6);
- studies of the changing composition of the labor force done at *Fortune* that drew on Clark's classification of employment into three sectors (primary, secondary, and tertiary) (1957) and a subsequent study by Foote and Hatt (1953) that extended the idea into quaternary and quinary sectors;
- a reading of Schumpeter (1942) that turned his mind to technological forecasting; and
- a paper by a historian of science, Gerald Holton (1962), that emphasized that the path of innovation in science was best reflected in the codifications of theory.

The post-industrial-society concept put these ideas, a new ruling elite, the movement of the labor force into service sectors, technology as the driving force of change and theory as the most important type of knowledge, into an entirely novel and challenging sociological account of changing social structure.

Before proceeding to an outline of the theory it needs to be located generally within the three-realms paradigm. Bell insists throughout his analysis, and against the understandings of many of his critics, that it is only the techno-economic realm of society, the realm that he often calls the "social structure," that can become post-industrial. Social structure can become post-industrial regardless of political regime or cultural configuration. Indeed, he goes further in distinguishing two dimensions *within* social structure, the socio-economic (patterns of economic ownership) and the socio-technical, and it is only in the second of these that the transition to post-industrialism can occur (COPIS: ix-xii). The issue of whether a society is post-industrial is, therefore, not only independent of whether it is Christian or Islamic, democratic or totalitarian, but also of whether it is capitalist or socialist. Indeed, if these dimensions are truly autonomous, one might presumably encounter a feudal post-industrial society or even a tribal post-industrial society (although Bell does not admit to either of these possibilities). The line Bell takes is not only an attack on the holistic and deterministic theories to which he is opposed, but also serves to defend him against critics who accuse him of constructing a convergence thesis.

THE CONCEPTUAL PRISM

The "post-industrial society," then, is a theory of social change. It argues that contemporary societies are or will be going through a shift so that the post-industrial society that emerges will be as different from industrial society as industrial society is from pre-industrial *society*. We can perhaps begin by considering the distinctions that Bell makes between these three (COPIS: 116–19, 126–9). It must be remembered that Bell intends this distinction only to be analytic, which, in his terms, means that while societies may appear different when viewed through this particular "prism" or typology they may be similar when viewed through another. Also, Bell does not argue that one type displaces the preceding one but that rather: "Like palimpsests, the new developments overlie the previous layers, erasing some features and thickening the texture of society as a whole" (COPIS: xvi).

A *pre-industrial society* can be characterized as "a game against nature" that centers on attempts to extract resources from the natural environment. Primary-sector occupations and industries (hunting, foraging, farming, fishing, mining, forestry) dominate its economy. Economic activity is carried out according to custom and tradition and faces severe limitations from the supply of land and resources. The level of economic activity varies according to the seasons and to global fluctuations in demand. The possession of land determines the pattern of stratification. The unit of social life is the extended household which, above the level of manual labor, often includes a relatively large number of domestic servants.

An *industrial society* is "a game against fabricated nature" that centers on human-machine relationships and applies energy to the transformation of the natural into a technical environment. Economic activity focuses on the manufacturing and processing of tangible goods. The central occupations are the secondary sector ones of semi-skilled factory worker and engineer. The chief economic problem is the mobilization of sufficient capital to establish manufacturing enterprises. By contrast, the main social problem is located in the stratification system. That system depends on the differential ownership of capital and is likely to give rise to industrial or class conflict about the distribution of returns to capital and labor. So another key problem is the coordination of differentiated activities and interests around machine technology.

By contrast, a *post-industrial society* is "a 'game between persons' in which an 'intellectual technology,' based on information, rises alongside of machine technology" (COPIS: 116). The post-industrial society involves industries from three sectors: the tertiary industries of transportation and utilities; the quaternary industries of trade, finance and capital exchange; and the quinary industries of health, education, research, public administration, and leisure. Among these, the last is definitive because the key occupations are the professional and technical ones, with scientists at the core. Given that the generation of information is the key problem and that science is the most important source of information, the organization of the institutions of science, the universities and research institutes is the central problem in the post-industrial society. The strength of nations is given in their scientific capacity and: "For this reason the nature and kinds of state support for science, the politicization of science, the sociological problems of the organization of work by science teams, all become central policy issues in a post-industrial society" (COPIS: 117–18).

Bell elaborates his ideal-typical construct of the post-industrial society in terms of five dimensions, a methodology that presumably emulates Weber's dimensions of the ideal type of bureaucratic administrative staff. They are as follows (COPIS: 14–33):

- *Creation of a service economy.* Here Bell conceptualizes social change in terms of what Miles and Gershuny (1986) call "a march through the sectors." The techno-economic structure of a society changes according to an economizing principle in which more efficient and productive techniques and production systems replace less efficient and productive ones. Drawing on Clark (1957), Bell argues that change, therefore, involves unilinear progression between the sectors (primary through quinary) and a corresponding shift in the labor force. Accordingly: "the first and simplest characteristic of a post-industrial society is that the majority of the labor force is no longer engaged in agriculture or manufacturing but in services, which are defined, residually, as trade, finance, transport, health, recreation, research, education, and government" (COPIS: 15). On this criterion the United States had the first service economy by the mid-1950s but it has now been joined by much of the Western world, Japan and some of the Asian dragons. Bell cautions about the particular use that he gives to the word "services" (against misreadings by such critics as Kumar 1978: 242ff). He intends it to apply not to personal and manual services but only those found in health, education, research and public administration.
- *The preeminence of the professional and technical class.* Here Bell tells us that the predominant, although not necessarily the majority of, occupations in the society will be professional and technical occupations requiring a tertiary level of education. The core will be scientists and engineers and together they will become a knowledge class that displaces the propertied bourgeoisie.
- *The primacy of theoretical knowledge.* This is the defining "axial principle" of the post-industrial society, the organization of the society around knowledge that becomes the basis for social control, the direction of innovation and the political management of new social relationships. Bell stresses that in a post-industrial society knowledge is theoretical, rather than traditional or practical, in character. It involves the codification of knowledge into abstract symbolic systems that can be. The scientist displaces the inventor; the econometrician displaces the political economist.
- *The planning of technology.* The advance of theoretical knowledge allows technological forecasting, that is, the planning of change, including forward assessments of its risks, costs and advantages. The control and regulation of the future introduction of technologies becomes feasible.
- *The rise of a new intellectual technology.* Against usual understandings of technology as physical, as to do with tools or machines, Bell introduces

the idea of an intellectual technology, a system of abstract symbols that can model those "games between people" and allow one to make decisions without intuition: "An intellectual technology is the substitution of algorithms (problem-solving rules) for intuitive judgements" (COPIS: 29). The computer is a physical technology that is necessary to this development because only by the use of a computer can the multiple complexities involved be calculated. However, the critical intellectual technology is the software and the statistical or logical formulae that are entered into the computer.

In a foreword written for a new edition of COPIS published in 1978 Bell alters this list of dimensions. The planning dimension is eliminated and seven new dimensions are added. These are (COPIS: xvi–xix):

- *A change in the character of work.* Work focuses not on the manipulation of objects but on an engagement in relationships with other people.
- *The role of women.* The expansion of the services sector provides a basis for the economic independence of women that had not previously been available.
- *Science as the imago.* Scientific institutions and their relationship with other institutions are the central, emergent, and "perfect" feature of the post-industrial society.
- *Situses as political units.* A situs is defined as a vertical order of a society, as opposed to the horizontal orders of classes or strata. Bell specifies four functional situses (scientific, technological, administrative, and cultural) and five institutional situses (business, government, university/research, social welfare, and military). Major conflicts will occur between situses rather than between classes and, indeed, class formation may well be prevented.
- *Meritocracy.* Position is allocated on the basis of education and skill rather than wealth or cultural advantage.
- *The end of scarcity?* Scarcity of goods will disappear in favor of scarcities of information and time. A key problem may be the allocation of leisure time.
- *The economics of information.* Because information is essentially a collective rather than a private good, it will be necessary to follow a co-operative, rather than an individualistic strategy in the generation and use of information (perhaps the creation of a "public household."

The dimensions are now multiplying like rabbits and Bell seeks to bring us back to the core of his proposal by specifying that there are two "large" dimensions by which one decides whether a social structure has yet entered a post-industrial phase. These are, the centrality of theoretical knowledge (including by implication, the employment of science as a means to technological change) and the expansion of the quinary service sector. We can now move on to examine the consequences of these two shifts in some detail.

A SERVICE SOCIETY

Bell disentangles the move towards a service economy into several components (COPIS: 127–9). First, industrial society itself presupposes an expansion of certain "manual" service industries, transportation, communication, public utilities, and wholesale and retail distribution. Second, white-collar employment grows in the "co-ordinating" sectors of the economy, banking and finance. Third, as goods production begins to exceed immediate needs and as individual incomes rise, personal and leisure services (grooming, dining, leisure travel, entertainment, sport, etc.) expand. Fourth, the conception of rights to health and education expands. Last, the increasing complexity of society and the increasing politicization of rights and entitlements leads to an expansion of public-sector services. In so far as the United States is the emerging post-industrial society, Bell (COPIS: 129–33) can now move on to examine the march through the sectors in that society. The overall picture confirms the existence of such a trend: in 1900, 30 percent of American workers were employed in service-sector industries (tertiary, quaternary, quinary); in 1940, 50 percent were so employed; and by 1980 the proportion had reached 70 percent. Until 1920 this development was the consequence of declining agricultural employment and service employment grew only in the tertiary sector. Thereafter, the share of secondary sector employment itself began to shrink, even though its absolute numbers increased. After 1947 the most important area of service employment growth was government, so that by 1980 it accounted for about 16 percent of the labor force although a major component of this was the expansion in the area of education. Bell is also acutely aware that sectoral distribution does not necessarily inform us about the distribution of manual versus non-manual labor. Many employees in the service sector are manual workers and about one-third of the manufacturing employees are non-manual. He forecasts that not only will the secondary-sector share of employment decline but that the proportion of manual workers in manufacturing will also decline as automation takes hold.

This leads Bell (COPIS: 134–7) into an analysis of the occupational distribution of the American labor force. The proportion of the labor force in white-collar (excluding personal service) occupations rose from 17 percent in 1900 to 50 percent in 1980. He admits that much of this change has been due to the absorption of women into routine white-collar employment. However, even if one looks solely at male employment the transformation has been remarkable; the share in white-collar occupations increased from 15 to 42 percent between 1900 and 1970. By comparison, blue-collar (manual-industrial) occupations peaked at about 40 percent in 1940 before declining to 32 percent in 1980; and agricultural employment slid from 37 percent in 1900 to 2 percent in 1980. A key element in Bell's argument is that the fastest-growing occupational group of all is the professional and technical group. It was less than a million in 1890 and now numbers over 12 million, or 16 percent of the labor force. Four million of these are teachers and health workers but 2.3 million are in science and engineering.

This development poses severe difficulties for the trade union movement which Bell clearly regards as a phenomenon of industrial society (COPIS: 137–42). American union membership advanced rapidly between 1935 and 1947 but since then the level of union density has declined from 30 to 27 percent in 1980. This slight shift masks some considerable internal redistributions of membership. The causes of the reduction lie in declining blue-collar employment (where unionization continues to stand at about 60 percent) and in rising female employment. The only real area of union growth is in the area of government employment, but private-sector, white-collar employment is a difficult arena of recruitment. Financial service employees remain largely unorganized.

Bell can now examine some of the issues that arise from the emergence of a service labor force and that differentiate it from an industrial labor force. He discusses five such issues, focusing on their implications for social division and conflict:

- *Education and status* (COPIS: 143–5) The post-industrial labor force is highly educated and, in so far as it is decreasingly fed by migration, culturally homogeneous. This allows Bell to ask whether this might provide the basis for the emergence of a new proletarian consciousness of a type envisioned by Marx, but he remains agnostic on the issue. Indeed, he is agnostic on the exact form of labor organization that new professional employees will set up.
- *Blacks* (COPIS: 145) Bell recalls that in his first specification of the post-industrial-society concept in 1962 he had suggested that class would disappear in favor of a system of social inequality based primarily on race. In 1973 he sees little reason to change his mind, although the stress of post-industrial occupations on performance criteria has provided a slightly increased measure of equality.
- *Women* (COPIS: 146) The service economy is highly feminized. About half the workers in the services sector are women, compared with 20 percent of employees in the goods-producing sectors. Women employees present a particular recruitment problem for organized labor that historically has excluded them.
- *The non-profit sector* (COPIS: 146–7) The non-profit sector of the service economy is growing much faster than the private sector. Indeed, it is the major area for the net growth of new jobs, so that by 1980 about 20 percent of the labor force was in non-profit-sector jobs. In so far as many of these workers are middle class they will have both an increased appetite for cultural products and a more liberal set of social and political attitudes.
- *The "new" working class* (COPIS: 148–54) The educated and professionalized sections of the working class are unlikely to become a militant and

radicalized vanguard for the rest of the (disappearing) proletariat. Rather, they are likely to be drawn into the system of professional situses which is a more likely possibility for socio-economic conflict.

Bell sums up the character of the emerging service economy in the following passage: [W]hat is central to the new relationship is encounter or communication, and the response of ego to alter, and back—from the irritation of a customer at an airline-ticket office to the sympathetic or harassed response of teacher and student. But the fact that individuals now talk to other individuals rather than interact with a machine, is the fundamental fact about work in the post-industrial society (COPIS: 163). For Bell, this means profound implications for the central conflicts and divisions in society. He recognizes the possibility that particular events, such as foreign competition, may occasionally heighten labor militancy but, in a return to an earlier theme, he thinks it unlikely that this will constitute ideologically organized class warfare. Politics is likely to focus on what he calls communal issues—health, education, the environment, and crime—on which labor may often be divided or, indeed, allied with capital.

A KNOWLEDGE SOCIETY

We can now turn to the second "large dimension" of the post-industrial society, the centrality of theoretical knowledge and the institutions of science. In an unusual step Bell gives a formal definition of knowledge, "a set of organized statements of facts or ideas, presenting a reasoned judgement or an experimental result, which is transmitted to others through some communication medium in some systematic form" (COPIS: 175; italics deleted). However, because he proposes to measure the growth of knowledge, he needs an operational rather than a formal definition, which he also offers: "Knowledge is that which is objectively known, an intellectual property, attached to a name or group of names and certified by copyright or some other form of social recognition (e.g. publication)" (COPIS: 176). He insists that such knowledge is social, as opposed to individual, in terms of both its production and cost and in terms of its evaluation by the market.

Bell more or less accepts a formulation from Price that the rate of growth of scientific papers and of books has always been exponential rather than lineal, with a doubling time of about fifteen years. However, growth in any field of science always hits limits and outputs of knowledge actually increase as the consequence of the differentiation or "branching" of science, "the creation of new and numerous subdivisions or specialties within fields" (COPIS: 186). This happens continuously: in 1948 the *National Register of Scientific and Technical Personnel* listed 54 scientific specializations; by 1968 there were 900.

Technology has grown equally rapidly. Bell surveys several estimates of the rate of technological change, measured largely by general increases in productivity (average output per worker). Productivity typically increases by roughly 2 percent

per year, give or take 0.5 percent. Before the Second World War it was usually below 2 percent, and after that war it was usually above 2 percent (COPIS: 189–95).
However, Bell claims that in the post-industrial society something radically new is
occurring in the area of technology, "the changed relationship between science
and technology, and the incorporation of science through the institutionalization
of research into the ongoing structure of the economy . . . as a normal part of
business organization" (COPIS: 196). Research is becoming organized systematically rather than operating on a piecemeal basis and industries are becoming more
science-based. Productivity is therefore likely to escalate.

Taking these developments together Bell argues that the post-industrial society is a knowledge society. In a knowledge society science and technology become
intimately related because technology is driven by theoretical as opposed to
practical knowledge; and the shares of employment of GDP in the knowledge
field become relatively large (COPIS: 212). Bell seeks to show that the United
States is moving into just such a configuration. For example, the proportion of
GDP devoted to education doubled from 3.5 to 7.5 percent between 1949 and
1969 (COPIS: 216–20). More impressively, the proportion of GNP devoted to
research and development multiplied fifteen times between 1948 and 1965 to
reach 3 percent. Most of this funding came from government, so that a large proportion was committed to defence and atomic energy research. However, almost
all of the rest went into physical and medical sciences. Spending in these areas
is growing much faster than in defence and atomic energy research (COPIS:
250–62).

The development of a knowledge society incorporates "a democratization of
higher education on a scale that the world has never seen before." The proportion
of 18- to 21-year-olds enrolled in education doubled between 1946 and 1964 to
44 percent. The average doubling time for the American university population is
20 years (since 1879), but since the Second World War the rate of increase accelerated rapidly by virtue of enrollments in graduate degrees. So by 1970 the doubling time had come down to ten years. Importantly, while only about a quarter of
first degrees are in science, more than half the doctorates are in natural science
and mathematics (COPIS: 216–20). From a sociological point of view, Bell makes
a more important claim that those who work in the knowledge sectors come to
constitute a "knowledge class." The members are some of those he has already
discussed in his analysis of the service economy—teachers, engineers, technicians,
and scientists. The last is the most "crucial group." Whereas the workforce increased by 50 percent between 1930 and 1975, and the number of engineers increased by 370 percent, the number of scientists increased by 930 percent
(475,000). In 1970 the "scientific population" was about four million or 4.7 percent of the work-force (COPIS: 216–17).

Bell works through a conceptual filtering process to identify the scientific
elite, the equivalent of the capitalist bourgeoisie, by progressively eliminating
teachers, those without doctorates, and those not engaged in research. The resulting select group of perhaps 120,000 scientific and technical personnel is very different from the population as a whole in so far as less than a quarter are employed

in (industrial) business and more than a half in universities. Here he shows that he really does mean that this elite is a knowledge *class:*

> *If one believes . . . that the expansion of science and scientifically based technology is creating the framework for a new social order that will erode capitalism, as the activities of the merchants and the bourgeois outside the landed economy undermined feudalism, then the significant fact is that most of the activities of science are outside the business system and the organiza-tion of science policy is not, in the first instance, responsive to business de-mand. The necessary foundation for any new class is to have an independent institutional base outside the old dominant order. For the scientist this base has been the university (COPIS: 232).*

While Bell is in no doubt that scientists constitute a new class he remains un-certain about whether they can maintain sufficient independence ever to under-mine capitalism. It follows though that the university is a critical institution. Certainly, current rates of expansion might give Bell cause to believe that an insti-tutional base for the knowledge class will continue to be available. More impor-tantly, he is able to isolate a smallish group of largish universities, perhaps 100 or 150 of the 2,500 in the United States, that teach most of the undergraduates and do nearly all the graduate teaching and research. Indeed, twenty-one such univer-sities carried out 54 percent of the research. It is critical to the preeminence of the knowledge class that this core should maintain the relatively high level of auton-omy that derives from private sources of funding, and Bell sees a threat to such autonomy in the declining share of enrollment received by the major private uni-versities (Harvard, Stanford, etc.).

A COMMUNAL SOCIETY

Bell's claims about the rise of a knowledge class appear problematic to many sociologists. The argument that social inequality might be based on the intangi-bles of theory and information rather than on the solidities of material property or even occupation runs counter to a century of sociological tradition. In a nutshell, Bell's stratification claim is twofold: first, that the basis of stratification in the post-industrial society will shift from property to knowledge, and, thus, from class to status, so that the knowledge "class" becomes the most powerful status-group in society; and second, that there will be intersecting dimensions of inequal-ity such that no particular cleavage can be regarded as fundamental. Society will come to approximate a community not merely because inequalities cross-cut but because the form of decision-making changes as social structures enter the post-in-dustrial phase. Industrial society is organized as a market in which the intersection of multiple individual choices determines outcomes, but the post-industrial society requires social decisions, that is, consensus on planning future developments. However, as the discussion of Bell's concept of the public household indicates, consensus is extraordinarily difficult to achieve in the context of an escalation of claims and entitlements. A conflict between populist claims and professional expertise is a real possibility. So the post-industrial society need not be communal in the sense that it realizes a utopian harmony, "If the struggle between capitalist and worker, in the locus of the factory, was the hallmark of industrial society, the clash between the professional and the populace, in the organization and in the community is the hallmark of conflict in the post-industrial society" (COPIS: 129). Rather, it is a community only in so far as many of its decisions need to be made by collectivized groups.

We can now examine these claims in more detail. At the gross level of the ideal type, the sources of power and who wields it are quite clear. In an industrial society the key issue is control of capital plant and machinery and it is the business class that controls these, exercising political power through indirect influence on governmental decisions and reproducing itself through direct inheritance, patronage, and educational inheritance. In a post-industrial society the key resource is knowledge and this is under the control of scientists and researchers influencing political processes by being engaged and incorporated in governmental decisions and reproducing itself largely through education (COPIS: 359). However, because contemporary social structure is not completely post-industrial it combines a mixture of power and mobility mechanisms including wealth and property, political position, and credentialized skill. Nevertheless, two features of this complex confirm a shift in the power structure: the common interest of the scientific elite in promoting professional or ethical rather than material outcomes; and the reconstitution of individual and private property into organizational property (COPIS: 360–2).

These developments do not imply that politics will become less important but rather the reverse. The reasons are that: society must be organized on a national rather than a regional or local basis if planning and co-ordination are to prove effective; and multiplying claims for entitlements are made through politics. Decisions about planning and entitlements cannot be made simply on the basis of technical rationality but imply political value-judgments (COPIS: 364). Politics, therefore, becomes the "cockpit" of the post-industrial society, the visible hand that coordinates where the market no longer can be effective. Its activities have been enlarged and problematized by five developments (COPIS: 468–71):

- the openness of government has increased and avenues for access have multiplied;
- telecommunications have increased the frequency of interaction between the members of society;
- families are more mobile and more technologized so their members engage in more frequent exchanges with others;
- there is an increased need for planning; and
- advancing levels of consumption make imperative an increased regulation of competition between individuals and groups for resources.

It follows from this that, "In terms of status (esteem and recognition, and possibly income) the knowledge class may be the highest class in the new society, but there is no intrinsic reason [that it should] become a new economic interest class, or a new political class which would bid for power" (COPIS: 374–5).

Bell's overall scheme for the "societal structure" of the post-industrial society, therefore, includes three dimensions that are somewhat reminiscent of Weber's class-status-party triplet. These are status, situs and control, although in Bell they are all dimensions of "the classes." Status is the "horizontal" dimension that sets up the knowledge strata. There are four such strata: the professional class, technicians and semi-professionals, clerical and sales workers, and craftsmen and semi-skilled workers. In a mix-and-match of stratification terminology, the professional "class" is subdivided into four "estates": scientific, that develops basic knowledge and is autonomous; technical, that applies knowledge to practical problems; administrative that manages organizations; and cultural, that is involved with the expressive symbolization of forms and meanings. Conflict is possible between these estates on the basis of ethical differences: for example between a professional ethos and an ethos of self-interest; or between a rational ethos and an expressive ethos (COPIS: 375–6).

Bell uses the term "situs" to indicate the "vertical" structures of society that are "the actual locuses of occupational activities and interests." There are five: economic enterprises; government; universities and research institutes; social service organizations; and the military. A peculiar feature of the post-industrial society is that statuses are not concentrated within situses but are scattered across them. In an industrial society, capital and labor are defined by the economic situs alone, but scientists in a post-industrial society can be found in any situs.

As the preceding discussion indicates, a new feature of post-industrial society is the importance of government. Whereas, in previous configurations, distributional disputes were fought out between capital and labor in the economic enterprise they are now being fought out within the "control system" between an expanded number of interest groups that are frequently situs-based. The control system is broadly divided between a "directorate" of senior government officials and "the polities" including parties, non-governmental elites, interest and lobby groups, and mobilized claimants (COPIS: 375–7).

CONCLUSION

One of the reasons that Weber's work has had a particularly seminal effect is that, although he often engages in a tedious semanticism, his work is also often loose and incomplete as well as being extraordinarily suggestive and insightful. Neo-Weberians can spend many happy hours, indeed whole careers, of scholarship chasing down alternative possible conceptualizations and typological arrangements. Bell offers those who study him similar opportunities and nowhere is this more true than in the case of the post-industrial society. To be frank, the concept is slippery, not through any attempt at dissimulation but rather because the essayistic style that Bell adopts encourages expressiveness at the possible expense of analytic precision.

Analytic imprecision is not difficult to find. The very term "post-industrial society" is imprecise because Bell frequently insists that he is not arguing about all three realms of society but only about the techno-economic or social structure. The polity and the culture are supposed to turn through their own cycles in blissful isolation. Even so, Bell cannot resist telling us that the form of the polity will be communal in the post-industrial society. Equally we cannot be entirely clear about his methodology. Perhaps the clearest statement of intent is on the first page of the 1978 Foreword, where he says that it is a speculative construct that identifies emergent features against which future reality can be measured. But there is an awful lot of straightforward narrative and description in the book that has little to do with ideal types or prisms and a lot to do with the peculiarities of American social development. Another inconsistency surrounds the discussion of axial principles and structures. In the three-realms argument (published in full after COPIS), the axial principle of the TES is economizing and its axial structure is bureaucracy. However, bureaucracy loses top billing in COPIS to the collegial structures of the university and the axial principle is variously specified as "intellectual technology" (COPIS: ix), "the centrality of theoretical knowledge" (COPIS: 115), or both (COPIS: 212). We can easily find other inconsistencies, about whether the post-industrial society has actually arrived or is merely a typological construct, and, if it has arrived, when it began, or about the usage of such terms as "class," "status," and "polity," but this would be fruitless because the importance of the book lies in its capacity to sensitize us to a significant social shift rather than in laying out an analytical grid.

This sort of quibbling is common in relation to Bell and in relation to this book in particular and frequently tempts somewhat uncharitable responses (See Archer 1990; Kumar 1978; Miller 1975; Pahl 1975). If we are to criticize we might more profitably concentrate on whatever theoretical weakness there is in the argument. These seem to be twofold. First, as Nichols (1975: 350) has it, Bell by assertion shuts tight all the doors on any claim that he is theorizing an end to capitalism and class, especially in so far as he claims that technology is on a different dimension from property ownership. However, throughout the book, and particularly in the sections on stratification, it is clear that, in Bell's view, neither society as a whole nor the TES alone will be structured by capital accumulation in the future. This formulation surely must be designed to deny the reality of business power in a claim that is perhaps a little too anti-Marxist. Second, Bell forecasts the development of an enlarged communal state as if it can only happen in some future society. In fact, liberal corporatist states have long existed elsewhere than in the United States that have frequently successfully managed to balance claims within a reasoned political philosophy. The underdevelopment of the state has been both the poverty and the strength of American society, but it should not be taken to be a general feature of all advanced societies.

Notwithstanding these qualifications, the force of much of the argument cannot be denied. As Bell himself says, almost with surprise, the phrase "post-industrial society" has passed quickly into the sociological literature (COPIS: ix). The argument must be regarded as strongest in its stress on the emergence of the quinary service sector and the development of information as a resource, and perhaps weakest in its claims for a scientocracy and the centrality of universities. Certainly, few scientists would see themselves as members of a dominant or even rising social group, and universities twist and turn in the winds of governmental and private-sector funding flows. These strengths and weaknesses are perhaps reflected in the ways in which sociologists conventionally use the term. Every sociologist knows that "post-industrialization" means the displacement of manufacturing occupations by service occupations, and indeed the description of such jobs as "post-industrial occupations" is common parlance.

12

Planning for an Uncertain Future: Socializing Information

Simon Nora and Alain Minc

In an often cited study commissioned by the French government, two students on modern social issues addressed the problem of what to do about the new age of information. More than simply a French perspective, this publication stimulated a great deal of debate about national policies. The French government was very interested in information economics because during the 1970s and 1980s it aggressively sought to exploit changing conditions to encourage a national computer industry, apply information technology to enhance its telephone system, and to take the lead in Europe's emerging information economy.

AN UNCERTAIN FUTURE

The liberal and Marxist approaches, contemporaries of the production-based society, are rendered questionable by its demise. The liberal approach tends to confuse history with economic laws. It only considers conflicts in terms of the market and tends to return them to this field if they escape. Thus, management aims at limiting the field of ideology and at expanding that of the market. Politics—insofar as it deals with the perception and handling of struggles for power—is apparently rejected. Actually, it is conjured away: it becomes less the field of deliberate and explicit action than the field of what is left unsaid. The vision of the future ends with a tranquilized postindustrial society. It assumes that affluence

From *The Computerization of Society: A Report to the President of France* (Cambridge, MA: The MIT Press, 1980): 133–141. The original French edition appeared in 1978 as *L'Informatisation de la societe* (Paris: La Documentation Francaise).

and the growing equality of standards of living will make it possible to build the nation around an immense culturally homogeneous middle class, and to overcome tensions.

The Marxist analysis recognizes conflicts, but it relates their evolution to the single opposition between two classes organized by relations of production. Arising from the suffering of the primitive accumulation of capital, it rests upon a simplistic, all-encompassing, and rigid view of power relationships, incapable of integrating the increasing complexity of modern societies. It is not surprising that the goal of history, arrival of the classless society, is reached quite simply by the collective appropriation of the means of production. It is a vision at least as mystifying as the post-industrial society.

The information society does not fit these analyses and predictions. Going beyond the world of production, it fashions its new requirements according to its own plan, its own regulatory patterns, and its own cultural model. It is the locus of an infinite number of decentralized, unexpressed conflicts that do not respond to a unifying analysis. Certainly, the systems approach can better explain a multipolar society, but the latter can have no prior strategy. Even its values will be the subject of multiple rivalries, and the results will be uncertain—it will be an uncertain society. The longer history continues, the more people make it, and the less they know what history they are fashioning. Thus, the future no longer depends on the approach but on the quality of the collective plan and on the nature of the regulations on which it is based.

UNTIL NOW: REGULATION WITHOUT PLAN, PLAN WITHOUT REGULATION

Liberalism produces mercantile societies: it is a system of regulation without a plan. Marxist management creates—but it is not the only one—protective societies: they constitute plans without regulation. Both reduce society to the level of the poor information on which they are based. In the liberal world, competition and its result, the price system, play the roles of both information and decision. They assure, for better or for worse, the adjustment of individual plans capable of solution. The entire society is measured by the single standard of commercial value; the market becomes the only "overall" value of society, and the supreme judge of values. This view has the advantage of offering an approximate guideline for interpretation and action, insofar as it is applied to the flows of information governing the behavior of producers and consumers. But it is useless in confronting what goes beyond commercial activities, that which depends on the cultural model, on the "formative matrix."

The constraints arising from long-term strategies, which exceed the strength and the stakes of individuals and of groups, are layered. The hierarchy of individual or collective choices cannot be discussed *ex ante*. Its *ex post* implementation will never be the sum total of preferences but an adjustment suffered unevenly. In such a system, each individual can only measure the unfulfilled part of his initial desire and blame the others for his unfulfillment. No mechanism of political participation can compensate for the resulting feeling of alienation and frustration. Marxist management, as practiced in the Eastern countries, is led to regard "indoctrination-information" as a tool for bringing reality within an imaginary framework, for reducing society to its ideological model. It tends to create protective systems and for that purpose only needs information from below. Information from above will be in the form of orders. The intention is not to take into account decentralized plans, but to give to each group and to each individual its allotted role in the implementation of the collective plan.

All regulation by decree seeks integration by a mystical participation. Sometimes, it can be obtained. Starting from the statement that the "principal plan of the center" ontologically and in the long run expresses the collective essence of individual desires, it justifies its present difficulties by its historical purposes and attempts to establish a system of representation that creates an emotional link between the collective plan and individual behavior. The weakness of such a system rests upon its internal contradiction. Civil society does not speak. Its only expression lies in the gaps, in the interstices. Thus, the logic of the center tends to drift away from reality. Having, on principle, suffocated the expression of desires and needs (even prices are no longer barometers but commands), the information from below, needed by the center to establish its plan, becomes only the mirror image of its own desire. By insisting upon erasing the signals and information that might be transmitted by the many facets of real society, the "apparatchiks" only manage the nightmares their fallow citizens, their own dreams, or their own interests. In a highly productive society, rich and well-distributed information must be able to make the spontaneity of social groups and the inevitable burden of constraints compatible.

SOCIALIZING INFORMATION

In an ideal world of fully informed "wise men," organization would coincide with spontaneity: a perfect market society, in which education and information would make each person conscious of the collective constraints, and a fully planned society, in which the center would receive from each unit at the base correct messages concerning its order of preferences and would have the same structure and the same attitude. Information and participation advance together. As long as it is up to citizens to express their quantifiable desires and up to the public authorities to perform their short-term regulatory activities, the market remains an effective forum for confrontations. But the groups' plans are increasingly expressing social and cultural aspirations. Simultaneously, external pressures will increase. Public authorities must preserve the future of society: the great disruptions in the international division of labor will require decisions by the government. Decentralized indicators and spontaneous reactions will not make it possible to prepare for massive scarcities, which can be forecast in the long run but which are only barely hinted at by current prices. Similarly, no individual forecast will determine the limit of national sovereignty beyond which all freedom of choice for the community will disappear. Only an authority possessing the appropriate information can promote development and guarantee the independence of the country: it is the mediator of vital constraints. A smooth functioning of society requires that social groups be able to express their aspirations and their dislikes, but that at the same time information concerning the constraints be received and accepted. There is no spontaneity without regulation and no regulation without a hierarchical system. A self-managed and self-sufficient society will remain marginally dissident. In order to contribute to the transformation of the entire society, it must accept a strategy of participation.

Therefore socializing information means establishing the mechanisms whereby constraints and freedoms, the prerogative plan and the aspirations of independent groups, are managed and harmonized. It means promoting the preparation of data on the basis of which the strategy of the center and the desires of the periphery may reach agreement whereby Society and the State not only support each other but produce each other. In order to do so, however, it is necessary to eliminate a basic contradiction: if information appears at the level of the decentralized units, it cannot be used as such for most of their decisions. It assumes its significance only through syntheses in which it confronts the long-term difficulties and the collective plan. It must then be returned in such a form that it will spontaneously produce correct reactions. This requires it to appear legitimate and effective, and its circulation must be institutionalized.

The British say that a fact must be respected like the "lord mayor." But what would be the weight of this dictum in a country in which the legitimacy of the lords mayor is contested? Legitimacy is the result of the procedure whereby they are appointed: all those who will be subjected to their authority participate in it. At present, information from above is not well received because it is resented as an extension of power, as a manipulation; it will be increasingly necessary to call its recipients to participate in its preparation, so that the recipients are also the transmitters and the transmissions take conditions for receiving into account. This participation will only be accepted if rival groups are equally capable of producing, processing, and transmitting their own information. This requires that most citizens be able to form communities or associations, public or private, and equip themselves to collect and use the information that justifies their plans.

But what type of information is involved? The people in charge will have to establish properly arranged sets of factual data, showing the constraints of the government, the purpose of the collective project, and whether it constitutes a plan or not. Effectiveness requires that the data be prepared by cross-examination, that their format render them easy to transmit, and that easy access make it possible to criticize them. It is not sufficient for them to be generally accepted as objective. Each group must also be able, on the basis of the same constraints, to reach an original reconciliation with its own projects, and the debate must produce alternative solutions. This requires that information can be exchanged with others and that it take into account environmental constraints, those resulting from the objectives of other groups and those arising from the common center, the public authorities. Information that only teaches technical solutions, that lists facts without putting them into a perspective and without structuring them into a coherent project, and, on the other hand, information that proclaims ideals without inserting them into the practical development of society will increasingly be regarded as pseudo-information. Making information useful, therefore, means reaching a minimum agreement on the structure that transforms it into coherent and accepted thought.

Furthermore, the resulting project must be inserted within a system of communications and concerted action. At the present time, information basically goes from the top to the bottom. Only the market constitutes a network, and a poor one, for horizontal communication. The information society requires focusing on the center of the desires of the independent groups and an unlimited multiplication of lateral communications. This must make it possible to compare formalized items of information to reveal those projects deriving from the base that exceed the quantified data from the market. The massive computerization of society will have to be utilized to create this new "network," in which each homogeneous community will be able to communicate with its counterparts and with the center. Oral communication, with its rituals, gave the village its stability. Processed communication, and its codes, must recreate an "informational agora" expanded to the size of the modern nation. Thus, agreements and compromises will gradually be reached. They will express a consensus involving ever larger communities, and increasingly long-range views.

Stability in a computerized society is difficult to achieve. In outline, national life will be organized at three levels, corresponding to three functions, to three regulatory systems, and, therefore, to three information systems. The sovereign state itself is where the collective plan will be established; the public authorities will determine the relative importance of the constraints to which society is subjected. They may use the market, but they must not retreat before a direct command or direct control. Here, regulation is essentially based on political mechanisms. The stage at which social and cultural programs will be organized and confront one another will be the field of the "informational agora." The market stage, based on the price system, will be where the spontaneous desires of groups are expressed and decided, insofar as they concern marketable goods and are quantifiable. Actually, these stages will interfere: as the constraints imposed by the common interest and by cultural aspirations are better expressed, they will tend to affect the market. The latter may stop being a metaphysical entity and become a tool. It will reflect exchange values increasingly dominated by motivations that go beyond them. It will be a quasi-market, which will recover a temporal scope and a range of desires that until then will have eluded it.

This dynamic, in which each regulatory system is enriched by the information originating from the other two, is the royal road that could be followed by a country that has generalized communication and thereby expanded participation. But the society that it produces is fragile; built to favor the formation of a consensus, it presupposes its existence and it is blocked if it cannot obtain it. Excessive or poorly accepted constraints would only enable it to recover its stability by an increase in authoritarianism. An irresponsible promotion of social and cultural aspirations, incompatible with the constraints, would reduce the collective plan to its proper size or would cause a strong reaction on the part of the advocates of sovereign power. This would be a prelude to a compromise in favor of checking the movement of history.

In order to make the information society possible, it is necessary to have knowledge, but also to have time. The reciprocal learning process of disciplines and aspirations takes place slowly: it operates through the generations, by transforming cultural patterns—families, universities, media, and so on. Data processing has falsely crystallized our concerns. They rise again, more general and stronger, at the end of this analysis. Will the urgency and scope of the constraints to which French society will be subjected grant it the time required for this vital learning process?

13

Employment in the Information Society

European Commission

Knowledge work is not unique to the United States, it also is emerging in Europe and in East Asia. The European Union is concerned about the role of knowledge work and commissioned a study of the issue. The document from which the selection below came explored how work was being organized in an information society, identifying challenges for people and organizations, while describing implications for job training, employment, and skills. The paper is an excellent summary of the concerns of workers and governments.

THE CONCERNS: JOBLESS GROWTH AND THE END OF WORK?

The main economic, social, and political problem in Europe is high and persistent unemployment. Some 18 million people are unemployed, half of them have been out of work for a year or more. There are at least nine million more discouraged workers who would look for a job if they thought the work existed. This depressing situation has led to a debate on the "end of work" and of "jobless growth" linked to the effects of ICTs on working life. Several major studies have been undertaken by the International Labour Organization (ILO) and the Organization for Economic Cooperation and Development (OECD) as well as by the EU (European Union) during the last few years to gain a better understanding of the nature of the employment problem in Europe, focusing on specific issues such as the relationship between technology and employment, as well as the more general relationship between macro economic and structural policies.

From *Living and Working in the Information Society: People First Green Paper* (Luxembourg: Office for Official Publications of the European Communities, 1996): 14–20.

The transition towards the information society is already taking place, and this will inevitably provoke significant changes in the living and working patterns of European citizens. The challenge is to shape the emerging information society so that we neither miss out in the global stakes nor weaken the solidarity of Europeans.

There are three aspects that deserve special attention in this Green Paper:

- The overall effect of ICT on employment;
- more effective management of the process of job transformation; and
- the effect on labor markets in terms of supply and demand of skills and competencies.

THE FACTS: STEADY EMPLOYMENT GROWTH SINCE 1960

It is well recognized that the EU has had, on average, a much lower rate of employment than the United States and Japan over the past two decades—some 60 percent compared with 70 percent or more—and that, in contrast to those countries, the EU's level of unemployment has remained stubbornly close to 10 percent over much of the last decade. However, it can also be observed that the rate of employment growth has remained almost unchanged over the last three-and-a-half decades across different areas of the developed world, albeit at different rates—at around 2 percent in the United States, around 1 percent in Japan, and 0.3 percent in Europe. It is worth noting that the rate of employment growth has not significantly slowed since 1973, the year of the first oil shock and the starting point for the slowdown of economic growth. Hence, far from reflecting a decline in the amount of work provided, the rise in European unemployment is largely related to the fact that employment growth (0.3 percent on average per year) lagged behind labor force growth (0.6 percent on average per year). The steadiness of employment growth over the whole period from 1960 to 1995 does not support the view that jobs are inexorably disappearing, only that employment failed to grow sufficiently to keep up with the growth in the labor force.

Contrary to some claims that technical progress can only be labor saving, existing data suggest growth has become slightly more rather than less job-intensive, with the pace of job creation remaining steady in the face of the sharply reduced rate of economic growth in the 1970s and 1980s. The data also suggest that the relative capacities of United States and European economies to create employment have not changed since 1973. Until then, annual growth of 4.3 percent was required for the economy to start creating employment in Europe, and 2 percent was required in the United States. New jobs are now being created as soon as growth reaches 2 percent in Europe, and 0.6 percent in the United States. This new growth and employment pattern is reflected in the slowdown in measured productivity growth after 1973. The rate of growth of productivity and GDP fell, even though more and more ICTs were introduced, while the growth in employment continued at much the same speed as before. Whatever the detailed explanation of this paradox—and debate and analysis continues—it is clear that the aggregate data do not support the thesis of "the end of work" or even the beginning of jobless growth. The more successful employment performance in the United States, Canada, and Japan, cannot be explained by less use of labor saving ICTs.

On the contrary, the development and introduction of ICTs have, in general, been more extensive in these countries—and particularly the United States—than in the European countries. Moreover, within the EU the Member States, which are more advanced in terms of ICTs, also tend to have the highest employment rates. As with all technological change, the spread of ICTs is a growth factor, and there is a positive link between technological progress, productivity, and economic growth which offers the potential for the growth of new forms of employment. Technological progress spurs innovation, thus, creating the potential for new entrepreneurial opportunities, especially for SMEs. This higher growth potential must be exploited if unemployment is to be reduced and the European economies are not to fall behind in the global stakes.

The main impact of ICTs in relation to employment is a radical restructuring of jobs and the world of work. Manufacturing industry has declined, but this decline has not been uniform. Within manufacturing, low-technology, low-skill, and low-wage jobs have been shed. High-technology, high-skill, and high-wage employment has expanded. The main source for employment growth is the service sector. Job gains are coming both from the dynamic part and from the more traditional part. Employment gains associated with new technologies have more than compensated for any labor displacement. In fact, employment growth in services has been faster in those countries which have invested most in the application of new technologies. So far, employment growth in the European core ICT industries has been quite flat, due to the downturn in the business cycle. But this hides quite heterogeneous developments. Employment in consumer electronics, data processing, and telecommunications equipment manufacturing has clearly declined. Employment levels in the components industry and telecommunications services has remained stable. By contrast, employment in software and computer services has seen steady growth, almost tripling its size since 1980 and employing nowadays around 750,000 workers in the Union. This sector remains an area in which there are particularly high hopes for employment growth, especially in new high-skill, knowledge-intensive services, such as multimedia software and end-user training.

Overall, these trends are expected to be maintained in the short run, with the exception of telecommunication services, where expected job losses due to digitalization and liberalization will not be compensated by the new entrants job creation in the short term. However, these trends do not take account of job creation in other areas related to the information society. Audiovisual services have shown a noticeable employment growth, with a 37 percent increase over the period 1983 to 1992, and the prospects are also good for further job growth. Additional ICT-related job creation has taken place in areas such as teleservices, telebanking, and retail distribution, but precise figures are difficult to trace statistically. The statistical observation of these new developments in the economy, and especially in the related service industries, is a challenge for the statistical system.

In addition, the positive employment effects of the information society are not expected to be concentrated only in the ICT and other IS sectors. Research undertaken by the Commission is showing that liberalization of telecommunications combined with a rapid adoption of ICTs will lead to job creation and improved welfare in the rest of the economy. The boost of investment in new telecommunication and data processing equipment, combined with the general price reductions and the real income increases resulting from the reductions in telecommunications tariffs, will yield positive effects in terms of employment and value added in the rest of the economy in the medium and long term. These job gains will largely compensate for any job losses that could take place in the telecommunication sector. This mechanism applies not only to telecommunications but also to the diffusion of all ICTs. The problem, however, is in managing the time lag between these processes, and in helping individuals adapt to the new challenges and opportunities of the labor market.

Though the longer term patterns of job creation in the information society are difficult to quantify, forecasts show that new jobs will be created in the whole economy, not only in the ICT industry and in new and emerging multimedia services, but also in all the other services and industrial sectors, including traditional and declining ones. There is a plethora of examples where the introduction and use of ICTs in enterprises has had substantial positive impact on employment. Over the period 1985 to 1994 employment in the service sector in the EU grew by some ten million. Although 80 percent of this overall growth in employment took place in the period 1985 to 1990, the second half of the period still saw a growth of two million jobs in business, computers, and research, the same increase as in the earlier period—with 0.6 million extra jobs in education, and 0.9 million jobs in health and sanitation—all sectors where ICT has an important impact.

The only significant area of service sector job loss in the 1990 to 1994 period was in wholesaling and retailing, where the decline in employment has been primarily due to lack of demand, not increased productivity. These new employment patterns are also affecting the gender balance of the labor market. The growth in the service sector has offered new opportunities for women entering the labor market. Employment for women has been increasing from the middle of the 1960s to the beginning of the 1990s. Women have increased their share in the workforce, and a significant proportion of the new female jobs are part-time jobs. In contrast to the long-term trend for female employment growth, employment for men has been decreasing ever since 1965, except for some years at the end of the 1980s.

THE FIRST CHALLENGE: TO PREVENT BEGGAR-THY-NEIGHBOR POLICIES

Across the labor market, one conclusion which must be drawn from past developments is that weak employment growth in Europe, around 0.3 percent a year, and concomitant high and persistent unemployment, must be explained by factors other than technological ones. Unemployment in Europe started to increase in the middle of the 1970s. Until 1985, a significant number of jobs were lost, at the same time as the labor force grew faster than ever. Ten million new jobs were created during the long growth period of the second half of the 1980s. However, half of the new jobs were lost during 1992 to 1993.

A number of factors—including macroeconomic developments—played a role in the emergence and scale of unemployment. However, it is important to understand the structural aspects. The high level of unemployment is due to the lengthening of unemployment spells. Unemployment has been turned into long-term unemployment and social exclusion as a consequence of the passivity of labor market policies, offering mainly income support to the majority of the unemployed, but no new skills for a restart in the new, more skill- and qualification-based labor market.

With the single market, Europe is taking a great leap forward in the modernization of the economy. It is not only a huge structural improvement. It also offers new conditions for growth and employment-oriented macroeconomic policies. Member States must make better use of the multiplier effect, as emphasized in the Commission's "Action for Employment in Europe—A Confidence Pact." It highlights the potential of the integration process. This potential has not yet been used to optimum effect. This is especially true in the fight for jobs.

The high degree of European economic integration and interdependence has intensified. Consequently, sustained coordinated action gives more value-added than the sum of individual, disparate, measures in each Member State. This approach will be addressed in the policy report being prepared at the request of the European Council in Florence, on the capacity of the European Union as an entity for employment policy. This involves replacing the zero-sum game of beggar-thy-neighbour policies with a plus-sum game of coordinated growth policy, creating confidence among consumers and investors. Such a growth-oriented policy would substantially improve the conditions for the development of jobs in the information society.

THE SECOND CHALLENGE: MORE EFFECTIVE MANAGEMENT OF THE JOB TRANSFORMATION PROCESS

Job destruction and job creation are an integral part of the process of structural change resulting from the introduction of ICTs. Enterprises can do much to absorb these shocks by planning employment requirements, and there are now many examples of imaginative policies negotiated between social partners. These involve not only education and training, as set out below, but also working time, wage moderation in order to maintain jobs, issues of equity in the process of change, and compensating job creation in local and regional economies.

In order to manage effectively the process of change, all economic and institutional actors—employers, workers, public authorities at all levels, education and training institutions, and business support services—have to be involved. Forward-looking enterprise behavior needs in many cases to be externally supported

and help for this process may come from the development of inter-firm cooperative agreements and partnerships as well as private-public partnerships to enhance
local business support structures. This is particularly relevant for SMEs, which
need to be supported and involved in networks to enhance their capacities to in-
novate, define business strategies and anticipate their skill needs. The Structural
Funds, and in particular Objective 4 and the ADAPT and SME Community initiatives, can also be used to facilitate these changes.

The bottom line is that if workers are to cooperate in the process of continuing change that the information society requires, new ways of handling the job
transformation process have to be found. This is a responsibility both for governments and social partners.

THE THIRD CHALLENGE: TO OVERCOME THE SKILLS GAP

The ICT revolution plays an important role in the functioning of the labor
market, through the reshaping of work, skill structures, and the organization of
work. As the new technology is an information technology, it requires not only
stronger basic skills in numeracy and literacy, but also a new form of basic skill,
the skill of interaction with the new technology, let us call it "informacy."

Technological developments and competition between enterprises are stimulating the speed of structural change. Each year, on average, more than 10 percent
of all jobs disappear and are replaced by different jobs in new processes, in new
enterprises, generally requiring new, higher, or broader skills. There is a much
slower pace on the supply side in the acquisition of new skills. Each year, one age
cohort, 2 to 3 percent of the labor force, leaves working life because of age and
other reasons, and a new one enters, with new education and training, with new
skills. The high speed of transformation of enterprises, and the limited supply of
new skills, leads to a severe mismatch, "a two-speed labor market," with the re-
dundancy of old skills and bottlenecks for new skills.

The real challenge for the transformation and upgrading of skills lies in the
readaptation of those who are already in the labor force to the new requirements
of the information society. However, many in the workforce have limited basic
skills in numeracy and literacy, skills even more necessary in the information society, and a great number have no education and training in informacy. People with
outdated or inadequate vocational training find it difficult to re-enter the workforce. Most training and retraining is organized for the young, not for people already in the workplace, nor for those who have been working for 10, 20, or 30
years and have lost their jobs. Most of them are offered only income support until
a new job turns up, or while awaiting early retirement. But new jobs, demanding
old skills, are not turning up. The new jobs require new skills. The gap will continue to grow, unless governments and employers embark upon a new, much more
radical policy to provide people with new skills and competencies, linked to the
development of new forms of work organization and the introduction of new
technologies.

This poses a major challenge to governments and to the social partners, enterprises and workers, the scale of which can be illustrated by the forecasts of a continued high speed of technological renewal and an ageing population. Ten years on, 80 percent of the technology we operate today will be obsolete, and replaced with new, more advanced technologies. By that time, 80 percent of the workforce will be working on the basis of formal education and training more than ten years old. Significant changes in the demographic profile serve only to highlight the scale of the challenge. The workforce is ageing, and the technology is getting younger.

OVERHAULING EDUCATION AND TRAINING TO MATCH THE ICT REVOLUTION

What Europe needs is a substantial overhaul of education and training that can match the ICT revolution and keep pace with the continued ICT development during the years to come. We need a new interplay between work and training, instead of the old interplay between work and non-work, a new interplay which gives the individual the opportunity to develop skills and competencies and to grow in tune with the permanent revolution of skills that accompanies ICTs.

In the long term, the underlying need is for Europe to develop a new architecture of life-long education and training, involving all parts of education and training systems, including schools, and designed and delivered in more appropriate ways, with particular regard to gender, but also by engaging more effectively older people and those with disabilities. This effort is now being initiated by the 1996 European Year of Lifelong Learning and the White Paper on teaching and learning. But the urgent need is to arrest the growing skill obsolescence of the adult working population through a proactive approach to industrial adaptation and change. Speed and foresight are of the essence, because all the evidence points to a vicious downward spiral of job destruction, long-term unemployment, and skill obsolescence which is harder to correct the longer it goes on.

Four areas are of great importance in enhancing employability.

Laying the best foundations: the foundations of our knowledge and skills are laid during the first years of education, and the processes involved will evolve as the IS develops. The quality and the organization of pre-school and school education will be profoundly affected. Teachers and trainers in particular must be targeted, and the quality of their initial training and continuing professional development secured to exploit new ICTs. The programs and infrastructure to link schools into the full networking potential of the IS, especially in the more remote regions where infrastructure is at risk, are of special importance. Member States, which have unambiguous responsibility for the organization and content of school education, should continue to mount suitable programs which take the IS into account and the EU can assist in supporting pooling of experience, particularly involving the less-favored regions. In addition, the European Council in Florence asked the Commission to elaborate quickly an action plan on "Learning in the information society," which will include the interconnection of school networks at European level, the promotion of multimedia educational content, and the stimulation of awareness and training of teachers and trainers to the use of new information society tools.

From teaching to learning: education and training must, according to the first annual report from the information society forum, be swiftly reoriented so that learning institutions are much more responsive to changes in the skill needs of business and industry. This is crucial to job creation and productivity growth. Higher education institutions have begun to lay the foundations for the learning communities of the future, and their efforts should be strengthened through the ties of partnerships with local industry and services recommended in the Ciampi report on competitiveness and piloted successfully in the Comett and Leonardo da Vinci programs. The compulsory school system has also seen important initiatives, many spurred by EU programs, but still needs considerable support and resources to build the necessary alliances with the world of work. This raises issues of investment capacity, methodology, and curricular development, with particular regard to learner needs. More broadly, since learning retention is much higher by "doing" (80 percent) rather than reading or hearing (5 to 10 percent), the potential for self-learning using ICTs is immense, and if shaped correctly, could be a key tool for closing the knowledge gap itself. The basic principles of education and training have to be based more on the notion of learning capacities, rather than formal education and training.

Using ICTs in Schools

Some Member States have launched plans for bringing their education systems in line with the dynamics of the information society. The German Ministry of Education recently announced one such initiative, Schulen ans Netz, through which 10,000 out of Germany's 52,000 schools over a three-year period will be connected to national and international networks and multimedia services. In some of the German *Länder,* it has been decided to connect all schools, a goal which in the longer term is shared by the Federal Government. The Schulen ans Netz initiative is made possible by an innovative partnership between government and private enterprises. Similar initiatives have been launched in other countries such as the United Kingdom, France, Italy, Denmark, Sweden, Portugal, and Finland.

Learning by doing: "the learning company" must emerge as a vital component of the learning society. People who work in such a company will be using their electronic access to knowledge and information to update their skills. This requires new forms of partnership between business, other organizations, and educators, to ensure that the new and changing skills required are made available. In this perspective, it is easy to understand that renewing education within working time will be more important than reduction in working time itself. The crux of this approach is continually to reinforce the employability of the workforce through training. The risk is that as firms develop more flexible employment contracts, with lower levels of job security, so as to adjust rapidly to changes in labor demand, the rationale for investment in the training of a principal labor force may be weaker rather than stronger. For example, the propensity of large Japanese firms to invest in training may be explained by the policy of life-long employment, which means that the returns on training are kept within the firm. In Europe, therefore, it should not be assumed that flexibility and job insecurity are one and the same thing. Indeed, the capacity of enterprises to adjust continually to market and technological change depends on the cooperation of a core, stable and loyal labor force. Enterprises should be encouraged to invest more in the training of their core labor force, and special incentives and arrangements should be provided to extend these instruments to the peripheral labor force.

Retraining instead of deskilling: the most critical question is how people who have lost their old jobs are reintegrated into working life. Member States have mostly failed, during the last 20 years, to offer restarts for the unemployed. Tackling this problem is one of the central tasks of the Essen reemployment strategy, further underlined by the Heads of State or Government at the European Council in Madrid in 1995. Instead of having nine million people in long-term unemployment and deskilling, the most expensive form of public spending, with the lowest return to the economy or the individual, and many more millions on their way to long-term unemployment, the Member States should have nine million involved in upgrading, maintaining, and improving their skills in literacy, numeracy and informacy. It should be a right, and an obligation, for all unemployed to maintain and develop basic skills for the information society and have them imbued with relevance to the real, dynamic, labor market. Reintegration should start long before people become long-term unemployed and discouraged. That is the fundamental difference between active and passive policies. In this framework, governments have to find ways to transform expenditures for passive labor market policies into active policies, preparing job seekers for a more knowledge-based pattern of production of goods and services. Focusing more of these financial resources on training grants and new skills, not merely cash assistance, will help in improving the dynamism of the labor market and of public finances overall. In this context, placement services also need to move towards the provision of more personalized ICT-based support for job seekers.

THE PLATFORM: NEW PRIORITIES IN THE CONVERGENCE PROGRAMS

There is now broad consensus in Europe that education and training play a fundamental role in a modern employment policy. This is why the Commission particularly welcomes the new emphasis given in the conclusions of the European Council in Florence to investment in human resources, in infrastructure, and in research and development. In this way, the ministers for labor and employment, education and training, research and development, transport and communication have a new platform for initiatives which are important for growth and employment.

Presenting education and training as a central element for a new re-employment policy can meet with opposition. The argument is that the deep-rooted employment problem in Europe cannot be solved through education and training if there are no new jobs to find after training. This argument is true, but misses the point. The purpose of education and training is not to replace macroeconomic policies for growth and new jobs. The purpose of a new education and training policy is to bring about a positive flexibility in enterprises and in the labor market that allows a more growth-oriented macroeconomic policy to be pursued. That is why the key to employment growth is the development of an integrated approach between structural and macroeconomic measures, as outlined in the broad economic guidelines and why education and training should be shaped to learner needs, with particular regard to combating inequality and disadvantage, in order to unlock the productive potential of the whole population.

QUESTIONS FOR FURTHER REFLECTION

These challenges raise a number of questions that need to be addressed, notably in the framework of the Essen employment process (the joint employment report to the Dublin summit and the 1997 multiannual programs). They concern:

- the capacity of education and training; against the perspective of the skills needs of the information society, what are the Member States' plans for the next five years?;
- the design and quality of education and training; how to reshape education and training to adjust to the existing and emerging needs of the information society during the next 5 to 10 years;
- the capacity for retraining those unemployed, which presently constitutes the weakest point in our system for education and training; how to give people who have lost their jobs a new start in working life; and,
- the degree to which equality of opportunity and access can be secured in order to ensure realization of the productive potential of the whole active population.

There are also some questions, where the social partners have a special responsibility, which need to be addressed in the framework of the social dialogue.

- What joint initiatives are the social partners prepared to take in the field of human resources to secure a continuous upgrading of skill and competence of workers to meet the needs of "the flexible firm" during the next five to ten years?
- What initiatives are the social partners prepared to take to give young people that have finished education and training a start in the real labor market, and opportunities to maintain and develop the basic skills required for the information society?

14

The White-Collar Body in History

Shoshana Zuboff

A Harvard University sociologist studied the impact of computers and automation among workers, particularly in the paper manufacturing industry. Her very important book, *In the Age of the Smart Machine,* provides one of the most thorough and influential examination of the effect of computing on the nature of work and power. In the selection below, Zuboff takes many of the issues introduced in the previous essays and places them in historical context. She also discusses in detail the evolution of the work of managers, a subject not fully explored in the selections above.

THE UNIQUE ETIOLOGY OF "WHITE-COLLAR" WORK

The use of the term *white collar* is, in a way, out of keeping with the argument I have thus far presented. As the work of the sentient body is displaced by the newer demands of intellective effort, who is to tell the "white collars" from the "blue collars?" But it is precisely the way in which these terms are dated that I want to draw upon in this chapter. The difference they refer to is one that must be understood if we are to explore the consequences of an informating technology for bureaucratic coordination—that is, the work of white-collared middle managers and their clerks.

Before closing in on the difference captured by these terms, we can note their similarity. Both are about *collars*—about how people dress. They evoke images of costume, physical bearing, and self-presentation. In each case, the term recognizes a body and the choices about how it is to be clothed. The difference between "white collar" and "blue collar" tells us much about what those bodies are likely to be up to. A blue collar indicates the probability of being soiled, while the white

From *In the Age of the Smart Machine: The Future of Work and Power* (New York: Basic Books, 1988): 97–123. Reprinted with permission.

collar communicates the proud assumption that whatever stresses the white-collar body may endure, it will not be required to face the dirt and muscular exertion of animal effort.

It is evident that information technology can eliminate the utility of the blue-collar designation, the weight and consequence of which can be grasped only in light of the long, sometimes proud and sometimes sorry, history of the laboring body. It may well be that those individuals who remain in the manufacturing sector of the work force will be able to trade in their blue collars for ones that are gleaming white. However, this historical trajectory of the blue-collar body does little to inform our understanding of what has been white-collar work and what it is likely to become.

The evolution of white-collar work has followed a historical path that is in many ways the precise opposite of that taken by blue-collar work. Manufacturing has its roots in the work of skilled craft. In most cases, that work was successively gutted of the elements that made it skillful—leaving behind jobs that were simplified and routinized. An examination of work at the various levels of the management hierarchy reveals a different process. Elements of managerial work most easily subjected to rationalization were "carved out" of the manager's activities. The foundational example of this process is the rationalization of executive work, which was accomplished by ejecting those elements that could be explicated and systematized, preserving intact the skills that comprise executive craft. It was the carving out of such elements that created the array of functions we now associate with middle management. A similar process accounts for the origins of clerical work. In each case, the most easily rationalized features of the activities at one level were carved out, pushed downward, and used to create wholly new lower-level jobs. In this process, higher-level positions were not eliminated; on the contrary, they came to be seen more than ever as the depository of the organization's skills.

The role of the body in white-collar work is a further counterpoint to the experience of workers in manufacturing. Blue-collar workers used their bodies in the service of *acting-on,* to transform materials and utilize equipment. White-collar employees used their bodies, too, but in the service of *acting-with,* for interpersonal communication and coordination. It was not until the intensive introduction of office machinery, and with it scientific management, that this distinct orientation was challenged. During this period, an effort was made to invent a new kind of clerical work—work that more closely resembled the laboring body continually *acting-on* the inanimate objects, paper and equipment, that were coming to define modern office work. Automation in the factory had diverse effects, frequently limiting human effort and physical suffering, though sometimes exacerbating it. But the discontinuity in the nature of clerical work introduced with office machinery, together with the application of Tayloristic forms of work organization, did much to increase the physical suffering of the clerk. While it remained possible to keep a white collar clean, the clerk's position was severed from its earlier responsibilities of social coordination and was converted instead to an emphasis on regularity of physical effort and mental concentration. In order to trace the unique etiology of white-collar work and the more recent discontinuities in the nature of clerical activity, it is necessary to start not only at the beginning but also at the top. It is in the nature of executive action that we can see the skillful domain from which middle-management functions were extracted. Similarly, the diversity and continued complexity of middle management provides the point of origin for clerical work as it once was and as it has become.

EXECUTIVE MANAGEMENT AS A CRAFT

The first generations of industrial capitalists were owner-employers whose comprehensive, action-oriented, and undocumented know-how absorbed a wide range of management functions. As Sidney Pollard said of the early British entrepreneurs who founded many of the most important industrial works, "The typical entrepreneur was his own manager." Or as Reinhard Bendix put it, "At one time individual entrepreneurs performed a large variety of routine administrative tasks in addition to their 'distinct economic function of undertaking new things.'" These owner-managers were engaged in activities ranging from invention to finance to direct supervision of their factories. Their know-how was wrung from trial-and-error experience during a time when there were few resources for practical training. In fact, the term *management* had little meaning until well into the nineteenth century. Alfred Chandler reports that the owner-managers of that period were so immersed in the daily operation of their enterprises that they had little time or inclination left for objective evaluation and long-range planning: "The owner-managers prided themselves on their knowledge of a business they had done so much to build. They continued to be absorbed in the details of day-to-day operation. They personally reviewed the departmental reports and the statistical data. They had little or no staff to collect information and to provide expert advice. . . . Long-term planning was also highly personal . . . their moves were personal responses to new needs and opportunities."

The dependence on oral communication was even more pronounced in a world where written documentation and correspondence were stored in boxes, pigeonholes, and difficult-to-read press books (bound volumes of tissue paper sheets onto which copies of letters had been impressed). Most business enterprises were small enough that orders, instructions, and reports could be given orally. The treasurer of one enterprise in 1887 defended the lack of written documentation in his organization: "We do not think printed rules amount to anything unless there is somebody around constantly to enforce them and if such a person is around printed forms can be dispensed with."

The resistance to written communication is illustrated in a popular book published in 1896 by Seymour Eaton and called *How to Do Business as Business Is Done in Great Commercial Centers*. The volume is crammed with "hints and helps for Young Business Men," from banking and margin trading, to character, will, and cheerfulness, to grammar, arithmetic, or how to fold a letter, and his admonitions provide a clue to typical patterns of behavior. Eaton tries to cajole his

readers to rely more upon written communication. "A letter is but a talk on paper," he says. "Things worth talking about are worth writing about." The resistance to written communication must have been considerable if eager young businessmen required such encouragement to put pen to paper. Most calculations associated with commercial accounting were done mentally and communicated orally. Many successful merchants and entrepreneurs were well known for the speed of their mental calculations, and Eaton's how-to book provides a chapter on tricks and shortcuts to aid in rapid mental arithmetic. Owner-managers frequently surrounded themselves with sons, nephews, and cousins—a move that facilitated oral communication through shared meaning and context and eased the pressure for written documentation.

Detailed empirical studies of modern executives' work, several of which have been published over the last thirty years, are greeted with the curiosity and fascination usually reserved for anthropological accounts of obscure primitive societies. It is as if these researchers had brought back accounts from an organizational region that is concealed from observation and protected from rational analysis. Perhaps this sense of mystery surrounds top management activities because they derive from a set of skills that are embedded in individual action, in much the same way as those of the craftsperson. In both cases, skilled performance is characterized by sentient participation, contextuality, action-dependence, and personalism.

What is different is that the craftsperson used action-centered skills in the service of *acting-on* materials and equipment, while the top manager's action-centered skills are applied in the service of *acting-with*. Like the seventeenth-century courtier, the top manager uses his or her bodily presence as an instrument of interpersonal power, influence, learning, and communication. The know-how that is developed in the course of managerial experience in *acting-with* remains largely implicit: managers themselves have difficulty describing what they do. Only the cleverest research can translate such embedded practice into explicated material suitable for analysis and discussion.

In 1938, Chester Barnard, the executive turned scholar, wrote a lengthy treatise, *The Functions of the Executive,* that eloquently discussed the implicit, experience-based, action-centered quality of executive skills. In a summary description of the executive process, he wrote: "The process is the sensing of the organization as a whole and the total situation relevant to it. It transcends the capacity of merely intellectual methods, and the techniques of discriminating the factors of the situation. The terms pertinent to it are 'feeling,' 'judgment,' 'sense,' 'proportion,' 'balance,' and 'appropriateness.' It is a matter of art rather than science, and is aesthetic rather than logical. For this reason it is recognized rather than described and is known by its effects rather than by analysis."

Barnard believed that communication was the dominant function of management and, as he put it, "the immediate origin of executive organization." When he discussed an organization's communication system, however, he did not refer to technological devices, reporting procedures, or other methods of information gathering and dissemination. For him, there were only two components of organized communication—the *means* and the *system*. In his view, people were the means of communication, and the positions they held constituted its system: "The center of communication is the organization service of a person at a place." His reasoning, to put it in the language of this discussion, was that an executive's place gave him or her exposure to a particular action context. Each executive, thus, was responsible for grasping that context and communicating it to the others. Executive communication depended on each member of this small group giving voice to a facet of the organization and so contributing to a shared sense of the whole. Executive communication was expected to be largely oral, face-to-face, and informal. For this reason, Barnard also emphasized the executive's bodily presence in its physical and characterological aspects, as an instrument of *acting-with*:

> *The general method of maintaining an informal executive organization is to operate and to select and promote executives so that a general condition of compatibility of personnel is maintained. Perhaps often and certainly occasionally, men cannot be promoted or selected, or even must be relieved, because they cannot function, because they "do not fit," where there is no question of formal competence. This question of "fitness" involves such matters as education, experience, age, sex, personal distinctions, prestige, race, nationality, faith, politics, and sectional antecedents; and such very specific personal traits as manners, speech, personal appearance, and so on. It goes by few if any rules, except those based at least nominally on other, formal, considerations. It represents in its best sense the political aspects of personal relationships in formal organization.*

The preeminence of action-centered skill has been stressed in several recent studies of executive managers. John Kotter studied the daily behavior of fifteen general managers and found that they spent most of their time developing networks of relationships that provided the insights they needed to develop their strategic agendas. Kotter stresses the implicit quality of the general managers' knowledge, noting that their agendas tended to be informal, nonquantitative, mental road maps highly related to "people" issues, rather than systematic, formal planning documents.

Daniel Isenberg's research on "how senior managers think" has penetrated another layer of this, usually inarticulate, domain of executive management. Isenberg found that top managers think in ways that are highly "intuitive" and integrated with action. He concluded that the intuitive nature of executive behavior results from the inseparability of their thinking from their actions: "Since managers, often 'know' what is right before they can analyze and explain it, they frequently act first and think later. Thinking is inextricably tied to action. . . . Managers develop thought about their companies and organizations not by analyzing a problematic situation and then acting, but by thinking and acting in close concert." One manager described his own immersion in the action cycle: "It's as if your arms, your feet, and your body just move instinctively. You have a preoccupation with working capital, a preoccupation with capital expenditure, a preoccupation with people . . . and all this goes so fast that you don't even know whether it's completely rational, or it's part rational, part intuitive."

Rosabeth Kanter's descriptive study of corporate life also underscored the salience of bodily presence in shared action contexts as the core of the manager's world. Visible participation in the meanings and values of one's immediate group helps to build a joint experience base. In this way, managers can assume that they share a common language and understanding, which provides many shortcuts for communication in a pressured, rapid-fire world. Most of the managers she studied spent about half of their time in face-to-face communication. Kanter concluded that the manager's ability to "win acceptance" and to communicate was often more important than any substantive knowledge of the business. The feelings of comfort, efficiency, and trust that come with such shared meaning are triggered in a variety of ways by the manager's comportment. The nuances of nonverbal behavior and the signals embedded in physical appearance are an important aspect of such group participation. Because the tasks at the highest levels of the corporation are the most ambiguous, senior executives come to rely most heavily on the communicative ease that results from this shared intuitive world.

Henry Mintzberg authored a pathfinding empirical study of top managers' work in 1973. He identified three role domains that account for most managerial activity: the interpersonal, the informational, and the decision-making roles. While there are intellective demands associated with each set of roles, the overwhelming emphasis in Mintzberg's data is on the action-centered skills that are at the core of each domain.

The interpersonal role, for example, relies upon the manager's bodily presence as an instrument of *acting-with*. Mintzberg stresses that actual leadership activity, as distinguished from the formal power derived from organizational status, is inseparable from the top manager's daily flow of interaction and communication. The most subtle elements of nonverbal behavior are treated as a window that exposes the manager's attitudes, values, and expectations. "In virtually everything he does, the manager's actions are screened by subordinates searching for leadership clues. In answering a request for authorization, he may encourage or inhibit a subordinate, and even in his form of greeting, messages (perhaps nonexistent ones) may be read by anxious subordinates." Network building is based upon the manager's sociability in direct oral communication as he or she nurtures the goodwill of others.

Action-centered skills are no less critical in the informational and decision-making roles. While top managers receive, through formal channels, a great deal of information that he or she must analyze and consider, the real work of monitoring the organization depends upon current information culled from personal contact, both face-to-face interactions and telephone conversations. Top managers rely on gossip, hearsay, and speculation gathered from these informal oral exchanges. Moreover, top managers were found to prefer what Mintzberg calls "trigger information"—concrete stimuli including specific events, conversations, and problems. The personal, idiosyncratic, and oral nature of top managers' most important information presents a problem when it comes to dissemination. The kind of information that derives from personal contact can be communicated only through personal contact, thus limiting most top managers' efficiency as disseminators of important organizational data. Success in the informational role depends upon the quality of the top manager's social, nonverbal, and oral conduct.

In the decision-making role, Mintzberg found that top managers rely on "tangible information in the form of stimuli—specific events and ad hoc data—rather than the gradual trends displayed in routine reports." The organizational disturbances that the top manager is required to handle typically arise in an unpredictable, ad hoc manner and are reacted to quickly with methods that frequently involve immediate oral exchange, discussion, persuasion, and negotiation. Mintzberg stresses that a top manager's plans tend to be flexible and largely implicit, in order to allow room for a dynamic response to the immediate environment: "My own impression is that the manager's plans are not explicit, documented in detail in the organization's files for all to see. Rather, crude plans seem to exist in the manager's mind in the form of a set of improvement projects that he would one day like to initiate."

Mintzberg summarizes the characteristics of managerial activity that run through each role domain. There is, he notes, a strong preference for live action: "The job breeds adaptive information-manipulators who prefer the live concrete situation. The manager works in an environment of stimulus-response, and he develops in his work a clear preference for live action." Another general trait is the attraction to oral, as opposed to written, communication. Mintzberg concurs with several other studies of managerial behavior in his finding that most of the top manager's time is spent in face-to-face communication, the telephone being the second preferred mode of interaction: "Documented communication requires the use of a formal subset of language, and involves long feedback delays. All verbal media can transmit, in addition to the messages contained in the words used, messages sent by voice inflection and by delays in reaction. In addition, face-to-face media carry information transmitted by facial expression and by gesture. . . . The manager's productive output can be measured primarily in terms of verbally transmitted information."

Top management activity is also relationship-intensive. Direct contact with subordinates and with actors external to the organization each require one-third to one-half of the top manager's time. Finally, Mintzberg, like others who have studied the management function, concludes that the job is physically taxing. Top managers' days and nights are filled to the breaking point with a myriad of activities, contacts, events, discussions, and meetings, which tend to be brief, rapid, and fragmented. Many students of managerial activity have proposed ways in which top managers could limit the demands on their time from the constant flow of interruptions. Mintzberg, however, takes another tack, pointing out that most top managers prefer to have their time organized this way, precisely because it keeps them in touch with the live action context of the organization. "They frequently interrupted their desk work to place telephone calls or to request that subordinates come by. One chief executive located his desk so that he could look down a long hallway. The door was usually open, and his subordinates were continually coming into his office." Though the top manager's work certainly has its intellective challenges, action-centered skill defines the core of each role domain. The same characteristics of action-centered skill as those encountered in craft work can be identified here:

1. *Sentience.* Top managers rely on seeing and hearing the people who constitute their relationship network. They seek ways to develop a "feel" for situations and actors.
2. *Action-dependence.* Top managers' skills are developed and conveyed in action. Their most critical activities demand bodily presence. Their experience tends to be organized into brief but intense action episodes. Learning and influence occurs primarily through action.
3. *Context-dependence.* Nonverbal communication is an important communication medium and is inherently context-dependent. Top managers require trigger information—concrete stimuli, rooted in an action context, which convey problems and issues. Personal knowledge is most efficiently communicated in face-to-face settings, where individuals share contextual meanings.
4. *Personalism.* Most of what the manager knows remains implicit and, thus, personal. The top manager's responses are of necessity filtered through his or her personality and style. Personal charisma and sociability are likely to be an important influence on the quality of the top manager's relationship network.

The skills of the top manager are not explicitly taught or explicitly learned; rather, they are assimilated through years of experience in the action context of the organization. As Mintzberg summarizes, "Today managing is an art, not a science. Most of the methods managers use are not properly understood; hence they are not taught or analyzed in any formal sense." Minztberg laments the fact that management science has shed relatively little analytical light on top management activities. As a result, professional education does a better job of training specialists and middle managers whose work involves a greater degree of explicit knowledge than it does in teaching these skills associated with the executive process. As Barnard had concluded, "We know very little about how to do it." The key obstacle facing the management scientist who would seek to analyze and then rationalize top management work lies in the implicit, embodied nature of executive know-how: "The manager is the nerve center of his organization, with unique access to a wide variety of internal and external contacts that provide privileged information. But most of this information is not documented, and much of it is unsubstantiated and nonquantitative. As a result, the manager lacks a systematic method for passing it on to the management scientist, and most of it never reaches him. . . . Today the manager is the real data bank. . . . Unfortunately he is a walking and a talking data bank, but not a writing one. When he is busy, information ceases to flow. When he departs, so does the data bank." Lodged in the body and dependent upon presence and active display, the implicit heart of the executive's special genius appears to evade rationalization.

HOW EXECUTIVE WORK WAS RATIONALIZED

This evasion has left many observers, including Mintzberg, quite frustrated. Reflecting on his findings concerning the implicit quality of top management know-how, Mintzberg hypothesized that management science would eventually arrive at the door of these managers, ready to apply the same principles of "scientific research" that Taylor's disciples had applied to the shop floor. It was just a matter of time before rational analysis would decompose managerial work and "reprogram" that work more efficiently. In this Mintzberg concurs with other scholars who have used the deskilling of craft work as the paradigmatic illustration of the rationalization of work. My own interpretation of the relationship between top management work and the process of rationalization is a different one. Top management work has now undergone almost a century of rationalization—and in a manner that is the precise opposite of the craft-work experience. In the case of executive activity, those elements most accessible to explication, and therefore rationalization, were carved out of the executive's immediate domain of concern. These more analytical or routine activities were projected into the functions of middle management, just as those functions were also absorbing new responsibilities for planning and coordination that had resulted from systematic analysis of the production process. Thus, the activities that made the executive most special, based on action-centered skill, were left intact, while the more explicit and even routine aspects of executive responsibilities were pushed downward and materialized in a variety of middle-management functions. This contrasts with the case of craft workers, in which the action-centered skills that had made them so special were researched, systematized, and expropriated upward. To put it bluntly, workers lost what was best in their jobs, the body as skill in the service of *acting-on,* while executives lost what was worst in their jobs, retaining full enjoyment of the skilled body as an instrument of *acting-with.*

To say that executive work can be rationalized is, thus, misleading. It may be that the future holds an increasingly diminished core of top management activity, but the work of the executive has been, by definition, work that is not subject to rationalization. Once managerial activity became subject to that procedure, it was no longer considered executive work. In fact, the more executive activity was projected downward and materialized in more rationalized processes, the more the executive was freed to indulge in the essence of his or her craft—the artful expression of knowledge in action. Executive power has been, among other things, a means by which to preserve the ultimate ineffability of this inner core of implicit knowledge—a power that most skilled workers did not enjoy. This process of carving out and rationalizing aspects of executive activity underlies the structural articulation of the modern organization. For example, in his discussion of the bureaucratization of the economic enterprise, Reinhard Bendix observes that "seen historically, bureaucratization may be interpreted as the increasing subdivision of the functions which the owner-managers of the early enterprises had performed personally in the course of their daily routine. These functions may be divided into labor management, technical staff work, administrative management and mercantile functions of purchasing, sales, and finance. As the work involved became more extensive and complex . . . it came to be delegated to subordinates."

The theme is sounded again in Chandler's discussion of the emergence of middle management in the American corporate enterprise. He notes that while owner-managers were reluctant to become more systematic about their own activities, they eventually hired salaried executives who "pioneered" the development of middle-management functions. These new managers provided the infrastructure of their firms as they literally invented the methods and systems of administrative coordination and, in the process, gave definition to a wide range of functions such as finance, collection, service, marketing, distribution, purchasing, inventory control, transportation, production, accounting, pricing, sales, training, and labor management. Peter Drucker has railed against owner-managers like Henry Ford and Werner von Siemens precisely because they refused to recognize the necessity of middle-management functions, insisting instead on surrounding themselves with "helpers" who were dependent upon the boss's implicit knowledge, directives, and whims.

During the 1920s and 1930s, there were earnest interpreters of business practice who, flushed with the success and rational appeal of scientific management, argued strenuously that executive activity should be subjected to the analytic rigors of Taylor's principles. One of these was Mary Parker Follett. In 1925 she told a conference of personnel administrators in New York City that "the next step business management should take is to organize the body of knowledge on which it should rest . . . The recording of executive experience . . . should have . . . our immediate attention . . . We need executive conferences with carefully worked out methods for comparing experience which has been scientifically recorded, analyzed, and organized. . . . From such experimenting and from the comparison of experience, I think certain standards would emerge."

Mary Parker Follett deplored the idea that executive leadership involved an "intangible capacity" or that executives relied on "hunches" in making decisions. She praised the still-youthful trend toward functional management based upon expert knowledge. Ten years later a prominent management consultant, Harry Hopf, presented a paper to the Sixth International Congress for Scientific Management, in which he proposed that the next great step in developing a science of management was the practice of "optimology"—the science of the optimum. In certain respects his notions foreshadowed the field of operations research. He complained that executives tend to be circumscribed in their thinking because they are limited to the concrete and contextual. "They could readily interpret their relations with others in terms of working understandings which had grown up among them and their immediate associates; but to project their minds beyond was difficult." He criticized executives who were guided primarily by "a strong speculative instinct" and insisted that successful management depended upon good planning: "Entering into the major aspects of planning and intimately associated with its manifestations, are the processes of analysis, simplification, and standardization. The ultimate realization of optimal conditions in a business enterprise is predicated upon adequate employment of these processes."

If we accept the portraits of executive activity that emerge from the work of Barnard, Kotter, Isenberg, Kanter, and Mintzberg, then we are led to the conclusion that these earlier criticisms of the implicit action-oriented quality of top management work did not succeed in eliminating its artful core. Rather, these critiques were part of a larger movement toward the development of a new stratum of managerial functions that systematized important aspects of executive activity and, in so doing, extended its reach.

MIDDLE MANAGEMENT AND THE DEMANDS OF *ACTING-WITH*

The case should not be drawn too starkly. The executive role involves its share of intellective endeavor that demands explicit, data-based, conceptual reasoning. Conversely, the middle-management role, with regard to both line and staff positions, retains much of the political and interpersonal activity associated with the requirements of general management. The world of the middle manager is unrelenting in its demand for skill in *acting-with*. Success and mobility depend upon working through one's subordinates and working well with one's peers. Like their superiors, middle managers must communicate, influence, motivate, persuade, and confront. The necessity for these fundamental encounters with others has been a critical part of all but the most specialized and technical managerial roles.

Moreover, middle management is the primary training ground for future executives. Since executive skill is experience-based, it follows that those middle managers who excel in *acting-with* are likely to be considered as executive material and their years in the ranks of middle management provide the opportunity to develop those skills. Throughout the century young managers have been advised to perfect their bodies as instruments in the subtleties of interpersonal influence. As early as 1902, a "how-to" book written for young aspirants to business success warned, "Be manly, and look it. Appear the gentleman, and be the gentleman. What's the good of unknown good? Negotiable intrinsic value must have the appearance of intrinsic worth."

Objective criteria for judging the future potential of managers were virtually nonexistent. One study of the emergence of the white-collar occupational category in the Krupp Steel Casting Works before 1900 found that there was a great deal of upward mobility from the lower ranks of white-collar employment to the highest management level. However, advancement tended to occur within areas of functional exposure, highlighting experience as a qualification for managerial work, which was still relatively uncodified. Advancement also depended less upon formal criteria than upon such factors as "the impressions of an official, private connections, or kinship." Another recent study, exploring the emergence of business schools at the turn of the century and how they attempted to meet the needs of the emerging class of middle managers, explained that "while the earlier version of the success theme had set forth ownership of large enterprises as the ultimate goal, now the focus was on rising into the managerial elite. Schooling took on new value, and the more one could obtain the better. Less emphasis was put on improving 'character' and more on improving on 'personality'; to get ahead, one had to get along with others, conquer self-created fear, and develop personal efficiency."

The classic text among the success literature of the period was written by Dale Carnegie. Originally published in 1926 as *Public Speaking and Influencing Men in Business,* the now familiar title, *How to Win Friends and Influence People,* appeared on a new edition brought out ten years later. The book was used as the official textbook for training aspiring management recruits in a variety of major organizations, such as the New York Telephone Company and the American Institute of Banking. Carnegie told his readers that their success or failure depended upon the impressions they made in the four kinds of contacts that people have: "We are evaluated and classified by four things: by what we do, by how we look, by what we say, and how we say it."

By 1938 Chester Barnard was telling his readers that "learning the organization ropes" was a matter of learning the "who's who, what's what, why's why, of its informal society." Nor has the importance of this knowledge diminished in the fifty years since Barnard's observation. In Kanter's study of corporate men and women, she observed that it is generally the individual with the most intense aspiration for mobility who devotes the greatest share of his or her energy for learning to master organizational politics. In the context of the interpersonal demands of the modern organization, this is a rational investment. Like the court societies of preindustrial Europe, bureaucratic leaders "often rely on outward manifestations to determine who is the 'right sort of person.'" It is worth reviewing Kanter's description of this situation:

> There were other examples of the difficulty in pinning down what made a good manager. . . . The traits were so vague as to be almost meaningless, and they included a large number of elements subject to social interpretation: "empathy; integrity; acceptance of accountability; ambition; makes decisions; intelligent; takes appropriate risks; smart; uses the organization through trust and delegation; a good communicator; a good track record." A group of junior managers also made a list. . . . If anything the young managers' list increased the judgmental, interpretive social components: "good communicator; well organized; good interpersonal skills; a successful performer; high peer acceptance; a risk taker; highly visible to other managers; able to recognize opportunities; results oriented; and possessing the requisite amount of prior experience in the company and in the function."

The emphasis in middle management on action-centered skill in the arena of *acting-with* has been both a rehearsal for a more comprehensive executive role and a measure of the integration between middle-management and executive functions. Though middle management developed as an exteriorization of those aspects of most executive activity most accessible to rationalization, it was also necessary for a certain amount of the implicit action-centered skill characteristic of the executive process to be subsumed by successively lower ranks of management. Complex organizations are composed of complicated webs of relationships, and management requires motivation and coordination within this system of interdependencies. Management is fundamentally something that occurs between human beings and, as such, has employed all of the most artful methods that humans have devised for dealing with one another in order to get something done. In this way, every manager of subordinates must, to some extent, enact the executive role. Even managers in more specialized staff positions must know how to communicate and influence if their point of view is to be heard or their recommendations are to be implemented.

Again, the issue is a matter of emphasis. The research on executive activity cited earlier suggests that the core of that function involves the action-centered skills associated with *acting-with*. High-ranking middle-management functions are likely to involve considerably more extensive intellective work as well as action-centered skill. At successively lower management levels, the intellective component tends to become more routinized—standard reports, collection of daily operating data, and so forth—but some degree of action-centered skill remains crucial. Indeed, many studies have found that the position of foreman or first line supervisor is one of the most interpersonally demanding jobs in an organization. Thus, while the bulk of rigorous intellective activity has tended to be concentrated in the middle ranks of the management organization, in varying degrees in line and staff positions, the requirements for action-centered skills related to the interpersonal world of the organization have also filtered down from the executive role.

The precipitation or diffusion of the executive process has tended to be a source of social cohesion among the various levels of management. It has provided a basis upon which these various groups could generate a rationale for a coincidence of interests between them, even where there is a considerable disparity in wages between the upper and lower levels of the managerial hierarchy. At every level, managers are united in their assumption of accountability for the organization's performance. Because organizations are, above all, configurations of persons, this accountability has inevitably required some immersion in the methods and manners of interpersonal presence and action.

THE ORIGINS OF CLERICAL WORK

The process by which activities subject to rationalization are projected downward and materialized in new functions, and the parallel, though more restricted, precipitation of interpersonal aspects of the executive process also account for the origin of clerical employment. The rationalization of office work during the course of this century has been viewed as another version of the deskilling process that transformed industrial work. Instead, the routinization of clerical work can be viewed as the result of a continual extrusion of middle-management activities as they became subject to further rationalization through the introduction of new technology and new techniques. These extrusions were the occasion for the creation of new organizational functions and strata, in much the same way that middle management first emerged as a rationalization of activities that were once integrated in the executive process.

This interpretation helps to explain why the activities of today's high-status clerical workers tend to have a great deal in common with those of an earlier generation. In both cases, these positions are close enough to the management domain to have absorbed some measure of the executive process as it trickled down the corporate hierarchy. It also helps explain why the rationalization of office work has resulted less in the displacement of old functions than in the creation of a vast number of new, highly differentiated low-status clerical positions.

David Lockwood used nineteenth-century pamphlets and periodicals to construct a description of the early British office. According to his study, *The Black-Coated Worker*, the first clerks were men, and their positions often served as entry points into management careers. The distinction between clerical and managerial functions was not rigidly drawn, and bookkeepers frequently were required to assume responsibilities that would now be considered managerial. In 1871 an observer described clerical work as requiring "knowledge of languages, skills in accounts, familiarity with even minute details of business, energy, promptitude, tact, delicacy of perception." Pollard has noted that in those industrial enterprises where craft know-how was not considered crucial to the tasks of management, the position of accounting clerk was an important route for promotion into management. "The forte of such men would be their business and financial acumen and their relationship of trust to the employer, leaving technical know-how to be acquired later, as the less important consideration."

In Toni Pierenkemper's study of the internal differentiation of employment at the Krupp Steel Casting Works during the late nineteenth century, he found four status groupings of white-collar employees marked by the system of payment (monthly versus biweekly) and by the budget from which their salaries were drawn (top management budget versus shop management budget). The status gradations roughly corresponded to the degree of executive process that their positions had absorbed. Pierenkemper compares his own data to that of several other studies of white-collar employment at that time and concludes that "the evidence suggests that industrial white collar employees in the late nineteenth century were a distinct but heterogeneous group. They performed a broad range of tasks—at one extreme close to those of management, at the other difficult to distinguish from those of the blue-collar work force."

Another study documented the experiences of female clerks in the federal government during the later part of the nineteenth century. The testimony of one woman who worked as a clerk examining the accounts of Indian agents, reveals the range of her accountability: "For years I worked faithfully . . . the work being brain work of a character that requires a knowledge not only of the rulings of this Department, but also those of the Treasury, Second Auditor, Second Comptroller, and Revised Statutes; demanding the closest and most critical attention, together with a great deal of legal and business knowledge." The experiences of another clerk, Jane Seavey, have survived in her correspondence. As a clerk in the Internal

Revenue Bureau, she was put in charge of the recording room, where she was credited with introducing "a new system of organizing work in her section, a method of filing adopted throughout the Treasury Department and used as a model for other agencies as well."

As the size of enterprises grew, it became increasingly difficult to operate by word of mouth. Written communication was required in order to ensure clarity in both lateral and subordinate relationships. There was a growing need for internal documentation, record keeping, and external correspondence. People and systems were needed to produce, maintain, and access the burgeoning load of written information. More than any other single factor, the introduction of office machinery made it possible to relieve the pressure on the traditional office organization by carving out those functions subject to routinization from the more integrated activities of the early clerk. The most significant mechanical intervention was the typewriter, which was first introduced in the American market in the mid-1870s and was selling at rate of 60,000 per year by 1893. In 1919 the editors of the journal *Modern Business* published a list of thirty machines then commonly found in the office, ranging from the ubiquitous typewriter to mechanical messengers, envelope feeders, and statistical machines that punched and read cards. The introduction of typewriters, the bookkeeping machine, and other forms of office equipment made it possible to extract from the clerk's job the laborious manual tasks associated with copying, preparing and checking data, printing, preparing mail and internal correspondence, billing, timekeeping, and routine arithmetical calculations. These machines could be operated by individuals with far less training than the years of experience, general education, and business knowledge that had characterized the clerk. A vast number of women were employed to fill the new positions.

Several studies have documented the spread of office machinery and its impact on the routinization, fragmentation, and feminization of clerical work. I will not repeat the entirety of those findings here, but I will point to a few highlights. For example, the years from 1880 to 1890, when the typewriter was introduce to most American offices, saw the greatest increase of female clerical workers of any decade—a more than tenfold increase from 7,000 to 76,000. During the same year, the enrollment of women in commercial schools jumped from 2,770 to 23,040, an increase of 732 percent, compared with an increase of only 140 percent for male students during that decade. In 1890, 64 percent of all stenographers and typists were women; by 1920, the figure had risen to 92 percent.

As portions of the clerical function were carved out and routinized with a combination of lower-paid labor and mechanical support, the clerks who had functioned with quasi-managerial responsibilities typically were not displaced. Just as executives were freed to become more artful when middle managers absorbed a portion of their activities, so these traditional clerks were pushed further toward the managerial arena, often assimilating even more of the executive process as they now supervised the new, lower-status clerical workers. During the forty years from 1890 to 1930, typists and stenographers had grown to constitute 22 percent of the clerical labor force, but there was also an impressive growth in the numbers of bookkeepers, cashiers, and accountants, all high-status (and male) clerical positions. What changed was the proportion of these positions as a percentage of the total clerical population—it declined. These employees typically inherited supervisory responsibility over entire offices of clerks who performed some fragment of the earlier, more comprehensive clerical task, such as bookkeeping. Routinization created a vast new array of clerical employment opportunities, absorbing functions that had once been integrated at a higher status level but, largely because of the achievements of technology, had become accessible to rationalization. The zest for rationalization was also expressed in the development of new office systems and methods. Joanne Yates, in her historical account of the vertical filing system, found that by 1918, a twenty-seven-page bibliography of materials on office methods, primarily concerning filing systems, had appeared. In the list of general works on filing, the author listed forty-four sources, and an additional twenty-eight were listed as relevant to the specific task of filing correspondence. The French sociologist Michel Crozier summed up this historical transformation in the following way:

> This transformation has profound consequences, since the arrival of women, coinciding as it did with very great expansion, was superimposed on a process of mechanization and automation, whose effects upon males were, therefore, diminished. The latter were pushed toward more skilled occupations and toward executive positions, so that the general proletarianization of the white-collar group—which seems quite clear if one analyzes its composition, its remunerations, and its tasks in the abstract—was not experienced as such by those directly involved. To the old white-collar group which had pretty much retained its social status—when it had not improved it by technical and hierarchical promotions—was added a new group consisting in part of females with a distinctly inferior social status. To be sure, many white-collar employees were personally victims of these transformations, but many among them were, on the other hand, beneficiaries.

In 1925, the same year that Mary Parker Follett made her speech exhorting managers to become more scientific, William Henry Leffingwell published his well-known text, *Office Management: Principles and Practice,* which he dedicated to the Taylor Society in appreciation of its "inspirational and educational influence." Leffingwell presented a copy of his book to Carl Barth, one of Taylor's best-known disciples. That copy bore the following inscription: "It is with deep appreciation of the honor of knowing one of management's greatest minds that I sit at your feet and sign my name." Leffingwell was obsessed with the notion of bringing rational discipline to the office in much the same way that Taylor and his men were attempting to transform the shop floor. Though his was not the only treatise on the subject, it quickly became one of the most influential. In an earlier work, published in 1917, Leffingwell had discussed "mechanical applications of the principles of scientific management to the office." His new text was written to address the need for "original thought" concerning the fundamental principles of his discipline and their relationship to office management. Leffingwell summed up the message of his book with one sentence: "In a word, the aim of this new conception of office management is simplification."

Leffingwell recognized that clerical work had its origins in and derived its purposes from the managerial function. In an early chapter of his text, he set out to define "the elusive character of office work." He concluded that the purpose of clerical activity was "the facilitation of any business function." It was to this facilitative endeavor, which aptly characterized the comprehensive activities of the traditional clerk, that he applied his principle of simplification. Leffingwell wrote in detail about his work in the Curtis Publishing Company, which included a large mail-order operation. He had reorganized the flow of work so that five hundred pieces of mail could be handled each hour by one clerk, as compared to an earlier standard of one hundred. He used the same methods, with comparable results, in over five hundred other clerical operations. There was no aspect of the office that was too trivial for Leffingwell's attention. He not only addressed major functions like correspondence, record keeping, and communication but also applied his logic to the subjects of light, heat, ventilation, desks, chairs, tables, filing cabinets, forms, office supplies, mail, and office machinery of every variety. He considered work flow, measurement, standards, planning, and control for every aspect of the clerical day, hour, and minute.

The overwhelming purpose of Leffingwell's approach to simplification was to fill the clerical workday with activities that were linked to a concrete task and to eliminate time spent on coordination and communication. This concern runs through almost every chapter of his 850-page text; it is revealed most prominently in his minutely detailed discussions of the physical arrangement of the office and in his views on the organization, flow, planning, measurement, and control of office work.

Leffingwell advocated what he called "the straight-line flow of work" as the chief method by which to eliminate any requirement for communication or coordination. The ideal condition, he said, was that desks should be so arranged that work could be passed from one to the other "without the necessity of the clerk even rising from his seat . . . for where the work does not flow in this manner there is a constant tendency for clerks to do their own messenger work. . . . It should not be overlooked that while a clerk is not at his desk he may be working, but he is not doing clerical work effectively."

Leffingwell recognized that the growth in the size of the office was a major force that would increase the coordinative demands on the office worker, and he saw his own principles of organization, together with the appropriate use of mechanical devices, as the chief bulwark against the threat of inefficiency and chaos: "A larger volume of business requires a large force of clerks to handle it; . . . this . . . makes the necessary communication between them more difficult, and there will be much walking back and forth between them for this purpose, unless some means is adopted to prevent it and save the time thereby expended. . . . Routine . . . tends to reduce communication." Layout, standardization of methods, a well-organized messenger service, desk correspondence distributors, reliance on written instructions, delivery bags, pneumatic tubes, elevators, automatic conveyors, belt conveyors, cables, telautographs, telephones, phonographs, buzzers, bells, and horns—these were just some of the means Leffingwell advocated in order to insulate the clerk from extensive communicative demands.

These efforts illustrate how scientific management in the office tried to provoke a discontinuity between the new clerical activity and the traditional clerical work that had preceded it. Scientific management sought to reorient the office on a new axis, so that clerical jobs would no longer be able to absorb even vestigial elements of the executive process, with its requirements for action-centered skills in the service of interpersonal coordination. Before this reorganization, the functions of supervisors and their clerks had been ambiguously defined. Procedures were determined loosely enough that coordinative responsibility had to be shared, if only informally. The application of scientific management to the office sought to redefine clerical work and to set clear boundaries on the downward diffusion of coordinative responsibility. The new concept of clerical work tried to eliminate the remaining elements of action-centered skill related to *acting-with* (that is, interpersonal coordination and communication) in favor of tasks that were wholly devoted to *acting-on* (that is, direct action on materials and equipment).

The requirements of *acting-on* associated with these new clerical jobs demanded more from the body as a source of effort than from skilled action or intellective competence. It is only at this stage, and in the context of this discontinuity, that the fate of the clerical job can be fruitfully compared to that of skilled work in industry. Yet even such a comparison has its limits, as the distinct history of clerical work is charged with a peculiar set of tensions and biases. When the clerical job is enriched, it tends to resume its traditional position in a direct line of descent from the executive function. In such cases, clerks are reintegrated into the sphere of coordinative responsibility, with all of its implications for skilled *acting-with*.

The application of scientific management to the office, particularly as it combined with mechanization, had a far-reaching impact on clerical work in the industrial enterprise as well as in the service organizations that grew to support both industry and the economic power of its growing labor force. Frequently, the jobs that were created had the effect of driving office workers into the role of laboring bodies, engulfing them in the private sentience of physical effort. Complaints about these jobs became complaints about bodies in pain. In 1960 the International Labour Organization published a lengthy study of mechanization and automation in the office. The study documented changes in the physical environment of the clerical employee and the working conditions associated with these new environments. While acknowledging that in some cases the introduction of expensive equipment had motivated employers to improve the office environment, the report concluded: "Of far greater importance, however, were the negative effects of mechanization. . . . Machinery in offices created an entirely different atmosphere from that which had prevailed before. . . . In contrast to the mechanization of production processes, which often relieved workers of physically tiring jobs, mechanization introduced work of this nature into offices where it had not existed before. . . . Clerical workers often complained of muscular fatigue, backache, and other such ills as a result of the unaccustomed strain of operating machines. . . . Machine operation is still more tiring for many workers than straightforward manual methods of copying or calculating, and can in some cases be a serious drain of their physical resources.

The study identified the chief sources of physical complaints as follows: fatigue induced by the increased speed of output, heavy lifting, standing, bending, the intensity of work measurement made possible by mechanization, the noise level of machines, and eyestrain. Moreover, it found that the nervous tension generated by the new forms of office work were an even greater threat than the physical exertion. Clerks complained of being "treated like trained animals" because of the "uniformity and excessive simplification of the work of many machine operators." It also noted that these clerical jobs were peculiar in requiring a high degree of monotonous and repetitive activity coupled with the demand for continual attentiveness to the work at hand: "Tabulating machine operators, for instance, even when the controls are set for them and an automatic device stops the machine when something goes wrong, cannot let their attention flag. . . . The strain of this kind of close attentiveness to a repetitive operation has resulted in a rising number of cases of mental and nervous disorders among clerical workers . . . physical and intellectual debility; disturbances of an emotional nature such as irritability, nervousness, hypersensitivity; insomnia; various functional disturbances—headaches, digestive and heart troubles; state of depression, etc."

As widespread as these new forms of clerical work had become, the reach of scientific management and mechanization was still far from complete. Throughout the late 1960s and the 1970s, management periodicals continued to devote considerable attention to the urgent need for an engineering approach to office work. Productivity, they cautioned, would never increase in the service sector unless the techniques of industrial engineering were applied to the tasks of the clerk. One such periodical, *The Office,* featured an article in 1969 by the director of a New Jersey industrial engineering firm who said: "We know from our company's studies that manpower utilization in most offices—even those that are subject to work measurement controls—rarely exceeds 60 percent. In some operations the percentage of utilization may fall below 40 percent. At least 17 percent of the time, employees are literally doing nothing except walking around or talking. . . . While many companies have squeezed out much of the excess labor costs in their production operations, only a few have given serious attention to the so called indirect labor or service operations."

In 1970, *Business Week* reported that companies were reducing their payroll costs by millions, using factory techniques to measure "how office workers work." One industrial engineer quoted in the article indicated that 75 percent of his firm's work measurement jobs were in the office, as compared to 25 percent just five years earlier: "Clerical jobs are measured just like factory jobs. The analysts add together scientifically predetermined time standards for human motions to find the time standard for a specific job—the standard by which worker's efficiency then is measured." The progress of these efforts, however, continued to be confounded by the persistence of elements in the diverse repertoire of clerical work that could not be rationalized. Measurement efforts overwhelmed the lowest paid and most routinized clerical jobs, while it tended to bypass higher-paid jobs entirely—jobs that continued to absorb, however weakly, both interpersonal and intellective aspects of the managerial function. As *Business Week* put it, "The trouble is that, with higher pay, routine lessens, and there is more decision-making of increasing complexity. The MTM [Methods, Time, Measurement] Assn . . . is sponsoring research on decision times at the University of Michigan. But data now available are primitive, and those who seek a time fix on the work of, say, a loan processor, will for some time to come have to accept far less precision than for a keypuncher. . . . The developing discipline of work measurement does not face its only challenge from creative jobs. . . . Statistical clerks, mail girls, and ex-pediters are tough . . . and the job of a secretary is considered "unmeasurable."

The problem was that jobs could only be measured successfully once they were converted to the dimension of *acting-on* and insulated from activities related either to *acting-with* or to more complex intellective effort. In 1972 General Electric published its "Program for Clerical Cost Control" and implicitly acknowledged this problem: "The program is based wholly upon the use of time values . . . selected from scientifically prepared tables of the Motion Time Studies (MTS), which provide proven time values for each physical motion likely to be used in performing any operation. . . . Clerical costs can be controlled on any routine, that is, repetitive or semi-repetitive work. Non-repetitive tasks, such as research and development, cannot be economically measured. Similarly, jobs such as receptionists, confidential secretaries, etc., do not lend themselves to control."

Kanter's description of the secretarial function also illustrates the difference between clerical jobs as *acting-on* and clerical jobs as *acting-with*. She found two broad groupings of secretaries—those who worked in a "pool" and those who were assigned to a particular boss. Secretaries disliked working in the pool arrangement, where jobs could be measured by the amount of typed output. Managers tended to avoid interaction with these typists, treating them instead with a purely "utilitarian" attitude, like input-output devices. In contrast, secretaries who worked for a single boss were required to absorb many subtle responsibilities associated with coordination and communication. They "could stop worrying about their own skills and work on their relationship with the boss. They could orient their work life around their connection with this one person. Some executive secretaries acquired their own corps of typists to do routine work, devoting their time to the social and interpersonal aspects of their jobs. . . . They participated in the behind-the-scenes transformation of chaos into order, or rough ideas into polished, business-like letters and documents. . . . They set the stage for an atmosphere that was designed to awe or impress visitors. They served as a buffer between the boss and the rest of the world, controlling access and protecting him from callers. And on occasion, they were asked to collude in lies on behalf of this front." For secretaries, much like their bosses, the salience of these implicit, action-centered skills of *acting-with* also put a premium on the body as an expressive instrument of interpersonal politics. Personal secretaries were supposed to look and behave in a certain manner; dress, posture, and physical attractiveness were each considered significant.

Thus, clerical work entered the decade of the 1980s still marked by considerable diversity and internal contradiction. Some clerical jobs continued to represent the furthest reach of the executive process. Despite efforts at simplification, they continued to absorb elements of responsibility for coordination and communication that precipitated from the managerial function and can be traced to the executive role. In these cases, the "elusive character of office work" persists in requiring clerks to engage in activities related to *acting-with*—sharing the communicative and problem-solving burden of "facilitating business functions" with their supervisors and managers. However, the combination of scientific management and mechanization did succeed in creating a new sphere of clerical work discontinuous with this historical trajectory. These jobs reflect those aspects of middle management's coordinative responsibilities that were most readily rationalized. In this new scenario, office workers were decisively driven into the demands of *acting-on,* engulfed in the rhythms and exertions of the laboring body. How will the application of information technology further transform white-collar activities? Will it enlarge the sphere of "industrialized" clerical positions, or will it be a force to reintegrate clerical work with its managerial past? If so, what implication might this have for our current conceptions of the middle-management function? The first step in answering these questions turns upon the issue of skill. In the case of industrial workers, we saw the informating power of information technology driving out opportunities for action-centered skill in favor of intellective skill demands. As clerks and their managers are required to work through the computer medium, what kind of knowledge will they need? Will the demands for action-centered skills related to communication and coordination be reinvigorated? Will office workers or their managers face accelerated demands for intellective competence? Will clerks be pushed further into the sentient but mute terrain of fatigue and nervous exhaustion?

15

Toward an Ecology of Knowledge: On Discipline, Context, and History

Charles Rosenberg

Rosenberg, a professor of history at the University of Pennsylvania, is the author of a number of books on the nineteenth century. In this paper we get the perspective of an historian, who emphasizes different points than those of sociologists and economists. He examines the relationship between knowledge and society, suggesting what future scholars will be looking at. The value of Rosenberg's paper is to point out how the subject of knowledge management remains a relatively new field of study and experience.

America at the conclusion of World War I was vastly different from the nation that had stumbled through Reconstruction a half-century earlier. The book this chapter is taken from sought to illuminate one aspect of the cultural revolution that took place in the half-century before 1918: the changing nature of organized knowledge and the contexts in which it was elaborated, transmitted, and used.

For at least a half-century, historians and sociologists have employed such terms as urbanization, industrialization, bureaucratization, and most recently the even more inclusive—if elusive—term modernization to describe the interrelated changes that brought the mid-twentieth century Western world into being. Yet it is only within the past generation that American historians have sought to deal systematically with the multifaceted transformation of their society between the mid-nineteenth and early twentieth century—seeing it as a "response to industrialism" or a "search for order" in the phrases of two influential synthesizers. American historians are, thus, belatedly orienting themselves toward a major question of social interpretation, one that has concerned European students of society for at

From his paper of the same title in Alexandra Oleson and John Voss (eds), *The Organization of Knowledge in Modern America, 1860–1920* (Baltimore, MD: The Johns Hopkins University Press, copyrighted by The American Academy of Arts and Sciences, 1979): 440–451.

least a century. Marx, Durkheim, and Weber—to cite only the most obvious examples—all sought to understand the institutional and even existential consequences of technological and economic change. Specialization of work, for example, or changing attitudes toward family and community have already attracted generations of social and historical speculation. Indeed, the term modernization implies—if anything—the necessity of integrating every aspect of a culture in attempting to understand social change.

This volume constitutes a pioneering attempt to survey our present understanding of a particularly significant period in the shaping of new relationships between knowledge and society. New kinds of knowledge, new institutions for the support of learning, new modes of education and certification all established themselves in the half-century between the Civil War and the First World War. In their diversity, the contributions that make up the volume this chapter was taken from indicate the difficulty of locating knowledge in society and the still tentative quality of our understanding; yet their very existence implies a new awareness that the ecology of knowledge does indeed constitute a significant historical concern. The following remarks attempt not to summarize the content of those pages which precede them, but to suggest some directions for further research, especially in areas not elaborated in these essays.

Intellectual history and the history of particular areas of pure and applied learning have a long and often distinguished tradition. Yet the bulk of this work has been undertaken by practitioners of the relevant mystery—physicians concerning themselves with the history of medical ideas, or philosophers with the geneology of particular philosophical problems. Not surprisingly, they have been comparatively unconcerned with the social and institutional context in which the ideas they study were elaborated, and demands for such research have sometimes been derided as an imposition of the trivial and temporal into a purer realm of thought. On the other hand, institutional and social historians concerned with learning or the professions ordinarily lack sufficient training in the relevant disciplines to allow them to explore fully the interactions between ideas and institutions. In recent years, however, this conventional division between the intellectual and institutional seems decreasingly tenable. It may describe much of an existing canon; it cannot dictate a necessary division of historical labor. Virtually every contributor to the book this chapter is from is a practicing historian and this constitutes in itself a significant reality; within the past decade, American historians have shown a steadily increasing interest in knowledge and its social context. Indeed, something of a preliminary if informal consensus has emerged. We have become increasingly aware that even the internal logic of formal thought can be shaped by social needs and assumptions; the domain of seemingly value-free inquiry grows ever smaller. We have become aware as well that specific institutional structures mediate the relationship between men of learning and the society that supports them. In sum, we have become conscious of the need to integrate knowledge into a more general understanding of organizational and attitudinal trends.

Yet such assumptions imply an interpretative challenge. These developing relationships cannot be understood by affixing to them neat labels such as specialization or professionalization. It is not that such terms are deficient in content; quite the contrary. They describe a significant social reality—but in a schematized and potentially misleading way. Insofar as we ask such ideal types to serve as both description and explanation of change, we have to some extent chosen to mislead ourselves. Such terms tend to incorporate a largely unexamined model of uniform institutional development, an evolution, moreover, whose end is the shape assumed in mid-twentieth century by such professions as those of medicine and law. But as Laurence Veysey has so forcefully argued in his contribution to the book this chapter was taken from, most such definitions blur under careful historical scrutiny; diversity and inconsistency mark the professions and academic disciplines as much as commonality of value and institutional practice.

Certainly one can find parallels in the development undergone by the several professions and learned disciplines in the half-century between 1865 and 1915, yet to dwell on these parallels is to obscure as much as to clarify. The terms that we habitually employ to describe these uniformities of development—specialization, professionalization, bureaucratization—tend like any such synthetic formulations to obscure the real differences that characterized change in the several areas of organized knowledge; the differences between academic disciplines or among professions are, after all, at least as instructive as their similarities.

It is no more than a truism to observe that social scientists are trained to discern and formulate patterns that can be expressed in general terms, while the historian is tied by sensibility and socialization to the particular. But this is as much the historian's advantage as his limitation—especially when we remind ourselves that no currently available formulation of the stages and characteristics of the professionalization of knowledge is based on adequate historical investigation. To understand the relationship between knowledge and society, historians must move beyond the passive and taxonomic—are individuals professional or preprofessional? do they fulfill an appropriate number of characteristics in some sociologist's diagnostic checklist?—and try to understand the fine structure of interaction between knowledge and the society that supports its accumulators and practitioners. Generalizations about the characteristics of, let us say, professionalization might be likened to the bones that structure the body; they provide a necessary general framework. But to understand its anatomy and physiology—if I may be forgiven another biological metaphor—we must look at the flesh, the blood, and the connective tissue as well.

This is no utopian program. Formal thought is retrievable from surviving documents and its social context discernible with some precision (as is not the case with social values and attitudes, whose shifting forms and elusive social constituencies make the task of their would-be historian difficult indeed). The consumers and transmitters of academic and professional learning can be identified, their backgrounds evaluated, the formal content of their ideas retrieved from documents written with the specific intent of communicating these ideas. The place of knowledge in society is not only appropriate to the historian's concerns but clearly within the scope of his documentary resources. Nevertheless, historians must accept several assumptions—at once of substance and method—if they are to systematically pursue the relationship between knowledge and its social setting. This is, after all, the central agenda of the present chapter and a major theme generally in understanding the development of modern society. Let me mention each, then discuss them in somewhat greater detail. First, historians must assume that knowledge subsumes different kinds of relationships with society, that these are structured by diverse institutional contexts, that the interaction of discipline and context—be that context university, professional school, or applied research laboratory—is the stage upon which the needs of society interact with the specific norms and ideas of the several disciplines and professions. Second, knowledge itself must be seen as playing a significant *social* role within those institutions that shape the vocational lives of their members; specialized knowledge helps dictate the internal organization of academic disciplines and learned professions, defines needs, and rewards achievement. Third and finally, within the larger society, knowledge can define legitimacy, shape personal and vocational identity, imply and help to define social place. Individuals do not choose careers at random, nor does society support intellectual endeavor haphazardly. In a society like nineteenth-century America, moreover—undergoing rapid change and comparatively lacking in the sources of emotional reassurance available in traditional societies— the role of knowledge must be seen as potentially crucial, not only in bringing about social change, but in defining identities appropriate to a changed reality.

In studying the institutionalization of knowledge in late-nineteenth-century America, perhaps the most useful distinction to be made is that between the professions and the learned disciplines. Though the distinction cannot be defended as absolute, it is nevertheless useful not only because it reflects important substantive realities but because it implies differing strategies of historical analysis.

Probably the most important single distinction between the professions and academic disciplines lies in their relationship to the society that supports them. As they have grown in size and self-consciousness, in the past century, the learned disciplines have come to rely on indirect modes of support, primarily through universities but to some extent through foundations and private learned societies. The professions have related far more directly to their supporting social substrate; even today the line between academic law and medicine and the world of practice is shifting and often ill-defined. To understand the social underpinning of a profession we must, to some extent at least, see it as a marketplace phenomenon—or, relatedly, as an object of government policy. The contrast between, let us say, law and classical philology needs no elaboration.

This is not to suggest some absolute distinction between a university-based seeker after abstract knowledge and the more worldly professional. The various professions and academic disciplines might best be seen as occupying places along a continuum defined by the nature of their social support system. There are any number of ambiguous cases, each telling us something about the complexity of the relationship between ideas and society. Is an agronomist, for example, a professional or a member of an academic discipline? Or must one provide an answer depending on the agronomist's employer? Clearly the texture of interaction between his knowledge and the society that supports its accumulation is different from that confronting, for example, a professor of romance languages. These two are per-haps extreme cases but represent in their diversity both the difficulty of defending an absolute distinction between discipline and profession and the complex social realities that must be faced by the would-be historian of knowledge in American society. The study of each discipline or profession implies a somewhat different re-search strategy.

Support for the learned disciplines is filtered through exterior priorities and assumptions, initially those that determine how generously the university and learning generally are to be supported. Then, within the university itself, an inter-vening layer of decisions and decision-makers interposes itself between the larger society and the department structure. Thus, the historian of a particular discipline must, among other questions, deal with the exigencies of the departmental system and the priorities and perceptions that determine levels of support within the uni-versity. He must understand, as well, the division of authority between depart-ment and central administration. Who is to be hired or fired? What sorts of research are to be encouraged? How is teaching to be weighed against research? In each instance, the department plays a significant role, for it is the department that has come to mediate between the demands of the discipline and the realities of a particular university context. In some ways, indeed, the history of the university in the half-century between the Civil War and First World War is not only a history of growth in size and influence, but of a shift in structure—with the departments sharing power with a previously dominant executive.

Historians have concerned themselves little with the department; insofar as individual departments have been studied it is ordinarily with the pious enthusi-asm of the hagiographer. Yet it is the discipline that ultimately shapes the scholar's vocational identity. The confraternity of his acknowledged peers defines the scholar's aspirations, sets appropriate problems, and provides the intellectual tools with which to address them; finally, it is the discipline that rewards intellec-tual achievement. At the same time, his disciplinary identity helps structure the scholar or scientist's relationship to a particular institutional context. His profes-sional life becomes then a compromise defined by the sometimes consistent and sometimes conflicting demands of his discipline and the conditions of his employ-ment. The totality of any discipline or profession must be seen as a series of paral-lel intellectual activities being carried on in a variety of social contexts. Such rubrics as the "humanities," "life sciences," or "social sciences" mask diversity as much as they imply unity. A bacteriologist working at an agricultural experiment station or pharmaceutical firm deals with very different questions and in a very different work environment from a medical school bacteriologist or one attached to a research team at the Rockefeller University. At the end of the nineteenth century, indeed, bacteriology was not a field at all; it could be defined only in terms of botanists and mycologists, alert and ambitious pathologists, and employ-ees of state and municipal departments of public health. To write a history of the origins of bacteriology would imply an evaluation of all these contexts and the specific influence they had in shaping the work and aspirations of would-be bacteriologists.

In the opening years of the present century, to cite another example, American genetics grew as a discipline largely out of the work of biologists employed either by university departments of zoology or botany or in agricultural colleges and experiment stations (supported by an atypical federal commitment to the funding of farm-related research). Medicine had few resources to support laboratory investigation and little incentive to devote those it had to genetics, which seemed only marginally related to the physician's clinical realities. As Garland Allen notes in his discussion of T. H. Morgan, however, an existing university-based experimental tradition with a well-defined interest in embryology and cytology proved a natural intellectual context for the elaboration of the "next step" in shaping a new science of heredity. Biochemistry, on the other hand, and at roughly the same time, found substantial support and encouragement in the world of medicine. Chemistry had proved itself relevant in pharmacology, in pathology, and in clinical diagnosis. It was only natural that many elite physicians were convinced that meaningful questions might indeed be asked in the laboratory, that they saw in chemistry a means of solving long-standing clinical problems. But biochemistry had roots outside as well as inside the medical school. When America's first professional biochemical society was founded in 1906, its charter members were drawn from a variety of contexts: industry, agricultural colleges and experiment stations, university departments of physiology and physiological chemistry, as well as medical schools and hospitals. Diversity of context is a characteristic of almost all learned disciplines in twentieth-century America—in particular the sciences.

Indeed, certain conventional disciplinary categories—chemistry for example—are almost too inclusive to be analytically useful. The American Chemical Society includes a host of individuals occupying very different social locations and making use of very different bodies of knowledge. Its membership includes men employed in the most routine quality control as well as the directors of lavishly funded research teams. Nevertheless, scholars and scientists who identify themselves with a particular discipline, no matter how diverse their work places or marginal their commitment to the larger discipline, still feel some residual sense of common identity, still interact in professional associations, possibly even in editorial committees or positions of public responsibility. Even relatively small groups such as ecologists or limnologists may occupy radically different institutional positions, yet remain bound by an affinity growing out of a shared consciousness of disciplinary identity.

There are no simple cases. Even those disciplines with an almost exclusively academic setting may still be characterized by a complex and highly differentiated structure, differentiated not only in terms of varied institutional contexts—for even colleges and universities vary widely—but in terms of specialized intellectual relationships that create de facto subdisciplines. Research areas, that is, help shape a social as well as an intellectual identity; in many ways one's closest peers are the handful of individuals at work on the same or closely related areas of research. Each intellectual cluster of this type may constitute a distinct subculture within the larger discipline—plasma physics within physics, for example, or criminology within sociology—just as each learned discipline constitutes such a subculture within the world of learning generally.

A diversity at least equal characterizes the professions. Differing social functions imply differing patterns of organization, differing patterns of status and recruitment, and differing degrees of control over professional activities. The learned professions may all have traits in common, but clearly the differences between, let us say, medicine and engineering are no less enlightening than their similarities. Historically, most engineers have worked for large-scale enterprises, be it a canal, railroad, or industrial firm, and have to that extent been lacking in autonomy. Thus, there exists a conventional wisdom among engineers which contends that in order to attain success the engineer must stop working as an engineer and instead use his credentials as an entrée to an entrepreneurial or administrative career. This realization would help explain the creation by engineers in the early twentieth century of an ideology of efficiency; this ideology, glorifying the engineer and his alleged problem-solving skills, reflected not a consciousness of social influence but of increasing marginality.

American physicians, on the other hand, have always related directly to the consumers of their services. As they moved in the late nineteenth century into more institutionalized settings, physicians were able to retain, and indeed enlarge upon, that autonomy. With greater knowledge and a seemingly greater ability to heal, physicians began to control ever greater areas of their professional lives. A pattern of increasingly formal institutional ties coupled with greater control of their professional universe was consistent with organizational trends in society generally. In addition, the sacred, emotionally resonant quality of the doctor-patient relationship, its mediation at times of sickness and death, created another source of potential social leverage for the physician—one that other professions could not ordinarily draw upon in their claims to social autonomy.

Each profession constitutes a unique configuration of social need and intellectual and institutional tools, evolved through a unique historical development. Nursing, for example, failed to benefit to the same extent as medicine from the emotions surrounding sickness and death; other variables have shaped nursing as a social institution. Attitudes toward class, toward gender role, toward servile manual work, for example, as well as the very necessity for structured hierarchy implied by the need to work with medicine in the same social setting have all interacted to create a history of nursing very different from that which has shaped medicine. Indeed, knowledge itself has played a different role in nursing and medicine; nursing has never been clothed with the prestige-bearing mantle of innovation and the accumulation of esoteric knowledge. Thus, the historian must not only be aware of differences among the professions but of complex distinctions of function and status within each profession.

None of this is meant to deny the power of the professional model or the desire of occupational groups to see themselves and convince others that they are indeed a profession and entitled to its prerogatives. Librarians, teachers, optometrists, and undertakers, for example, have adhered as best they could to the program of professionalization, though with varying degrees of success. Would-be historians of knowledge must balance the general against the particular. They must, if I may be excused the analogy, commit themselves to an ethnology of knowledge—the unit of analysis being not the geographically isolated culture but the knowledge-defined discipline, subdiscipline, or learned profession. Like the ethnological field-worker, historians of knowledge must integrate formal intellectual content with social and institutional organization, systems of economic support, and finally, the values that sanction and reward the career choice of members of a particular intellectual subculture. Like ethnology itself at the beginning of this century, we must free ourselves from the domination of over-schematized developmental models and seek to understand the specific forms of particular cultures.

What the foregoing suggests is the necessity of seeing knowledge itself as a central element in shaping the structure of disciplinary cultures and subcultures. This is no more than common sense. The historian who hopes to study, let us say, late-nineteenth-century philosophy or chemistry must understand the ideas that scientists or philosophers regarded as the essential reality of their discipline. He must understand how such individuals evaluated the competence of their peers, how networks of personal and institutional relationships were predicated on shared goals and commonality of judgment. Without such intellectual competence, the historian can hardly hope to unravel the mechanisms through which status and power were distributed, or even the nature of institutional decision-making (why certain appointments were made, for example, or certain kinds of investigation underwritten) and the implications of such decisions for ultimate intellectual change.

The social contours of formal learning reflect not simply institutional arrangements—memberships in societies, editorships of journals and the like—but a less visible structure of group identity based on intellectual commitment. Ideas shape meaningful units of emotional identification: a sense of community based on common education, allegiance to the solution of parallel or identical problems with the same intellectual tools. The members of such groups are also likely to occupy similar positions and face parallel institutional problems. Despite the controversy surrounding Thomas Kuhn's much-debated term "paradigm," it is at the very least heuristically useful in pointing toward the need for disentangling such units of intellectual and institutional identity. The fine structure of any twentieth-century discipline is a mosaic of such clusters, the precise configuration of which defines not only the discipline's intellectual profile but its social shape as well. Ideas must be taken seriously and they must be understood—even by scholars concerned primarily with questions of social organization or the social impact of knowledge.

On the other hand, historians concerned primarily with explaining intellectual innovation or the lack of it must, by the same token, become historical sociologists of knowledge. Understanding the intellectual options facing a particular scholar or scientist is a prerequisite to understanding his role as innovator; in order to reconstruct those options, the historian must necessarily study his protagonist's initiation into a particular discipline at a particular time. He must try to read the textbooks his subject used and recreate the atmosphere of the seminars he attended; he must understand the institutional pressures he experienced, be they for specific kinds of teaching or particular emphases in research. All of this may seem commonsensical, but it has all-too-rarely guided historians in their study of men of learning.

The needs of society can and do intrude even upon the internal texture of academic discourse. Those critical spirits who urge a demystification of the professions and learned disciplines are often correct in scoffing at the claims toward value-free neutrality that may embellish the social pretensions of such groups. But to concede the existence of an inevitable give-and-take between the realm of intellect and the needs of society is hardly to advance our intellectual awareness; the difficulty lies in understanding how and when such interactions take place. Each discipline presents a different potential for social relevance—and, thus, a different order of sensitivity to social pressure. Obviously the internal logic of ideas in quantum physics is less prone to reflect such social demands than their counterparts in political science or sociology. Yet it would be naive to assume that quantum physics has not had a significant social impact, though perhaps of a different kind from that exerted by political science. It would be equally naive to assume that even in many areas of physics social priorities and perceptions did not play some role in shaping research support and, thus, effecting the differential plausibility of research options. Most cases are even more ambiguous.

Let me refer, by way of example, to an incident that took place in the years immediately preceding the First World War—an incident of both great practical and theoretical significance. Some years ago I was engaged in a study of American agricultural experiment stations before 1914 and was surprised to discover, in a generally undistinguished research canon, that two groups of American scientists had discovered vitamin A almost simultaneously. And this happened at a time when American agricultural research was notable more for assiduity in attracting support than eminence in achievement. How could this seeming anomaly be understood? The explanation is illuminating, for it illustrates nicely the interdependence of economic and social factors with intellectual and institutional ones.

The discovery of vitamin A grew out of the juxtaposition of a number of areas previously little-related; one was a sophisticated ability to work with the chemistry of proteins, another the use of small mammals as indices to the biological activity of chemicals of known composition, a third the skills of the pathologist. No existing discipline contained the configuration of tools and motivation appropriate to demonstrate that minute quantities of a previously unknown substance were necessary to the normal growth and development of men and animals. Protein chemists did not ordinarily work with the problems and tools of experimental pathology; agricultural scientists concerned with the comparative efficacy of diets lacked adequate biochemical skills; pathologists normally lacked the chemical skills and tradition of working in experimental situations (and were also distracted by an absorbing concern with the etiological role of microorganisms). Yet at both the Wisconsin and Connecticut agricultural experiment stations the force of economic necessity brought together an appropriate mixture of skills.

Prodded by the need to contribute to the economic well-being of dairymen and cattle-raisers, research administrators at these experiment stations created a novel intellectual context by bringing the skill of protein chemists to bear upon the problem of explaining experimentally-demonstrated inadequacies in seemingly complete diets, thus, transcending the limitations of conventional disciplinary training.

In other fields, of course, the problems implied by the need to exist within society assumed different guises. The social sciences, for example, were shaped to a large extent in the half-century before 1920 by conflicting tendencies toward social intervention and reform, on the one hand, and a value-free, neutral stance on the other. Though some of the most prominent leaders in the formative decades of American social science were imbued with an almost evangelical desire to intervene righteously in society, it soon became clear that such intervention could be dangerous, not only to the individuals involved but to the disciplinary needs of the nascent social sciences. Certainly one of the characteristic themes in all of the social sciences in the last-quarter of the nineteenth century and first-quarter of the twentieth was this very conflict between social consciousness and academic cautiousness. And social scientists did proceed with a growing caution in the twentieth century—or at least caution in expressing opinions potentially offensive to those who wielded social and economic power.

But how is one to interpret this shift? Were they paralyzed by a simple fear of reprisal from conservative trustees and administrators? Or were they intimidated instead by a growing respect for an increasingly complex body of empirical data and demands by their disciplinary peers for its mastery? Or did generational differences in recruitment imply a differing kind of vocational commitment among social scientists? Answers to such questions can never be one-dimensional or unambiguous, yet the questions must still be asked if we are to understand the evolution of the social sciences in America. For even if we do not concede a genuine decision-making power to the findings and deliberations of academic economists and sociologists, they nevertheless play a powerful legitimating role in society.

The humanities and social sciences have in some ways—as Dorothy Ross and Laurence Veysey suggest—played very different roles. While social scientists have to some extent assumed the task of guiding society, the theologian and philosopher have played decreasingly prominent public roles. The philosopher's evolution from moral teacher to discipline-oriented academician is particularly striking and instructive. Moral philosophy was still central to the learned man's intellectual world in 1865; by the 1920s academic philosophy had turned away from consideration of those eternal human problems that philosophy had always addressed. The increasingly internal orientation of the philosopher has made the products of their scholarship well-nigh unavailable to the society that supports his linguistic, logical, or mathematical investigations. In some ways, the differentiation of the moral philosopher's subject matter into a half-dozen specialized descendants—among them philosopher, economist, psychologist, political scientist, sociologist—provides an exemplary paradigm for all those shifts that marked the changing context of knowledge in the half-century between the Civil War and World War I.

Thus far, we have been discussing the role of knowledge within a particular discipline or profession. A second kind of question concerns the place of knowledge in the social order generally. What was the social value attached to the possession of knowledge? What did the mastery of a specific body of knowledge mean to its possessor? And how did his peers regard him? Such realities shaped not only recruitment into a particular discipline but also the willingness of society to accept that implicit evaluation and support its acolytes.

Laurence Veysey contends in his study of the humanities that one motivation for the embracing of humanistic knowledge was the status such a commitment implied to certain members of the older middle class. Such individuals, he maintains, found themselves sorely in need of the transcendence and moral stature implied by a seemingly selfless commitment to wisdom—not wealth. These late-nineteenth-century academic humanists sought as well a collegial atmosphere of like-thinking peers whose devotion to the same scholarly vocation served to forge a bond of emotional affinity in a world frequently lacking in such ties for the sensitive and introspective. Even in an egalitarian and supposedly pragmatic society, the nurturance of a seemingly unselfish, and in that sense spiritual, orientation toward scholarship implied the kind of moral elevation that seemed necessary to at least some Americans as they sought to contend with their own desires for achievement in a context in which most kinds of distinction were tied to the sordid compromises of the marketplace.

This commitment to scholarship is intimately related to another central aspect of this period: the growth of the research ethos, a development touched upon by almost every essay in the book this chapter is taken from and discussed in particular detail by Hugh Hawkins. Research and research-like activities not only grew to play an ever-increasing role in the actual work of scholars but gained greater acceptance in the public mind as well. Though research seemed selfless, it was at the same time consistent with the urges of romantic individualism. The search for truth could, thus, channel and domesticate the emotional need of at least some ambitious young men. In certain areas, moreover, research promised painless conflict resolution in society—while providing new knowledge and serving as an agent of change.

Considerations similar to that of the spiritual value attached to the possession of knowledge help us to understand certain kinds of behavior among professionals that do not lend themselves to purely economic analysis. Why, for example, did nineteenth-century physicians publish, perform autopsies, work indefatigably to improve medical school curricula? Was it simply a need to provide a more prestigious product in competing for a limited stock of consumers? The truth is far more complex. Individuals crave moral legitimacy—and in medicine, legitimacy has traditionally implied mastery of a particular body of knowledge; that possession of such knowledge implies or might bring with it economic advantage (or social status) does not mean that the motivation for acquiring it can be understood in exclusively economic terms. One could argue indeed that the very materialism of most physicians motivated an idealistic and distinction-hungry minority to embrace the search for knowledge. To orient themselves toward the approval of their peers in Paris and Berlin was at once to remove themselves from the confining standards of their own community and, paradoxically, to elevate themselves within it. Could it be doubted that a physician who sought earnestly after intellectual enlightenment occupied a higher moral status than a contemporary who sought simply to increase his "business?" Both traditional religious values and the internal values of the profession endorsed many of the same kinds of behavior.

Though only a small percentage of American physicians may have sought such intellectual mastery, they nevertheless played a disproportionate role in bringing about the changes that were to reshape the institutional structure and public status of their profession between the Civil War and World War I. Learning, as measured in publication and membership in specialized societies, was closely associated in late-nineteenth-century American medicine with status and influence—and in this association lay a structural basis for the leverage exerted by a comparatively small group of intellectual and institutional innovators. The desire to achieve intellectual distinction, to define one's aspirations in terms of the world of scientific medicine must be seen as a change agent in itself, a necessary ingredient not only in technical innovation but in the transmission of ideas such as the germ theory across the Atlantic. And it would be hard to overestimate the impact of such intellectual artifacts as the germ theory in ultimately reshaping the realities of even the humblest country practitioner; in this case, the link between high-culture ideas and their transforming social impact is unmistakable. Of course, the status and emotional fulfillment implied by the possession of specialized knowledge served as a change agent in fields other than medicine.

Index